Slot Car Bible

Bible

Robert Schleicher

MBI Publishing Company

First published in 2002 by MBI Publishing
Company, Galtier Plaza, Suite 200, 380 Jackson
Street, St. Paul, MN 55101-3885 USA

MBI Publishing Company books are also
available at discounts in bulk quantity for
industrial or sales-promotional use. For details
write to Special Sales Manager at Motorbooks
International Wholesalers & Distributors,
Galtier Plaza, Suite 200, 380 Jackson Street,
St. Paul, MN 55101-3885 USA.

Library of Congress Cataloging-in-Publication
Data Information Available
ISBN 0-7603-1153-6

Designed by LeAnn Kuhlmann
Edited by Dennis Pernu

Printed in China

On the front cover: An MRRC 427 Cobra leads a
Carrera 427 Corvette Stingray, a Carrera
Mercedes-Benz 300SLR, and a Ninco Ferrari
Tests Rossa down the corkscrew turn on the
Suzuka four-lane raceway for Carrera track
shown in Chapter 5. The Carrera track borders
have been painted with red and white rumble
strips, green "grass," and beige "sand." The tree
is a Life-Like number 1971 Super Giant Oak,
and the figures, from MRRC, painted by hand.

On the frontispiece: Four Mattel NASCAR
sedans—three Ford Tauruses and a Chevrolet
Monte Carlo—scream around a banked turn
on the HO scale Tomy A/FX Daytona
International Raceway detailed in Chapter 11.

On the title page: A Carrera BMW and a Fly
Panoz in a refueling pit stop scene. The
buildings are Scalextric and the figures are
from MRRC, handpainted to match the crew
at a vintage race.

On the back cover: *Top:* This 1/32 scale replica
of the Le Mans–wining XJR9 Jaguar has a Fly
chassis with a Pattos clear plastic body. Its
construction is detailed in Chapter 10.
Bottom: Axle washers can be used to increase a
car's magnetic downforce, forcing the magnet
further into its pocket (and hence, closer to the
track). In this way, model car racers can tweak
their car's downforce just as real racecar
mechanics adjust downforce with ground effects.

Author bio: Robert Schleicher is a veteran writer
and publisher in the hobby field, as well as the
author of the slot car classic *Model Road Racing
Handbook* (1967) and MBI Publishing
Company's *Racing and Collecting Slot Cars* and
101 Projects for Your Model Railroad. The
publisher of *Model Car Racing* magazine lives in
Niwot, Colorado.

Contents

Chapter One

RACING MODEL CARS

A 1/64 scale replica of the La Rascasse restaurant in Monaco, scratch-built from styrene sheet plastic, on Jason Boye's HO scale track. The harbor is in the background. The cars are all Boye's model resin bodies (hand painted by Boye) on Tyco chassis.

Electric model car racing allows you to re-create what you can only imagine: watching a race while being in complete control of the car you are watching. And you can view the action from the same vantage point you would watch a real race. This time, though, you are in full control of a model of a real car from your favorite period in motorsports racing on a replica of a real track—and you're racing it in your own home.

Four 1/32 scale Formula 1 cars set up for a power sliding drift around a tight hairpin turn. The cars are Ninco's 1998 Jordan, Pro Slot's 1999 Ferrari, Carrera's 1999 McLaren, and SCX's 2000 Arrows. The pit buildings and grandstands are Scalextric models with Preiser and MRRC people.

Top: These high-banked turns snap together from Carrera plastic track to assemble a replica of the Daytona International Speedway in chapter 5.

Center: This Rally/hillclimb track just fits on a 4x8 tabletop as shown in chapter 8.

Above: There's room on a 5x9-foot Ping-Pong tabletop for a variety of challenging and exciting raceways like those in chapter 3.

A 1/32 scale four-lane replica of the famous downhill Corkscrew turn at Laguna Seca Raceway near Monterey, California. The curve was assembled using a combination of flat and banked curve sections from Carrera. The cars include a Grand Sport Corvette (made from a Patto's clear plastic body on a Ninco Cobra chassis), a Ninco Cobra, an Any Slot brand Maserati Tipo 61 Birdcage, and a Ninco Ferrari Testa Rossa (modified as described in *Racing and Collecting Slot Cars*).

You Create the Action

When you watch a real automobile race in person or on television, you can only imagine you are driving the real car. With these models, however, you drive a real car that happens to be 1/32 or 1/64 the size of the real one. And it really is better than sitting in the cockpit of a real car because you see the entire car rather than just the dashboard and fenders.

The ability to create the racing action you witness as a spectator is the incredible experience you can get only with these model racing cars. You will discover that you are a spectator and a participant at the same time. Here's how: when you watch a real car race, the images that flow through the retinas of your eyes are just about the same size as these models, so what you see on a 1/32 scale race track is precisely the size of what you would see from trackside at, say, Laguna Seca's famous Turn 6 Corkscrew or in the esses at Le Mans. The smaller HO cars offer a similar image, it's just farther away—more like watching Formula 1 races or the Indianapolis 500 or going to Daytona. From your point of view, each of these models is an exact replica of the real thing, and you are the one who can make that race car perform just like the real thing.

Real Racing Car Action

You are in full control of these model cars. You accelerate away from the start, trying to control the wheelspin and thus minimize fishtailing. You hold the throttle on until the car enters the corner, then you use the brakes to set up the car for a power slide that you control right at the limits of the tires' adhesion. You must then finesse the application of evermore throttle for maximum acceleration out of the corner.

If you can do it driving a real race car, you can usually do it with a model race car: power slides, brake slides, understeer, oversteer are all real race car driving techniques you can master with these model cars. With a real car, you use the steering to set the car into the corner, then the throttle to control the car's path through the turn. With a slot car, the slot serves that turn-in function, but you still must steer the car around the corner with the throttle. There's more: you can actually tune your model car for more or less downforce to promote understeer or oversteer.

Radio Control and Video Game Racing

Racing these electric model cars differs from radio control model car racing in that you never have to reverse your vision when the car drives toward you. It's easy enough to determine that you should move the steering wheel on the radio control transmitter right or left to steer right or left when a radio control car is speeding away from you. When that car is turned and comes back toward you, however, the steering control

must be reversed. That action alone often breaks the spell of imagining you are driving a real race car. With slot cars, it is much easier to keep your imagination focused on the model car because the slot automatically decides right or left. All you must do is use the throttle (just as you would in a real car) to control the model car's slide through the corner.

Electric model car racing is even more realistic than the best of the video games because you see the car in three dimensions and see it as the same size image you would while watching it on a real track. And your control input has the same mechanical input-response feeling you would get controlling a real race car. Model racing cars are so accurate that the realism only gets better when the car slides through the turn and accelerates down the straight.

Your Dream Come True

Remember those incredible slot cars of the 1960s and 1970s? Memories have a way of becoming better as time passes—those slot cars were nowhere near as realistic as the models produced today.

You will probably be disappointed if you really do get your hands on one of those 1/32 scale Revell, Monogram, Cox, Varney, Atlas, Super Shells, Airfix, MRRC, or VIP slot cars you remember so well. (Nearly all are still available at

Carrera plastic sectional track was used to assemble this two-lane replica of the Suzuka Grand Prix circuit as shown in chapter 5.

A four-lane 9x14-foot re-creation of the Suzuka Grand Prix track using Carrera track as described in chapter 5.

Far left: Three NASCAR sedans roar through the esses on the three-lane Suzuka track routed from particleboard by the late Al Hetzel as shown in chapter 6.

Left: The 9x14-foot Suzuka Grand Prix track assembled from Scalextric and SCX track sections. The grandstands and the pits in the distance are Scalextric.

flea markets or on eBay, but expect to pay collector prices.) Frankly, not one of them is up to today's standards for detail and finish.

None of those model cars were painted and most were kits. You assembled them, then painted the body, painted the trim, and applied the decals. Today's cars are painted at the factory with pad-printed details like windshield frames and trim and sponsor decals. Only a handful of

modelers have the skills to finish a kit to match the level of detail that has become standard for the ready-to-run models. It is possible, however, and later in this book I'll show you techniques and secrets for painting and detailing a model car to those standards.

The details on today's ready-to-run cars include engine, visible chassis details, and full interiors, with perfectly even windshield frames and decals that look like they were printed on because they are printed on. Today's ready-to-run cars are far more realistic and far better detailed than even the contest-winning model cars of past decades. And you can have almost all you want without the need to find a professional modeler to build them!

Many of those 1/32 scale slot cars from the 1960s and 1970s are still available: MRRC has reissued the Monogram Ferrari 1964 Ferrari GTO, Cooper Cobra, and Porsche 904 with a new metal chassis that is very similar to the Revell chassis of the 1970s. Most of the Airfix 1/32 scale cars are still available from MRRC as well. Each year, SCX reintroduces a classic from the original SCX and/or Scalextric line. Be prepared for disappointment in the level of realism from any of these older models, however.

If it's the real car you remember and want to model, there are ways to fulfill that dream as well. Hundreds of new 1/32 scale models appear each year, but we can only show a few dozen in this book. Visit your local dealer or check some of the Websites to see what's now available (see the Resources section). Chances are you can get a 1/32 scale replica of the car of your dreams. If not, you can almost certainly find a clear plastic or cast-resin body and build a model for yourself. I'll show you how later in this book.

Affordable Racing Is Not an Oxymoron
Get two avid motorsports fans together with two racing cars and you are going to have a race. Having stated the obvious, the hobby of 1/32 and HO car racing is more about the cars (and the tracks) than about the races. We want to re-create the races we missed or, in some cases, the race we saw last weekend. The difference here is that you don't need to spend $300,000 for a car, $50,000 for a mechanic, $50,000 for a transporter, and $50,000 to get to and from the tracks. A typical 1/32 scale car costs about $40 to $60—about 1/10 of 1 percent of the real one. You can have an entire stable of exact-scale model racing cars—and effectively your choice of the best race tracks in the world—for $500 to $1,000!

Real Racing on Real Tracks
Model car racing is not limited to just watching cars zip around a two-lane figure eight. You can use sectional track pieces to assemble a track that matches your favorite race track from anywhere in the world. If you tire of racing on that track, change it to another. You can create a new

race track, especially if you have plans, in about an hour. There are plans in this book and additional plans in my previous book, *Racing and Collecting Slot Cars* (MBI Publishing Company, ISBN 0-7603-1024-6). Manufacturers in the industry also offer plans for both custom tracks and replicas of the world's race courses.

You really can drive those turns they talk about, like Laguna Seca's Corkscrew, Indianapolis' Turn 1 or Turn 13 (for the F1 cars), the Hairpin at Monaco, the Carousel at the Nürburgring, or just about any other corner and combination of corners on any track you've ever heard of. Driving what seem to be real cars on what seem to be real tracks brings an incredible element of realism to this hobby. You can carry that element further and re-create specific races with accurate scale models of the cars that raced on that track in that race. See for yourself if you could have driven Stirling Moss' Vanwall as fast as Juan Manuel Fangio's Maserati at Monaco, or if the Ferraris might just beat the Fords on your replica of Daytona International Speedway.

The stairs and buildings are all photo flats as described in chapter 4. The Carrera Aston Martin DB3 and Maserati A6GCS slide through the Station Hairpin on the Monaco Grand Prix track from chapter 5.

Which Scale?

The most popular size for electric racing cars is 1/32 that of the real car. Modelers call it 1/32 scale. And yes, each car is supposed to be precisely 1/32 the size of its real-life counterpart in every dimension. That's not always precisely true, but in general the cars are accurate models. You'll discover that Carrera's 1/32 scale replica of the Maserati A6GCS, for example, is a relatively tiny car compared to a 1/32 scale replica of the 1999 Le Mans–winning BMW from Ninco or Carrera, or SCX's 2000 Le Mans–winning Audi. Scalextric and SCX 1/32 scale models of the NASCAR sedans are larger yet, as are the real cars they duplicate.

The next most popular size is HO scale. Virtually all HO scale cars are the same size, even though the real cars they copy vary. Thus, the HO scale models of full-size sedans measure approximately 1/87 scale, the NASCAR sedan racers are about 1/64 scale, and the sports cars like the Ford GT40 are about 1/58 scale. The advantage is that all three sizes of cars fit on the same size chassis.

There is a following for 1/24 scale cars, particularly in Germany and among those who want to race on the high-speed eight-lane commercial tracks that were popular in the 1970s. The 1/32 scale cars you'll see in this book are really not designed to run on those large tracks but they certainly can—they just take a lot longer to get down the straightaways than the 1/24 scale cars. There are also some modelers who build 1/32

scale cars using the same type of lightweight frames and distorted bodies favored for most 1/24 scale racing. If you prefer speed above realism, you may want to investigate the commercial raceway shops where you can rent both track time and cars. In addition, Carrera offers a variety of 1/24 scale cars for use on the home raceways in this book.

11

You can squeeze an HO scale track onto a 2x4-foot board, but 4x8 feet is the minimum for a really enjoyable track. It is possible to fit a two-lane 1/32 scale track onto a 4x8 board, but a 5x9-foot Ping-Pong table is about the best minimum size space, while 9x12 or larger—up to about 9x20 feet—is even better. Most homes have room for a 4x8- or 5x9-foot tabletop, especially if it can be folded away for storage (as can portable Ping-Pong tables).

History

Although there were slot cars as early as about 1900, and although people raced model cars guided by rails throughout the 1930s, 1940s, and 1950s, the cars in this book are direct descendants of the slot cars produced by Scalextric, VIP, and Strombecker in the 1960s, as well as by dozens of other firms in the 1970s, including Monogram, Revell, Cox, and Eldon.

By the mid-1960s, there were about a dozen hobby shops offering four- or six-lane tracks that could be rented by the hour. By the late-1960s, the number of shops had increased to several hundred, and by 1970 there were more than 4,000 slot car raceways in the United States alone and about that many more in other countries. These shops featured massive 20x40-foot eight-lane tracks, mostly routed from sheets of particle- or chipboard. The price of a winning car escalated from about $20 in the mid-1960s to over $100 in 1970.

In the hobby's early years, the quest for speed outweighed the desire for realism, so both modelers and manufacturers produced machines that bore only a passing resemblance to real cars. Ironically, slot cars offered foot-wide tires (to scale, of course) and wedge-shaped bodies years before such designs became common on real sports, Formula, Championship Auto Racing Team (CART), and Indy cars. Slot car racers took the wedge a step further, however, when they added inch-high clear plastic air dams to the sides of the cars in order to direct the airflow and increase the aerodynamic downforce. The cars reached incredible speeds, lapping huge tracks—as long as 200 feet—in a half dozen seconds.

This form of what I call "commercial slot car racing" still exists and there are now about 200 commercial raceways in the United States. Incidentally, some hobby shops (that sell the 1/32 scale cars you'll see in this book) also offer tracks for rent, but they are assembled from the same sectional track you would use at home and are seldom larger than about 5x12 feet. In some ways, the hobby has come full circle, back to its roots of racing in your own home on your own track.

How Fast Do You Want To Go?

The upper limit for 1/32 and 1/24 scale slot car speeds was defined in the early 1980s by commercial raceway cars, those wedge-shaped flying shingles with air dams. These cars are no more suitable for racing on a home track than your 1/32 scale car is suitable for racing on a commercial raceway.

There is an absurdly high limit to how much speed you can get out of a slot car. The question is, "Why would you want to?" One of the reasons why today's 1/32 scale cars are so realistic is because their speeds and—to a degree that might surprise even an experienced road racer—their handling are very similar to the real cars that they duplicate. Those speeds are matched to the tracks you can build at home: most 1/32 scale cars reach top speed in less than a dozen feet of straightaway.

The good news is that you can actually tune your 1/32 and HO scale cars so that each is a match for the other. You can go a step further and tune each car so that both it and its competitors closely match the speed and handling of the real cars. I call adjusting the performance of model racing cars "performance

You can select race cars that are replicas of those from any of the major racing classes in the world, including German Touring Cars, like these two Ninco Mercedes CLK DTM racers.

parity" because it is an attempt to level the field so that driver skill and, in some cases, cunning (the best weapon of the older racer) rather than sheer car speed or handling win races (as they usually do in the real world). You would not expect, for example, a model of a 1956 Ferrari Testa Rossa to be as powerful or as quick around the corners as a 2000 Audi R8R Le Mans car. But by swapping traction magnets and sometimes motors and controllers, you can make replicas of all the cars that raced in 1958 equal to that Ferrari, and all the cars that are replicas of cars that raced in 2000 equal to that Audi's performance.

What Kind of Hobby Is This?

This hobby is not about speed alone. First, model car racing is a hobby for those who really love automobiles: their styles, their shapes, and their histories. And especially it's a hobby for those who love racing automobiles. The need for speed comes second for most of those who enjoy this hobby.

Most of us want the cars to look as much like the real cars as possible. So what passes for a "production car" in the Sports Car Club of America (SCCA), a Mustang in the current Trans-Am series, or a Prodsports car in Europe, is just not acceptable as a historic replica of a real car. If these full-size modified production cars appeal to you, you can buy clear plastic bodies that are distorted images of the original cars in much the same way as these real-life modified cars. You can obtain these cars as 1/32 or 1/24 scale models at the commercial raceways that house the huge eight-lane tracks. Generally, however, these caricatures of real cars are far, far faster than the scale models you see on these pages. If speed is what you seek from model car racing, then those commercial raceway models are the cars and the tracks that will fulfill your dreams.

For many enthusiasts, these commercial cars and tracks define the hobby of slot car racing. And that's why I really do not like to refer to the cars in this book as "slot cars" because they are so very different from the slot cars that are raced on eight-lane commercial raceways.

Automobiles, particularly racing automobiles, look their best in motion. Electric model car racing—call it slot racing if you must—provides the best possible means of putting dead-accurate replicas of those shapes into motion and

replicating the movement and speed of the real cars. For most of us, the hobby is very similar to full-size vintage car racing in that we are there to watch the cars in action, not to destroy them. The car owners who bring their machines to the Monterey Historics or to the Goodwood Revival are there to see their cars perform as they did when the cars were new. Sure, these are racing cars and they are racing, but the emphasis is on the action, not winning at all costs. Fortunately, you can purchase a stable of twenty 1/32 scale replicas of the most gorgeous race cars ever built and assemble a 40-foot four-lane track for less than the cost of a set of tires for a vintage race car.

The sweeping ess bends on the Suzuka track assembled from Carrera plastic track sections in chapter 5. The cars are a Carrera BMW, a Ninco BMW, a Fly Panoz, and an SCX Ferrari.

Chapter Two

TRACK FOR 1/32 RACERS

Broad ess bends and high banks are just part of what's possible with tabletop racing in 1/32 scale. This is the Daytona International Speedway four-lane track for Carrera from chapter 5.

When model car racing was a new hobby back in the 1960s, most serious racers built their own tracks by routing slots into a particleboard surface. Why? Because the plastic sectional track available from a host of makers, including Scalextric and Carrera, was just not as fun to race on as a track you could design yourself.

Most brands offered just a standard curve and an outer curve so you could assemble a four-lane track. Plans for the tracks you could assemble from 1960s-era Revell, Monogram, and Strombecker track sections are in chapter 5 as replicas of Monaco, Daytona, and Suzuka. It may not be apparent just from looking at the plans, but they were not all that exciting to drive. Within a few weeks of racing, even if a track configuration matches the shape of one of the world's greatest circuits, it really is just the same old right and left turns arranged in a different sequence—learn one and you knew them all. With a routed track, however, you can vary the size of the curves and even include increasing radius and decreasing radius turns—which is precisely what occurs on any road racing course in the world.

Why Plastic Track?

Today, the choice of plastic track sections is broad enough so you can assemble a track that is the rival of the best routed tracks. The routed tracks, however, are still the most exciting to drive, but not by much. A well-designed routed track can produce a flow from corner to corner—and perhaps a chicane, where the cars actually follow the "racing line" through the inside of the curve—that makes the movements of the cars as realistic as the cars themselves. Also, routed tracks can be less expensive than plastic tracks if you do the work yourself. Even a custom-made routed track won't cost more than about twice what a similar-size plastic track would cost. Plus, the track is solid and permanent, making it a substantial fixture.

And therein lies the problem: "substantial." Once you have completed a routed track it is, so to speak, part of the family. You don't particularly have to worry about creating a "bad" track because you can fix it. What I discovered, however, was that after less than a year I was bored with the track.

I admit to a personal prejudice, but the Paramount Ranch track in chapter 6 was and still is the best 1/32 scale track I have ever raced on. It had an incredible flow through the corners and it just felt like driving a real car on a real track. Within a year, however, I was bored. Worse, all the other racers were bored, too, so I gave the track to a friend.

We started racing on four-lane plastic tracks that were assembled on three or four portable 4x8-foot tables. We assembled a different track every month, using the plans from a series that appeared in the now-defunct *Model Car & Track* magazine, including the Monaco, Daytona, and Suzuka tracks for the Revell/Monogram/Strombecker track shown in chapter 5. We used Revell track and borders and cemented them together into four-lane "modules" of common 180-degree, 90-degree corners and 2-, 4-, and 6-foot four-lane straights, all with borders on both inside and out. With these modules, we could assemble a four-lane track in less than a half-hour and disassemble it even faster.

Unfortunately, the same old corners even made this system less exciting than a track routed from particleboard. What we wanted was a routed track that we could change as quickly as we did the Revell track. Well, now we have it. Scalextric Sport, Scalextric Classic, SCX, Ninco, and Carrera offer four different curves, and Carrera even has a choice of three different banked turns.

Why 10 Lanes?
The Scalextric Sport, Scalextric Classic, SCX, Ninco, and Carrera track available today includes enough different curves to build an eight-lane track. There's even a custom-made inner-inner curve for Carrera that allows 10 lanes of track. Carrera offers three different sizes of banked turns that are, in effect, different radii because they alter how the car corners compared to similar-size flat curves. Why would you care if you can have 10 or more different curves if you only want a two-lane track? So you can have up to 10 different curves, rather than just the single size that comes in most racing sets. In fact, my recommendation is that your second purchase (after a race set) be a circle of outer curves and perhaps four 1/4-sections so you can assemble

some really exciting tracks, including replicas of those increasing and decreasing radius turns. Later, you can buy more track sections that will even allow you to re-create downhill spirals like Laguna Seca's famous Corkscrew or the high banks of Daytona. You'll see all these in the plans in chapter 5.

Which Brand of Track Is the Best?
I can make a strong case for Sport, Carrera, Ninco, Scalextric, SCX, and Artin track each being the best, and not necessarily in that order. Yes, I have raced on all of them and built tracks from all of them, as well as from the old Revell, Monogram, and Strombecker track. And, yes, I do have a favorite, but only barely and I'm not about to share my personal prejudice because it is just that, personal. You will have your own. What's important to me in a track is included in the list of "Pros and Cons" (see sidebar). What's important to you will be in that list as well.

Scalextric Track
Scalextric actually offers two brands of track. The flexible plastic track with loops-over-pegs to join the sections is still available but it is now called "Scalextric Classic" track. This is the track that will interchange with SCX. Scalextric also makes "Scalextric Sport" track, which comes in exactly the same sizes as the Classic (and SCX), but is made of a stiffer plastic with snap-in connectors between sections, a deeper slot, and a smother surface. The footprint for each section of Scalextric Classic and Sport is identical, as is the footprint for SCX track, so any plan for any one of the three types of track can be used for any of the others. All three use 45 degrees as the

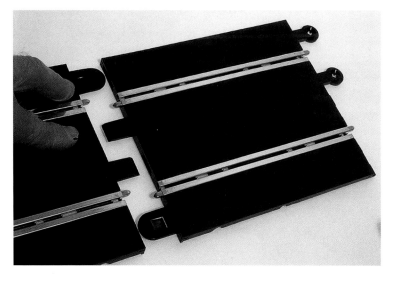

Sport track from Scalextric (left) has a plug-in connection system in place of the loop-and-peg system used by Scalextric Classic track (right). (SCX and Ninco use similar loop-and-peg systems.) This the Sport C8222 adaptor track section used to adapt Scalextric Classic track to Sport track.

standard geometry for turns, so it takes 8 or 16 sections (depending on the size of the curve) to make a full circle. Also, the lanes are spaced 3 inches apart for all three brands, so if you are running cars with correct scale track widths, there's little problem. Some of the wider cars, like SCX Formula 1 cars, can sometimes hit as they fishtail exiting a corner but, frankly, I do not feel the 3-inch spacing is a problem. Scalextric Sport track is the smoothest of these three brands but it is not quite as smooth as Carrera. SCX is the roughest but it is not quite as rough as Ninco.

Ninco Track

Ninco's track is also flexible, somewhat similar to Scalextric Sport, but it has the roughest surface of all the popular brands of track. The rough surface makes it relatively difficult to power slide cars, but some racers feel that is a major advantage. Ninco's track has 3-1/2-inch lane spacing, which is wider than Scalextric Sport, Scalextric Classic, and SCX, but not as wide as Carrera.

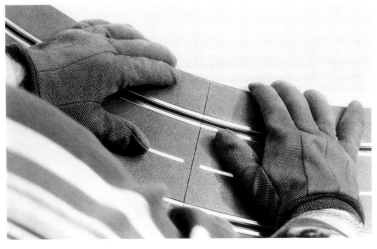

Carrera Track

Carrera track is made of relatively hard plastic with 4-inch lane spacing. It's wide enough to run 1/24 scale cars, but only Carrera makes truly realistic ready-to-run 1/24 scale cars. You can, however, use a variety of chassis to convert plastic display model kits or cast-resin kits into slot cars. Personally, I see the main benefit of the wider lane spacing being broader curves which, in turn, means the 1/32 scale cars appear to handle just a bit more like racing cars than go-karts. Carrera uses a special steel alloy that will not rust for the pickup rails, while the other makers use plated steel. As a result, any car that runs on Carrera track has about one-third the magnetic downforce it would if running on Scalextric, SCX, or Ninco track. That's not a particular problem because replacement magnets are available if you really want stronger downforce. Some racers feel it is easier to control a power slide on the rougher track surfaces, but I find it easier to control the slide on the smoother Carrera or Scalextric Sport track. Because of its surface and the wide choice of both flat and banked turns with borders to fit them all, Carrera is probably the closest you can get to duplicating the look and feel of a hand-routed track with plastic track.

Artin Track

Artin barely makes it as a hobby brand. It is really a toy, but it is very well-engineered and by far the least expensive. It has the same basic problem as the Revell, Monogram, and Strombecker track of the 1960s: there are only standard and outer curves, which limits your choice of track designs. In fact, Artin does not offer even half-straights or half-length inner curves, but you can learn how to cut your own half-sections later in this chapter. The Artin surface is about equal to Carrera's, with similar alloy-steel pickup rails. I cannot tell you where to buy it, because it is commonly sold in huge quantities to large retailers like JCPenney and the TV shopping channels. But because of its price and limited mass distribution, there's a lot of Artin track out there and it is cheap.

Riggen/Revell, Monogram, and Strombecker Track

Revell, Monogram, and Strombecker were the most popular brands of track in the 1960s. Today, REH produces Revell track in black plastic (the original was dark gray) under the Riggen label. REH also has a large supply of Strombecker track. Bachmann manufactured the Strombecker track in the early-1980s, of which REH has some supplies as well. Only standard curves and full-length straight track sections are available today for any of these brands, so your options are very limited. In addition, borders for these brands are extremely difficult to find anywhere. You may be able to search out used track on the Internet, but why? If you want a broad selection of track, any one of the current brands is at least as good as these older brands, and you have the valuable option of different curve sizes.

Interchanging Track Brands

My advice is simple: *don't mix brands of track!* The only exception is Scalextric Classic track and SCX track, which are very similar. Yes, Scalextric offers adapters to interchange Sport with Classic, but all it takes is one section of Classic on the track to lose the deeper-slot advantage that Sport track offers. Ninco sells an adapter to mate their track to Scalextric Classic or SCX, which means you can connect Sport track to Ninco by using both the Scalextric Sport adapter and the Scalextric Sport/Ninco adapter: it's an interesting exercise in using up all the track you may have accumulated.

I definitely applaud both Scalextric Sport and Ninco for offering the adapters because it means less of a financial shock if you decide to change from one brand to the other. During the interim period of the changeover, you can run some of each until you accumulate the funds for a complete changeover (even if you just buy a few sections a week of your new favorite). But it is very difficult to decide which brand is best and you may have to actually buy at least a figure-eight size set of the brands you are considering so you can try them yourself.

Banked Turns

Only Carrera offers true banked turns, with a choice of inner, middle, and outer curves, each of which is available with a border. The banked turns can be extremely effective in re-creating the character of circuits that have banked turns, including NASCAR ovals and tri-ovals, Indianapolis, and Monza. You will see banked turns on the Carrera versions of the Daytona tracks and the Indy F1 Grand Prix tracks in chapter 5. Scalextric Sport, Scalextric Classic, SCX, and Ninco track joints are flexible enough to allow you to force the track into a bank: simply make the straights just a

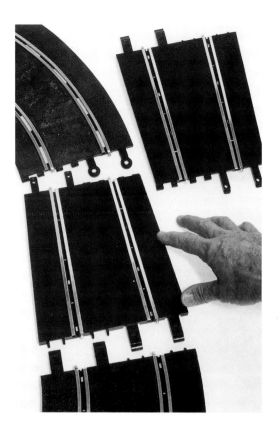

Ninco track (bottom) has a 3-1/2-inch lane spacing, while Scalextric Classic (top), Scalextric Sport, and SCX have a 3-inch lane spacing. Ninco offers a Number 10110 adapter track to join Scalextric or SCX track to Ninco. Scalextric Sport offers an adapter for Sport to Scalextric Classic or SCX—use that plus this adapter to connect Scalextric Sport track to Ninco.

fraction too short by assembling the last straight section from shorter sections. You will, however, need to support a four-lane track or a track with borders with 1/16-inch plywood or a similar thin sheet material to keep the side-by-side tracks and borders in alignment. It's far simpler and just about as effective to simply prop up the curve you want to be banked. But, again, it must be supported with thin plywood. The Carrera banks, on the other hand, are already molded into the proper shape and need be supported only with the posts that are supplied with Carrera bank turn track sections.

This four-lane banked turn from the Daytona International Speedway is assembled from Carrera middle and outer banked turns with borders as shown in chapter 5. The black tubular supports are furnished with the Carrera banked track sections.

Picking the Best Track: Pros and Cons

Scalextric Sport Track

Pros:

· Snap-together assembly and disassembly
· Locks together well on a solid floor or tabletop
· Good variety of different track sections
· Great-looking borders for all curves
· Borders for all curves are wide
· Great-looking guard rails
· Excellent low-cost lap counter/timers
· Plug-in option for reversing
· Highly recommended Pacer option to race against yourself
· Can be adapted to Scalextric Classic , SCX, and Ninco
· Connector track with built-in brakes, reversing, and individual lane power

Cons:

· Borders do not attach firmly enough for use on crossing bridges
· Lane spacing a bit close for modern Formula 1 and sports/GT cars
· No banked curves available

Scalextric Classic Track

Pros:

· Easiest track to assemble and disassemble
· Because of its ease of assembly, it is a good track for younger children
· Locks together well on a solid floor or tabletop
· Good compromise between too little and too much traction
· Best variety of different track sections
· Cars are less noisy on this relatively soft track
· Flexible enough to allow some misalignment
· Flexible enough to allow slight banking in turns
· Great-looking borders for standard curves
· Borders for all curves are wide enough
· Great-looking guard rails for standard curves
· Excellent low-cost lap counter/timers
· Plug-in option for reversing
· Highly recommended Pacer option allows you to race against yourself
· Interchanges with SCX and can be adapted to Scalextric Sport and Ninco

Cons:

· Track comes apart too easily to be moved without compete disassembly
· Borders do not attach firmly enough for use on crossing bridges
· Must buy second transformer and connector track for individual power supply to each lane
· Slot too shallow for many other brands of cars
· No outer-outer curves available
· Lane spacing a bit close for modern Formula 1 and sports/GT cars
· No banked curves available
· Color of outer curve and straight borders not realistic

SCX Track

Pros:

· See Scalextric Classic
· Outer-outer lanes available
· Best-looking borders of all the tracks

Cons:

· See Scalextric Classic
· Track surface too rough in some racers' opinions
· Borders are too narrow to be really useful
· Can be more difficult to find
· Must use Scalextric track section for individual lane power supply
· No self-racing program track available

Ninco Track

Pros:

· Track assembles easily and holds together well
· Offers outer-outer curves
· Slot deep enough to allow any brand of car to operate
· Cars are less noisy on this relatively soft track
· Flexible enough to allow some misalignment
· Flexible enough to allow some banking in turns
· Borders available for inside and outside of all curves
· Borders for outer curves are wide enough
· Individual lane power is standard
· Reversing is standard
· Brake feature is standard

Cons:

· Track surface too rough in some racers' opinions
· Can be more difficult to find
· Can be more expensive
· No banked track available
· Color of borders not realistic
· No self-racing program track available

Carrera Track

Pros:

· Track holds together tightly enough to operate on carpet and to move
· Offers outer-outer curves
· Offers borders for all curves
· Borders are wide enough for any 1/32 scale car
· Offers banked turns
· Connector track has built-in brake feature
· Slot is deep enough for any brand of car
· Individual lane power standard
· Brakes are standard

Cons:

· Can be difficult for those under 12 years old to disassemble
· Plastic tabs can break off if track is carelessly disassembled
· Track can break easily if stepped on
· No reversing available
· Borders are black with unrealistic "construction zone" yellow chevrons
· No self-racing program track available

Artin Track

Pros:

· Lowest cost of all brands
· Track locks together easily and firmly
· Borders attach easily and firmly

Cons:

· Can be difficult for those under 12 years old to disassemble
· Plastic tabs can break off if track is carelessly disassembled
· Track can easily break if stepped on
· No reversing available
· Borders are black with unrealistic "construction zone" yellow chevrons
· No self-racing program track available

Riggen (Revell) and Strombecker/Bachmann Track

Pros:

· Locks together tightly
· Lane spacing wide enough for cars to run side by side

Cons:

· Can be difficult for those under 12 years olds to disassemble
· No half inner curves available
· No half straights available
· No borders available
· Track can easily break if stepped on
· No self-racing program track available

Track Assembly Tricks

When assembling Carrera track with borders or for four-lanes, snap subassemblies of borders (or both lanes with their borders) together. It is nearly impossible to add borders or another lane: the side-to-side connections must be made first, then the end-to-end connections of each border/track subassembly. When I am designing a track of any brand on a tabletop, I usually try to have a few modules of 90-degree turns and four or five lengths of straight track assembled and, with Carrera track, locked together complete with borders. Chapter 3 shows one of the 9x12-foot tracks at this planning stage, with several assembled Carrera track modules.

Track Maintenance

Plastic track sections are rugged enough to last for decades of use without noticeable wear. The track does get dusty, however, so wipe over it with one of the new oil-free floor-cleaning rags designed to pick up lint. Use a vacuum cleaner with a hose attachment to vacuum out the slots (SCX makes a battery-powered vacuum for just this purpose). Never use steel wool to clean the pickup strips because the fibers can work their way into the motor magnets and short out the motor. Do not use a file or emery paper to clear the rails either, because they will just create rougher surfaces and can eat right through the plating on all but Carrera track. Clean the pickup rails with a hard rubber eraser. If the track has oil residue from the cars, wash it off with a sponge dampened with mild detergent or window cleaner like Windex. If you use detergent, wipe over the track again three or four times with another sponge dampened in clear water to rinse away the oily residue. Do not, however, literally flood the track because the edges of the rails can rust. If the track has been sitting for more than a week or so, wipe over the rails with a piece of tough cloth like canvas to remove traces of oxidation that can hinder electrical contact.

Troubleshooting Track

Usually if a car does not run, it is the fault of the pickup brushes on the car, so try another car or two that you know run properly. (For more information on troubleshooting cars, see chapter 7.) It is unusual for the metal contacts between track sections to be at fault, but it can happen. The three-tabs on the male portions of the track connections on most brands can become bent and slip over—rather than inside—the adjoining

track. Check the joints at both ends of any offending track section.

Carrera uses a slip-in metal clip at the terminal tracks rather than a soldered joint. If the Carrera terminal track is not functioning, remove the plastic plate from the bottom of the track section and gently pull the clips out of the metal rails. Polish the faces of the clips with a model railroad track-cleaning eraser to remove oxidation and pry the contacts apart slightly before reinserting them. If you want to be really sure they make contact, solder the wires to the pickup rails as shown in chapters 13 and 14.

It is not unusual for cars to jam in the slot with Scalextric Classic, SCX, or Ninco track. The trouble occurs near the ends of the track and results from the methods used to hold these track sections together (all three brands use a peg-and-loop system to join track sections). It is tempting to disassemble Scalextric, SCX, or Ninco track by pulling upward on the free end of the track so the loops snap off the pegs. It's quick, but if the loops hang up you can bend the track upward slightly at the ends. On Scalextric, SCX, and Ninco track, that usually forces the rails inward, and they can bend far enough to make the slot so narrow that the pickup will not fit.

Sometimes when the problem merely appears to be bumpy track, it's not the track that is at fault, but rather the pickup rails. Use finger pressure (you may want to wear gloves) to gently bend the rails downward so they are perfectly flush with the surface of the track. Use a large flat-head screwdriver to gently pry the rails apart so the slot is the same width for the full length of the track section. Sometimes the plastic sides of the slot on the ends of Ninco track sections can be permanently bent inward from improper track disassembly. You may be able shave away the protruding plastic with a hobby knife or single-edge razor blade. It's better, however, if you can spread the plastic on each side of the

Carrera connects terminal track wires to steel alloy rails with small copper clips that snap inside the rails. If the terminal track is not providing power, remove the clip and polish it, bend it out slightly for better contact, and reinsert it inside the rail.

Ninco slot apart and cement the plastic to the rails with Super Glue—just be certain not to use Super Glue when the track is joined to another track section.

Custom-Fit Borders

Carrera, Scalextric Sport and Classic, SCX, Ninco, and Artin all offer borders to extend the width of the track so power-sliding cars will not fall off the edge of the track. Each manufacturer has its own name for these track width–extending pieces, including "shoulders," "skid aprons," "aprons," and "inside tracks." "Borders" is the most common, so I will use that term in this book.

Borders definitely make model car racing more fun. I strongly recommend that you fit every corner with borders so you can, if you wish, power slide around each. You will also need borders for at least 2 feet down every straight to give the cars time to straighten out as they fishtail out of the corners. If you want to be able to run the track in both directions, you'll need to install borders for at least 2 feet from both ends of every straight. You will also need inside curve borders in any ess bends because the cars leaving the outer lane can easily fishtail right off the track as they swing through the ess from the outer lane to the adjoining inner lane in the middle of the ess. If you take a close look at the tracks in

Custom-cut borders for Carrera 1/3-straight, 1/4-straight, and 1/2-inner curve (an inner curve border Number 2051 cut in half with a razor saw).

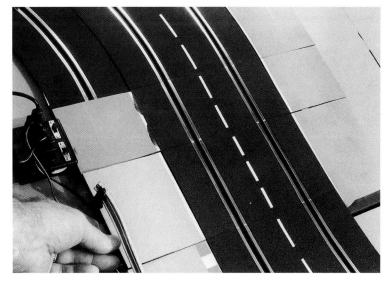

Top: Borders for 1/4-length (shown) and 1/3-length Carrera straight track can be cut from a full-length straight border. Plug the border into two sections of 1/4-straight as shown and mark where to cut the border with masking tape. Make the cuts with a razor saw.

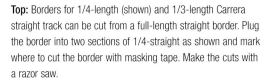

Above: The leftover pieces of Carrera border can be cemented together with metal-filled epoxy to make another 1/4-length border (left) in addition to the two with tabs (right). The leftover 1/4 border can also be used, supported by the tabs from adjacent borders.

Three custom-cut borders for Carrera track (top to bottom): an inner border for a 20572 middle curve cut from a piece of 20571 curve; a 1/4-length straight (built into a custom terminal connector track as shown in chapter 14); and a 1/3-straight. The red Carrera guardrails are painted a more realistic silver using chrome-colored automobile paint.

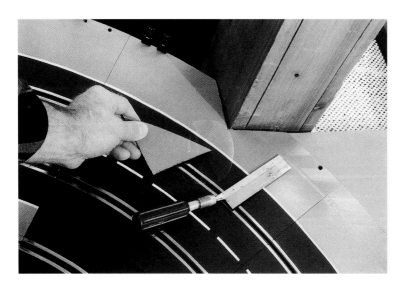

You can often fit a track plan in a tighter area if you are willing to sacrifice a border or two. I used the razor saw to cut this triangle from the Carrera curve border to fit the track closer to the pole. There's still ample room for the cars to slide around the curve.

Below left: To make a border to fit inside the Carrera Number 20572 middle-size curve, cut the smaller inner curve (Number 20571) in half using the dotted white lines as guides. Use a saber saw with a fine-tooth blade to make the cut

Far right: The outer half of the just-cut Carrera 20571 curve can be painted green to match all the other borders and fitted inside the 20571 curve. The plastic tabs Carrera offers for four-lane track connections can be used to attach the border if necessary.

chapters 5 and 8 you'll see that there are really very few places on the track that do *not* need borders. Yes, you can install the clip-on fences that come with the sets, but then the fence, not the driver, is controlling the car.

The borders for Scalextric Sport, Scalextric Classic, and SCX are interchangeable—and none of them grip the track tightly enough unless you tape on the border with duct tape or screw it to a tabletop. There are, however, some serious missing borders that you may want to custom-cut for yourself. "Missing borders" are those for the inside of curves, particularly on Carrera track. SCX offers inner borders for their curves that will also fit Scalextric Sport and Scalextric Classic track. Sport offers only half-length borders which, when used as two end-to-end, work nicely for full-length straights. Scalextric and Carrera do not offer inner borders for anything except the standard curved track included in most sets. Ninco makes borders to fit both inside and outside of every curve and every straight track section.

You can cut the missing borders from existing borders or track sections. Carrera borders are designed to plug into the side of the track, so you may loose that feature with some of the custom-cut borders. Carrera has tiny clips that help the borders snap tightly, but the tabs from adjacent borders will do most of the work. Because Scalextric Sport, Scalextric Classic, and SCX borders are held in place with tiny tabs that do not hold well, I recommend that you use duct tape to hold borders onto any of these three brands.

I'm going to show you how to custom cut borders for Carrera track; you can use the same techniques to cut Scalextric Sport, Scalextric Classic, and SCX borders. A single Carrera number 20560 border (Carrera calls them "shoulders") can provide the material for two borders on the number 20612 1/4-length or 20611 1/3-length straight track pieces. Plug the two tabs on the border into two of the short pieces of track. Use the edges of the track as guides to mark where to cut the border and make the cut with a razor saw. If you are cutting two 1/4-length aprons, the leftover ends can be joined to form a third 1/4-length border and the leftover middle is a fourth 1/4-length border. The tabs on the adjacent borders will support these short borders adequately. If you need to cut two Carrera 1/3-length borders, you can assemble the three leftover scraps into a single border. Cement the cut borders together with metal-filled epoxy—plastic cement will not make the joint strong enough. You may also need to cut one or two inside curve borders by simply sawing one of the Carrera 20551 borders in half.

Borders for the inside of the Carrera number 20572 middle curves, 20573 outer curves, and the 20578 outer-outer curves can be cut from the next smaller track section. Yes, you will waste some track, but you won't need many of

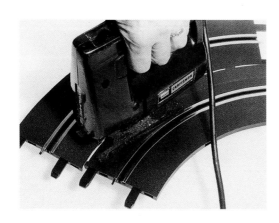

these inside curve borders. In fact, I have only actually needed about four inside curve borders, all for the inside edges of the 20572 curves. The leftover half can be used on the outside of the custom-made (number 0) curve from Brad's Tracks if you choose to obtain one of these track sections (see below). Use a saber saw with the finest-tooth blade you can find. You'll find that the blade melts and tears the plastic more than it cuts, so be prepared to file a bit to get the cut edge smooth.

One final note: I do not like the yellow stripes on the Carrera borders, they remind me of construction zones, not race tracks. It's easy enough to paint the borders a grass green or sand beige as shown in chapter 4 and in *Racing and Collecting Slot Cars*. Virtually all the Carrera borders you'll see in this book have been painted.

The Number 0 Curve

Carrera numbers their curves 1, 2, 3, and 4, with number 1 being the curve that's included in most sets. Carrera does not make an inner-inner curve to match the ones available from Scalextric Sport, Scalextric Classic, Ninco, and SCX. If Carrera did make such a curve, they would have to call it a "number 0." The innermost slot in the Brad's Tracks custom inner curve is moved closer to the outer slot for a larger radius, just as Scalextric Sport has done with their combination of C8201 Hairpin Turns and C8246 Sideswipe Straights. Brad's Tracks custom-made inner-inner turn for Carrera fits inside a 180-degree turn made from three 20571 curves and two 20509 standard straights. The smooth flow of the track into the 180-degree corner works with any car I've tried

Top: All these borders are Carrera, but they have been painted grass green or sand beige for more realism. The inner border for the left curve is the one cut from a 20571 curve.

Center: The most famous corner on the Monaco Grand Prix circuit, Loews Hairpin (or Station Hairpin as it was known in the 1960s), can be modeled with either Scalextric Sport or Carrera (shown) plastic track as described in chapter 5. This is the turn assembled from the smallest Number 20571 curves.

Right: Brad's Tracks offers a custom-made inner-inner curve for Carrera track to fit inside Carrera's smallest standard curve. The custom curve is a 180-degree turn with the innermost lane moved out to a more useful radius. This is the optional treatment for Loews Hairpin on the Monaco track from chapter 5.

(as it does on the Sport system). If you need borders for a Brad's Tracks inner curve on a two-lane track, like the Monaco track in chapter 5, they can be cut from the outer halves of Carrera 20571 curves and the leftover halves used as inside borders for 20572 curves as described earlier.

Custom-Cut Artin Half-Sections

Artin track has the same 30-degree geometry as Carrera track and the older Revell, Monogram, and Strombecker track. The inside curve covers a full 60-degrees, however, so it is impossible to make a 90-degree curve using inside Artin curves.

To make 1/2-length straight and curve sections from Artin (shown), Ninco, or SCX track, remove the 5-1/4-inch half from the middle of the track section (not the end), so you can retain the assembly tabs on the extreme ends. Use a hobby knife to scribe a line 2-5/8 inches in from each end of the track. Use a machinist's square or drafting triangle to get the line perfectly straight.

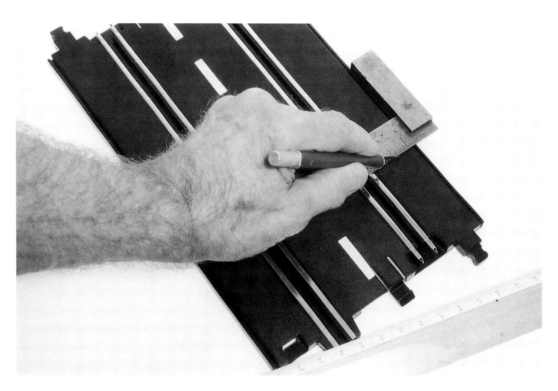

Turn the Artin track over and pry the tabs that attach the rails inward so you can push the rails from the track. Use a razor saw to slice along the lines you just scribed.

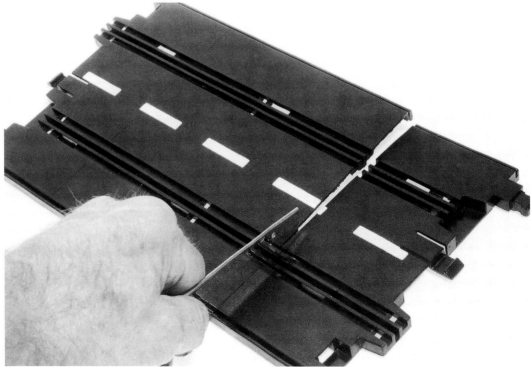

To make the Artin half-curve, remove half the length of the curve from the middle of the track section as you did for the half-straight. Mark the line 3-1/4 inches in from the outer edge of each end of the curve. Use the outer curve to guide a ruler when you scribe the cut line with a hobby knife. Remove the rails and cut along the scribed lines with a razor saw.

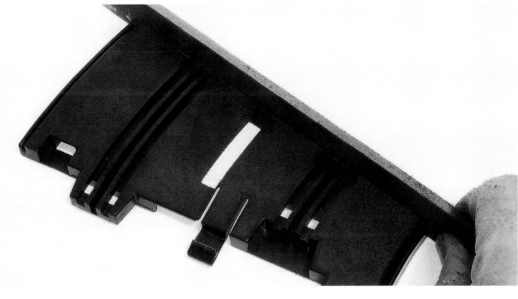

Use a flat machinist's file or a cabinetmaker's file to smooth the cut ends of the track.

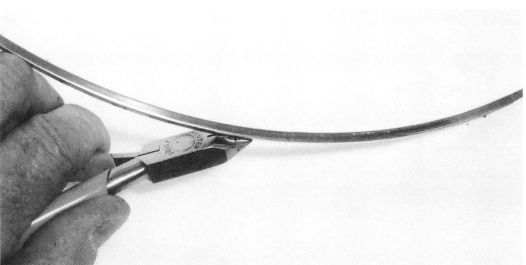

Use diagonal cutters to remove the tabs from the center of the rails.

The Artin outside curves are half the length of the inside curves, so three of them can be used to make a 90-degree turn. If you want to be able to create interesting race tracks out of Artin track, you will need at least two of their half-length standard curves. You will also discover that you need four or more half-length straights.

You can use a razor saw to cut the Artin straights and standard curves in half, but each full-length track section will only yield a single half-length section (the middle half is scrap). As with the custom-cut borders from Carrera track, use metal-filled epoxy to reassemble the cut sections. You will see both the curved and straight half-length sections in the Artin versions of the Daytona tri-oval and the Daytona road course in chapter 3.

Custom-Cut Ninco Half-Sections

Ninco uses the 45-degree curve geometry that is also the basis for the Scalextric Classic, Scalextric Sport, and SCX track systems. The Ninco track is a bit wider than these other three, but you can usually fit a complete Ninco racetrack in the same space as a Scalextric or SCX track, though you may need to add a few short lengths of straight track to get everything to properly line up. Ninco does not yet make a half-length (22-1/2 degree) curve, although they have suggested they might make one in the future. In the meantime, you cannot use Ninco track to assemble the plans for Scalextric track that require half inner curves (marked "H" on the plans) for Daytona (pages 36 and 84), Monaco (pages 63 and 64), Indy F1 (page 78), or Suzuka (pages 86 and 87), unless you are willing to make half-length Ninco standard curves. Use the same step-by-step techniques shown for cutting Artin track, dividing the 45-degree curve into four equal segments and removing the two inner segments, then rejoining the outer quarters to produce a 1/2-curve of 22-1/2 degrees. Ninco does make short straights, so only the 1/2–standard curves need to be custom cut.

SCX Half-Sections

SCX does not make half-length standard curve track sections, either. Fortunately, Scalextric Classic does offer the half-length standard straights, and the SCX system is interchangeable with the Scalextric Classic, so you can simply use the Scalextric C154 half-length standard curve section with SCX track.

Right: The rails will help hold the cut halves of the Artin plastic track together. Test fit the parts and double-check the length of the track sections to be sure they really are exactly half the length of the standard straight (shown) and curve tracks.

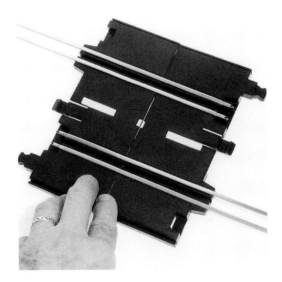

Below: Cover the track with a second piece of waxed paper and position some heavy weights (these are old cast-iron irons) to hold the track in alignment while the epoxy cures overnight.

Far right: Cover a piece of glass with a foot-square piece of waxed paper. Place the track face down on the waxed paper and apply a thick bead of metal-filled epoxy to the joint. Use a scrap of plastic to spread the epoxy evenly and to work it into the joint.

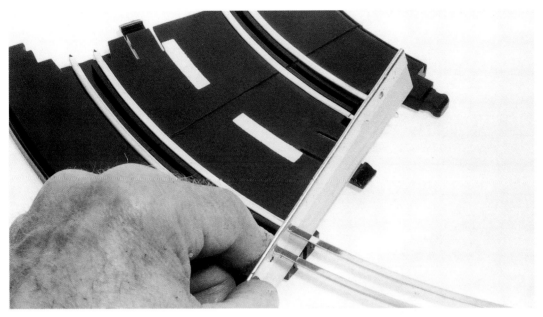

Use the razor saw to cut the plain ends of the rails (the opposite ends have the male connector plugs) flush with the end of the track.

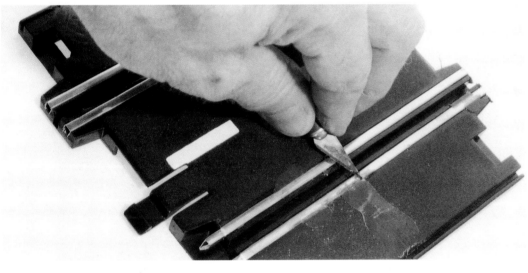

Some of the epoxy will flow over the rails: use a hobby knife to scrape away any excess epoxy so the pickup rails are perfectly clean. You may also need to whittle some blobs of epoxy from the slot so it is perfectly clear.

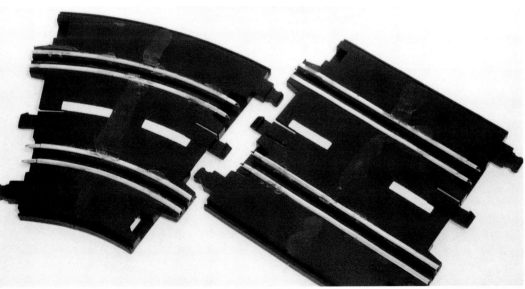

The two critical components of an Artin track system: a 1/2-standard curve and a 1/2-straight. Since Artin does not offer them you can make your own. I'd suggest making at least two 1/2-curves and four 1/2-straights, but some plans could require more.

Chapter Three

TRACKS FOR PING-PONG AND OTHER PORTABLE TABLES

There's plenty of room on a Ping-Pong table, even for a four-lane raceway.

Plastic track makes it possible for anyone to assemble an endless variety of race tracks in his or her home. It is also sturdy enough to set up on the floors of dens, living rooms, garages, and, in the summer, even on outside decks and patios. A table is definitely not a need. However, it is far more enjoyable to race your cars where you do not have to kneel or squat. If you assemble the sectional track on a table, you can stand. And, if you want trackside views, you can sit. What you might need, though, is a table that is as portable as the track.

Race Tracks for Portable Tables

Any of the tracks in this chapter will fit on a 5x9-foot Ping-Pong table, which also means they will

fit on a pair of 2-1/2-x10-foot conference tables set up side by side. In fact, you can even enlarge these 5x9-foot plans by adding another piece of straight track to all the tracks that parallel the long edges of the tracks. You can certainly purchase two or more Ping-Pong tables and/or a half-dozen conference tables to provide the portable tabletop space for the raceway of your dreams.

Racing in 4x8 Feet

It is possible to set up a 1/32 scale track on a sheet of 4x8-foot plywood, but it's very cramped (there are some tracks for Rally cars in chapter 8 that fit in a 4x8-foot area). However, the curves for 1/32 scale cars are small enough so you can easily fit a simple oval or rectangular Indy

500–style track in a 4x8-foot space. There's even enough room on a 4x8-foot board for a four-lane oval using Scalextric Sport, Scalextric Classic, SCX, Ninco, or Carrera standard and outer curves, with about three lengths of straight for the straightaways. The plans for six-lane ovals in 5x9-foot areas in *Racing and Collecting Slot Cars* work for a four-lane track in a 4x8-foot space if you assemble only the inner four lanes. Oval racing is far more fun than you might imagine, because the lanes are much more equal than you would expect. You'd be surprised at how many owners of garage-size tracks also set up a simple oval just to race with friends.

Four Lanes on a 5x9-Foot Ping-Pong Table

There's just enough room to fit a few different four-lane tracks on a Ping-Pong table. There are plans in this chapter for the Daytona International Speedway's tri-oval and road courses for both two lanes and four. In addition to the eight plans for 5x9-foot Ping-Pong table–size tracks in this book, there are seven track plans for two-lane 1/32 scale sectional track road racing courses in *Racing and Collecting Slot Cars*, including 5x9-foot Indy F1 tracks for Scalextric Sport, Scalextric Classic, SCX, and Carrera.

Track Section Key to 1/32 Scale Scalextric Sport, Scalextric Classic, SCX, and Ninco Track Plans

Each plan in this book has letters on every track section so you can identify the track sections that are required. This chart will show you which pieces are used. Scalextric numbers their curves starting with R1 for the inner, R2 for the standard used in most sets, R3 for the outer, and R4 for the outer-outer.

Key	Description	Sport Part No.	Scalextric Part No.	SCX Part No.	Sport Border	SCX Border
Z	Hairpin Curve	C8201	none	none	C8240 (x2)	none
U	1/2 Inner Curve	C8202	C152	84010	C8240	78940
I	Inner Curve	C8202 (x2)	C156	84010 (x2)	C8240 (x2)	none
H	1/2 Standard Curve	C8234	C154	none	C8239	none
S	Standard Curve	C8206	C151	84000	C8228	87930
O	Outer Curve	C8204	C153	84020	C8224	87950
OO	Outer-Outer Curve	C8235	none	84030	C8238	87960
E	1/4-Straight	C8200	C158	84040	none	none
D	1/2-Straight	C8222	C159	84050	C8223	none
B	Full-Straight	C8205	C160	84060	C8223 (x2)	87920
A	Connector	C8217	C8014	84240	C8223 (x2)	87920
	(Good location for plug-in controller track. Replace one standard straight, above)					
C	Chicane Track	C8246	C8031	84180	C18223 (x2)	87920
	(Good Location for chicane. Replace two standard straights, above)					

Note: Ninco utilizes the same 45-degree curve geometry and straight track length as Scalextric and SCX, so most of these plans can be adapted to use Ninco track. A slightly larger space will be required and some 1/4-straight sections may be needed to maintain track alignment. Ninco does not offer a half inner curve or a half standard curve, although you can custom-cut a Ninco standard curve to make a half-section using the techniques in chapter 2.

Track Section Key to 1/32 Scale Carrera and Artin Track Plans

Each plan in this book has letters on every track section to help you identify the track sections that are required. This chart will show you which pieces are used. Carrera numbers their curves with number 1 for the inner curve, number 2 for the middle curve, number 3 for the outer curve, and number 4 for the outer-outer curve. I have assigned a number 0 to the inner-inner curve custom-made by Brad's Tracks as shown in chapters 2 and 5. Carrera's banked curves occupy the same table space and they are assigned the same 1, 2, and 3 size numbers.

Key	Description	Carrera Part No.	Border Part No.	Artin Part No.	Border Part No.
I	Inner-Inner Curve	Custom-made. See chapters 2 and 5		none	none
H	1/2 Inner Curve	20577	20567	Custom-made. See chapter 2	
S	Inner Curve	20571	20561	5712	in set*
K	Banked Inner Curve	20574	20564	5714	in set*
O	Middle Curve	20572	20562	5718	in set*
M	Banked Middle Curve	20576	20565	none	none
OO	Outer Curve	20573	20563	none	none
OOO	Outer-Outer Curve	XXXXX	XXXXX	none	none
N	Banked Outer Curve	20575	20566	none	none
E	1/4-Straight	20612	none	See chapter 2 for custom-made 1/2-straight.	
D	1/3-Straight	20611	none	none	none
B	Full-Straight	20509	20560	5711	none
Q	Overpass Bridge (Crossing)	20545	none	none	none
R	1/2 of Overpass Bridge	20545	none	none	none
A	Connector (Good location for plug-in controller track. Replace one standard straight, above)	20515	20560	in set	none
C	Chicane Track (Good Location for chicane. Replace two standard straights, above)	20516	20560	5717	none

Note: Artin utilizes the same 30-degree curve geometry as Carrera, so some of these plans can be adapted to use Carrera track, although a slightly smaller space will be required. Artin does not offer 1/2 inner curve sections, so you must use outer curves anywhere a half-curve is required. Also, Artin does not offer 1/2-, 1/3-, or 1/4-length straight track sections, so you may not be able to make the track align properly for some of these plans unless you are willing to cut special sections to fit as shown in chapter 2.

In addition, Artin does not offer borders as accessories because they are included in most sets. Borders for two-lane standard curves are only available with two-lane sets. Curves for outer borders are only available in four-lane sets.

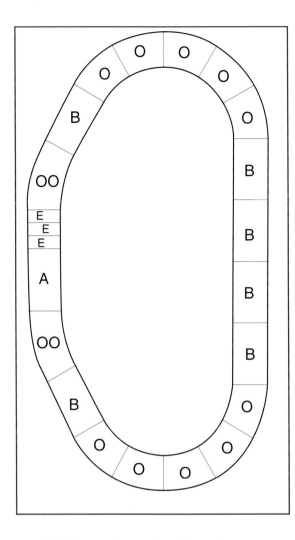

This two-lane version of the Daytona International Speedway tri-oval occupies less than 5x9-feet of area. You can set it up on the floor or on a Ping-Pong table.

5x9 Daytona International Speedway for Carrera

If you can find 5x9 feet of space, either on a Ping-Pong table or on the floor, you can assemble a reasonable replica of the Daytona International Speedway using Carrera track sections. Start with the two-lane version of the Daytona tri-oval for Carrera track. The track is shown here with flat curves on each end, but you can substitute the banked Carrera turns in the same space. It is also possible to fit Carrera inner curves, either flat or banked, inside the tri-oval shown here to create a four-lane track.

5x9 Daytona International Speedway for Scalextric and SCX

Scalextric Speedway sets include a two-lane tri-oval that will fit on a 5x9-foot Ping-Pong table. The Scalextric Super Speedway set has enough track to fit outside the Speedway set and thereby convert it to a four-lane tri-oval, but it requires nearly 6x10 feet of space.

LIST OF CARRERA TRACK REQUIRED FOR 5x9-FOOT DAYTONA TRI-OVAL

Key	Quantity	Description
H	0	1/2 Inner (1) Curve
I	0	Inner-Inner (0) Curve
S	0	Inner (1) Curve
K	0	Banked Inner (1) Curve
O	10	Middle (2) Curve
M	0	Banked Middle (2) Curve
OO	2	Outer-Outer (3) Curve
OOO	0	Outer-Outer-Outer (4) Curve
N	0	Banked Outer (3) Curve
E	3	1/4-Straight
D	0	1/3-Straight
B	6	Full-Straight
Q	0	Overpass Bridge
R	0	1/2 of Overpass Bridge
A	1	Connector Track
C	0	Chicane

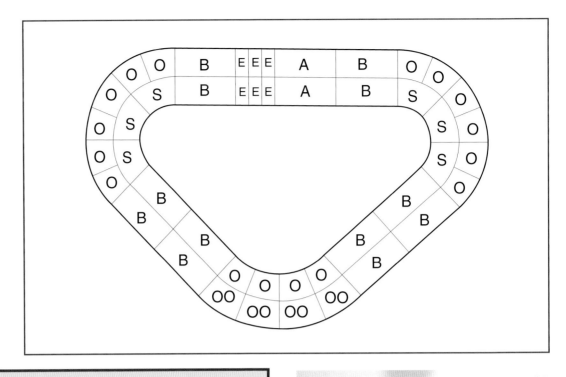

Lower right: Some Ping-Pong tables fold onto their own 2x5-foot dolly with casters. You can store the boxed track and portable scenery (see chapter 4) inside the folded-up table.

Bottom: You can assemble this four-lane Daytona International Speedway tri-oval on a Ping-Pong table using Scalextric Sport, Scalextric Classic, SCX, or Ninco track sections.

LIST OF SCALEXTRIC SPORT, SCALEXTRIC CLASSIC, OR SCX TRACK REQUIRED FOR 5x9-FOOT DAYTONA TRI-OVAL

Key	Quantity	Description
H	0	1/2 Standard (R2) Curve
I	0	Inner-Inner (R1) Curve
S	6	Standard (R2) Curve
O	16	Outer (R3) Curve
OO	4	Outer-Outer (R4) Curve
E	6	1/4-Straight
D	0	1/2-Straight
B	12	Full-Straight
V	0	Crossover Track
A	2	Connector Track
C	0	Chicane

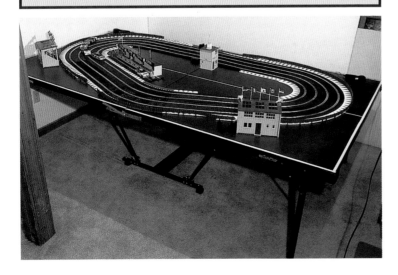

The Daytona tri-oval for Scalextric Sport, Scalextric Classic, and SCX track sections shown here utilizes outer-outer curves for the start-finish turn at the bottom of the track and allows four lanes of racing in a 5x9-foot area. A similar track can be assembled from Ninco track sections.

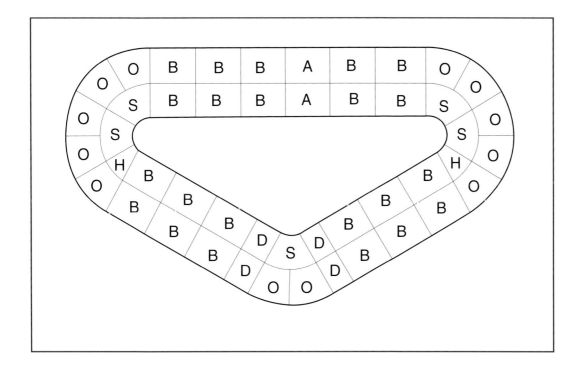

Artin only makes three useful track sections: a standard straight (B), a standard curve (S), and an outer curve (O) plus a terminal track (A). To assemble this track you will need to custom-cut two 1/2-standard curves (H) and four 1/2-straights (D) as shown in chapter 2.

5x9 Daytona International Speedway for Artin

Artin track out of the box will not fit this small of an area. However, if you are willing to cut a pair of half-length inner curves and four half-length straights as described in chapter 2, you can assemble a four-lane Daytona tri-oval from Artin track in a 5x9-foot area. If you are not willing to cut those half-length curves, you can assemble a track to include only the two outer lanes.

You can assemble the outer two lanes of this Artin Daytona tri-oval from standard Artin outer curves and straight track sections. The inner lane, however, requires two custom-cut, half-length curves and four half-length straights as described in chapter 2.

33

5x9 Daytona Road Race Course
for Scalextric and SCX

There is a plan of the real Daytona International Speedway's road racing circuit in chapter 5, as well as some larger versions of the track for 9x12 and up to 9x16-foot areas. However, you can squeeze a reasonable replica of the Daytona road course in just 5x9 feet. You can start with a two-lane track like the one in these plans and photos. You can expand the track to four lanes by fitting the third and fourth lanes inside this plan, but the infield curve must overlap the straight (as it does on the Carrera and Artin four-lane Daytona tracks in this chapter).

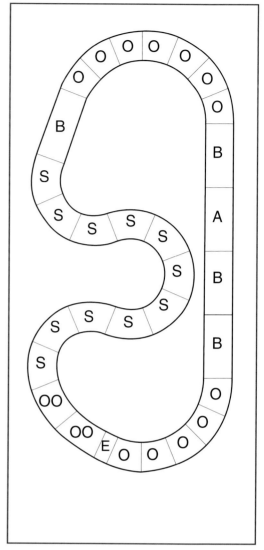

The two-lane road course at Daytona International Speedway assembled with Scalextric and SCX track on a Ping-Pong table.

	LIST OF SCALEXTRIC SPORT, SCALEXTRIC CLASSIC, OR SCX TRACK REQUIRED FOR 5x9-FOOT TWO-LANE DAYTONA ROAD COURSE		
Key	**Quantity**		**Description**
H	0		1/2 Standard (R2) Curve
I	0		Inner-Inner (R1) Curve
S	11		Standard (R2) Curve
O	12		Outer (R3) Curve
O	2		Outer-Outer (R4) Curve
E	1		1/4-Straight
D	0		1/2-Straight
B	4		Full-Straight
V	0		Crossover Track
A	1		Connector Track
C	0		Chicane

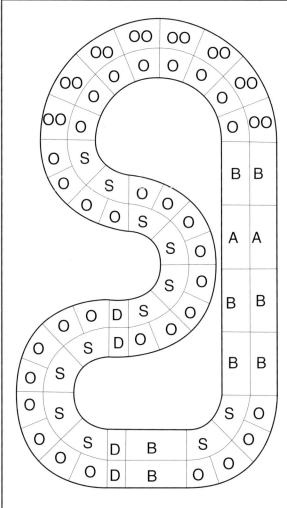

LIST OF SCALEXTRIC SPORT, SCALEXTRIC CLASSIC, OR SCX TRACK REQUIRED FOR 5x9-FOOT FOUR-LANE DAYTONA ROAD COURSE

Key	Quantity	Description
H	0	1/2 Standard (R2) Curve
I	0	Inner-Inner (R1) Curve
S	12	Standard (R2) Curve
O	32	Outer (R3) Curve
OO	8	Outer-Outer (R4) Curve
E	0	1/4-Straight
D	4	1/2-Straight
B	8	Full-Straight
V	0	Crossover Track
A	2	Connector Track
C	0	Chicane

5x9 Daytona Road Race Course for Carrera

There's enough room on a 5x9-foot Ping-Pong table for a two-lane version of the road course at Daytona. There is not enough room, however, to make effective use of the banked turns that Carrera offers: there is simply not enough length of straight track on both ends of the large curves for the track to flatten out for the center ess curves. Carrera's outer-outer curves are broad enough, however, to make this a very fast track indeed.

Carrera track is a bit wider than Ninco, Scalextric, and SCX. That extra width works well in a large space and is still compact enough for a two-lane track on a Ping-Pong table. It's a real squeeze, though, to fit four lanes of Carrera track in 5x9 feet; it can be done, as you can see by the plan, but the infield curve must overlap the middle of the main straight.

The four-lane Scalextric and SCX version of the road course at Daytona International Speedway. You can assemble any track in this book on the floor if you don't have a Ping-Pong table.

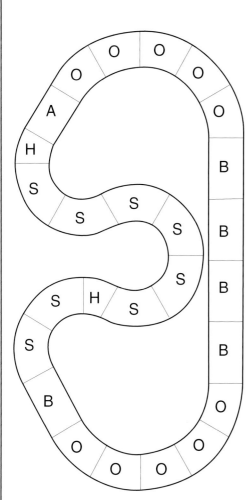

LIST OF CARRERA TRACK REQUIRED FOR 5x9-FOOT TWO-LANE DAYTONA ROAD COURSE

Key	Quantity	Description
H	2	1/2 Inner (1) Curve
I	0	Inner-Inner (0) Curve
S	8	Inner (1) Curve
K	0	Banked Inner (1) Curve
O	10	Middle (2) Curve
M	0	Banked Middle (2) Curve
O	0	Outer-Outer (3) Curve
OOO	0	Outer-Outer-Outer (4) Curve
N	0	Banked Outer (3) Curve
E	0	1/4-Straight
D	0	1/3-Straight
B	5	Full-Straight
Q	0	Overpass Bridge
R	0	1/2 of Overpass Bridge
A	1	Connector Track
C	0	Chicane

The two-lane version of the road course at the Daytona International Speedway for Carrera track fits nicely in a 5x9-foot area with no overlap of the infield ess bends or the main straight.

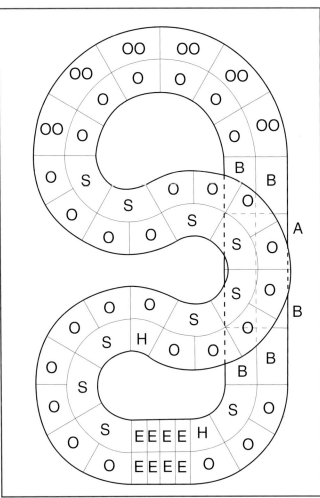

LIST OF CARRERA TRACK REQUIRED FOR 5x9-FOOT FOUR-LANE DAYTONA ROAD COURSE

Key	Quantity	Description
H	2	1/2 Inner (1) Curve
I	0	Inner-Inner (0) Curve
S	10	Inner (1) Curve
K	0	Banked Inner (1) Curve
O	28	Middle (2) Curve
M	0	Banked Middle (2) Curve
OO	6	Outer-Outer (3) Curve
OOO	0	Outer-Outer-Outer (4) Curve
N	0	Banked Outer (3) Curve
E	8	1/4-Straight
D	0	1/3-Straight
B	6	Full-Straight
Q	0	Overpass Bridge
R	0	1/2 of Overpass Bridge
A	2	Connector Track
C	0	Chicane

Above, left: The four-lane Carrera version of the road course at Daytona fits so tightly into a 5x9-foot area that the infield turn must overlap the main straight. It doesn't look much like Daytona, but thanks to the broad Carrera curves, it drives a lot like Daytona.

The road course at
Daytona International
for Artin track. The
ends of this track are
angled farther out than
for the tri-oval version.
This track will also
require four 1/2-
straights and two 1/2-
length standard curves
to be custom-cut as
described in chapter 2.

5x9 Daytona Road Race Course for Artin

Artin offers a very limited choice of track sections. You will need two half-length standard curves and four half-straights to assemble this 5x9-foot version of the road course at Daytona with Artin track. You can cut these sections from standard Artin track as shown in chapter 2.

Portable Track and Portable Tables

When it comes to portable tables, model-car racers have a wide selection. My first choice is a fold-up Ping-Pong table because it's large enough to hold a track all by itself and it is sturdy enough to withstand an excited racer grabbing across the table to re-slot his or her car. Fold-up Ping-Pong tables with self-contained storage platforms on casters sell for less than $300 and fold into a 2x5-foot space. There's even room to store the track sections inside the folded-up table so your 5x9-foot track need only occupy 2x5-feet of the room when it is stored. Once you have a plan you like, you can assemble it in less than a half-hour. I use a single Ping-Pong table as the anchor for the 9x14-foot portable tabletop you'll see later in this chapter.

Other excellent choices are conference tables with fold-up legs. Look for sales at office supply stores—you can often buy a 2-1/2x10-foot table for less than $50. Get two of them, set them up side by side, and you have a very sturdy 5x10-foot tabletop.

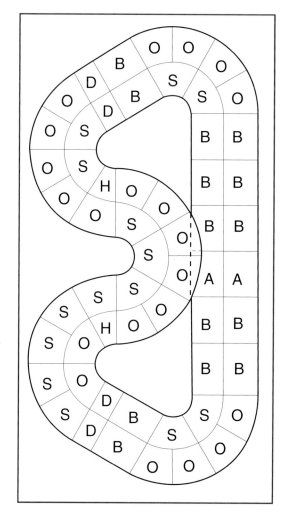

The Daytona road
course can be
assembled from Artin
track but, even for this
two-lane version, you
will need to cut two
1/2-length straights as
shown in chapter 2. To
complete the inner
lane, two more 1/2-
straights and two 1/2-
length curves will also
have to be custom-cut.

The third choice is to assemble a portable track by using the standard 4x8-foot sheets of 1/2-inch plywood.

Lightweight Portable Tabletops

All the tracks in chapter 5 were assembled on a portable 9x14-foot tabletop. The tabletop is actually four pieces: two 6x6-foot tabletops, a 3x6-foot tabletop, and a 2x4-foot tabletop. The two 6x6-foot tabletops are placed side by side with the joint between them supported by the Ping-Pong table. The outer ends of the 6x6 tabletops are supported on sawhorses, each with a 2x4 on the top to raise them to the height of the Ping-Pong table. The 3x6-foot piece rests on the 3-foot end of the Ping-Pong table that protrudes from the now 6x12-foot tabletop pieces. (If I were to do it again, I would make the 6x6 tabletops 6x7-feet. As it is, I made a 2x4-foot extension on one end of the table that is supported by a card table and some layers of blue Styrofoam.) This assembly completely fills the available space in my studio. You can obviously make smaller or larger combinations of tabletops and supports to fit the area you have available. If I had a basement or even a single garage stall to use, I would buy two Ping-Pong tables and one or two 2-1/2x10-foot conference tables and arrange them to suit whatever track I wanted.

I knew I wanted at least a 9x12-foot tabletop and I knew it would be massive and, therefore, extremely cumbersome if it were made from plywood or medium density fiberboard (MDF).

Above: The tabletop for the 9x14-foot layout is four pieces, two 6x6-foot tabletops, a 3x6-foot tabletop, and a 2x4-foot tabletop, all constructed from two layers of Gatorfoam.

My 9x14-foot track is supported by a single Ping-Pong table and two sawhorses, each with a 2x4 taped to the top to match the height of the table.

I opted to use 4x8 sheets of 1/2-inch-thick Gatorfoam (white expanded-Styrofoam sandwiched between plastic-treated cardboard outer faces). Gatorfoam can be ordered at most lumberyards, but it is easier to find at companies that specialize in materials for trade show displays. Search the Yellow Pages under "Displays—Design, Produce & Install" or "Displays—Fixtures & Materials" to find a source for the Gatorfoam panels.

I needed a 6x6-foot panel, but the Gatorfoam is only available in 4x8 sheets, so I elected to laminate two layers. I cut two pieces 4x6-feet and two more 2x6-feet. I placed the two 4x6-foot pieces on top of one another but at right angles so they formed a 6x6-foot "L." I then placed one of the 2x6-foot pieces beside each of the 4x6-foot pieces to fill in the two layers. To cement the two layers of Gatorfoam to one another, I used a caulking compound that did not require air in order to cure.

Gatorfoam has great bending strength but its edges are brittle and fragile and must be protected. The best material is a 1-inch extruded plastic channel designed to protect the edges of displays. The channel can be ordered from the same firms that supply Gatorfoam. I used white Gatorfoam with a black plastic channel. I painted

The edges of the Gatorfoam must be protected. I used 1-inch plastic channel from a trade show display supply company. Use a putty knife to guide the channel over the edge of the Gatorfoam.

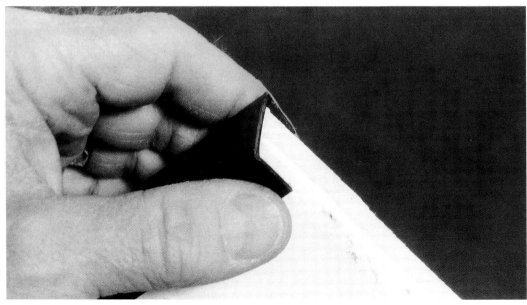

The 1-inch plastic channel is meant to snap on, but you must carefully lever it in place with a putty knife to avoid damaging the Gatorfoam.

the Gatorfoam with Sherwin-Williams Covent Garden green interior latex wall paint before installing the plastic channels, which dig into the Gatorfoam rather than snapping in place. First, cut the ends of the channels at 45-degree angles to fit the corners. Then, to install the channels, work one edge over the Gatorfoam, and insert a putty knife between the Gatorfoam and the second edge of the channel. Use the putty knife to spoon the channel over the Gatorfoam as you would use a tire iron to mount a tire. I spread a

bead of caulking compound inside the channel just before working it onto the Gatorfoam.

With the plastic edges in place, the Gatorfoam panels are nearly as strong as 1/2-inch plywood, and each 6x6 panel weighs just 19 pounds. The plastic edges have a strength of their own, especially when supported by the Gatorfoam: it all forms a foam-filled, double-layer monocoque that is quite strong. The only real weak point of this lightweight tabletop system is the Gatorfoam surface, which is relatively

One of the 6x6 tabletops is resting on the Ping-Pong table. The cloth is anti-skid pad for rugs to help hold the panels without the need for clamps or bolts.

The second 6x6 tabletop is in place and the third tabletop, the 3x6-foot piece, covers the closest end of the Ping-Pong table. The 3x6-foot piece can be moved about two feet in either direction to provide some variation in the shape of the available tabletop. A fourth 2x4-foot tabletop added to the far edge of the table behind the post is an option. The extension allows 9x14-foot tracks to completely fill the available space.

easy to dent. Since it is really only there to support the plastic track, dents are not a major issue. However, you must be careful when assembling track sections to not put too many dents or divots in the surface.

The panels simply rest on top of a Ping-Pong table for most of their support, with a single sawhorse at each of the extreme 12-foot ends. I cut a third 3x6-foot two-layer Gatorfoam panel to fill in the open end of the Ping-Pong table, and a fourth 2x4-foot panel to allow the option of extending the table from 9x12 to 9x14 feet. I also placed a layer of foam rubber carpet

Access for Corner Marshals

When you plan the table for your raceway, consider that you must be able to reach the de-slotted cars. The average person can only reach about 3 feet, which means a Ping-Pong-size table should be placed with the 5-foot end against the wall so marshals have access to both sides and need only reach 2-1/2 feet. You can extend your reach using the devices that are sold at drug stores to help the disabled reach beyond a wheelchair. These reachers have a pistol grip on the end of a 2- or 3-foot tube, with a pincher on the other end that closes by squeezing the trigger.

All the Scalextric/SCX and Carrera tracks in this book (except for the 9x16-foot Daytona track in chapter 5) and in *Racing and Collecting Slot Cars* were assembled on this tabletop. This is the four-lane Indy F1 track for Carrera in the design-by-doing stage.

anti-skid cloth on top of the Ping-Pong table to keep the panels from sliding around. I originally thought I would have to attach the panels to the Ping-Pong table and I even purchased some two-inch stove bolts, fender washers, and wing nuts for that purpose. But the panels barely move because they are wedged against the two outer walls of the room. If your track is an island or peninsula, you may need to use the bolts and wing nuts to keep the panels in place.

Remember: all these dimensions are for my particular area. The panels allow me to fill all the available space in a 9x14-foot room and still store the entire track, tables, and scenery in just 2x5 feet inside the folded-up Ping-Pong table.

Shop around because prices and designs vary somewhat. The most effective reachers have a suction cup on each of the pinchers that grip a model car nicely without much chance of breaking off a mirror or wing.

My 6x6-foot panels are not just squares: a 2x2-foot corner is cut off each panel to allow more access in my cramped studio. Since I cannot walk around three sides of the track for access, I also cut 2x2-foot access holes in the center of each panel. One of the panels has to fit around a post, so I cut a 6-inch-wide notch in that panel to allow it to thread around the post. On race nights, a corner marshal sits on a stool inside each of the access holes. When just three or four of us race, however, we use two of the reachers.

Above: The four-lane Indy F1 circuit assembled from Carrera track (as shown in chapter 5) on the 9x12-foot tabletop.

The Carrera track can be locked together so the track can be partially disassembled into modules for storage—it makes it quicker to reassemble the track. The modules of track can be stored inside the fold-up Ping-Pong table with loose track pieces and scenery in boxes.

The Daytona International Speedway for four-lane Revell track from chapter 5 in action in the late-1960s. This track was supported on four 4x8-foot ultra-lightweight tables made from 1x2 frames with burlap tabletops and screw-on legs. It really was not sturdy enough for the task.

Fred Martin's 8x26-foot tabletop has a framework welded together from 1-inch-square aluminum tubes with a trussed rectangle in the center for strength.

Portable 4x8-Foot Tables

If you prefer, you can build portable tables yourself using standard 4x8-foot pieces of 1/2-inch plywood. Install the same type of fold-up legs used for conference tables beneath one or more sheets of plywood. Finish the edges of the plywood with veneer or just sand and seal them thoroughly. You may even want to cut one or two 2x6-inch holes in the center of each of the sheets to make them easier to handle. I have assembled ultralight 4x8-foot tables with frames made of 1x2-inch lumber and burlap stretched across the top. The legs were the simple screw-on type. Frankly, they were just not sturdy enough for a race track: 1/2-inch plywood is the best choice for 4x8-foot tables. The Mona-co, Daytona, and Suzuka tracks for Revell, Monogram, or Strombecker track in chapter 5 are designed for groups of three or four 4x8-foot tables. Most of the 9x12-foot plans can be assembled on three 4x8 tables placed side by side with perhaps a 1x8-foot extension along the forward edge supported by another set of folding legs.

Martin's 8x26-foot tabletop is suspended by a system of cables, pulleys, and an electric winch. It is lowered by six cables to fit snugly over two 3x8-foot conference tables. The cables are unhooked after the table is in position.

All six cables are gathered into one adjustable block with a hook and pulley in the corner of the ceiling. The cables lead to an electric winch on a sturdy shelf.

8x26 Feet of Raceway in Zero Space

If your raceway must share space with other family or business uses, consider building a lift-up table like that made by Fred Martin for his Carrera track. He had a friend in the welding business assemble a pair of 8x13-foot tabletops supported by a trestle of 1-inch-square aluminum tubes. The two 8x13-foot tables are joined by sturdy aluminum plates attached with bolts and nuts to the 1-inch tubes so the tabletop can be transported if Fred decides to move. The supporting truss of tubes in the center of the table is spaced so it will fit around the tops of two 3x8-foot conference tables that supply the legs for the track. Six steel cables run from the sides of the layout to six pulleys on the ceiling, then across the ceiling to a single cable and pulley that leads down to an electric winch. All the pulleys are secured by 6-inch steel plates attached to 2x6-inch ceiling joists, and a single pulley leading to the winch is bolted to a steel I-beam supported by 2x6 joists.

If you decide on such a system, I strongly suggest that you talk to the theater arts department at your local college or university to determine if someone there can help you

Martin assembles a variety of Carrera tracks on his 8x26-foot tabletop. The tabletop itself is a layer of 1/2-inch Gatorfoam with the edges protected by aluminum angles.

design it so it will be safe and workable. I've seen it used for one or two other model car raceways and a half dozen model railroads, but it's not a job for guesswork. Between the aluminum support structure, the Gatorfoam, and the tabletop, everything possible has been done to save weight. But even at that, the track probably weighs close to 200 pounds.

As you can see, you *do* have space for a raceway somewhere in your home. It's wonderful if that space can be permanently devoted to a raceway, but one of these portable table systems can work for you if you need the raceway to be as portable as the track.

Chapter Four

SCENERY

A pair of older Scalextric Jaguars on the main straight of Russell Cox's Scalextric track during a nighttime endurance race.

Each of the cars that races around your track is an exact replica of a real car. If you assemble a track to match a plan in chapter 5 or custom-build a track to match a plan in chapter 6, the shape of your track and its corners will also be replicas of a real-world race track. Carry the illusion of reality just a bit further and include some scenery so the cars have a more realistic setting

Night Racing

The endurance races at Le Mans, Daytona, and Sebring are just a few real-world races that are run into the night and, thus, require lights. You can re-create the strange effects of night racing. More and more of the ready-to-run cars are now fitted with lights, and lights are standard on most 1/32 scale Rally cars. SCX even has a series

of trackside lights that plug into the track. If you want a set of floodlights, you can use Lionel toy train lighting accessories.

Race Cars in Context

You'll be surprised by how much more enjoyable racing can be after you have landscaped the edges of the track and the bare tabletop and installed a few buildings and trees. Now, the black plastic surface is a road because it is edged by curbs, grass, and sand just like a real race track.

You can simulate grass and sand by simply painting the tabletop to match the track borders. Scalextric Sport borders are sandy beige and SCX borders a grass green. You can paint Scalextric Sport borders green if you wish. The black and yellow borders on Carrera and Artin

Assemble just one large tree from the components meant for three trees in the Bachmann Plasticville 49001 Shade Tree kit.

track and the garish white and red stripes on Ninco borders can be far more realistic if painted grass green or sand beige. Paint the borders to match the green of the tabletop and you won't even notice where the borders end and the table begins. The curbs can be simple white lines or red and white rumble strips painted as shown in *Racing and Collecting Slot Cars*. Do not use dirt, ground foam, or sawdust to texture the grass or sand because the crashed cars will tear into the scenery and deposit the loose stuff on the track. Paint works just fine for simulating grass or sand.

A Forest Full of Trees

Most real race tracks are surrounded by trees, however far they may be from the edges of the track. When cars zip by the trees, their speeds seem much higher because you have something static to compare to the moving race cars. Trees can also help to place your track. If there are large groups of trees, the track is probably a circuit like Spa, Nürburgring, Silverstone, Road Atlanta, Road America, or one of a host of others that are set in the woods. If there are just a few trees, the track may be La-

guna Seca, Riverside, or Indianapolis. Palm trees suggest places like Daytona, Sebring, and Monaco.

Do not use any of the ready-built trees for model railroads that have leaves simulated with ground foam or sawdust. The loose material can get inside the gears and motors of any car. Life-Like's Number 1971 Super Giant Oak Tree with bundles of lichen for the leaves is perfect for a 1/32 scale raceway. There are about three dozen of them on the tracks in chapter 5.

Bachmann makes an all-plastic tree called a 49001 Shade Tree in their Plasticville series for O scale model railroads. Each tree kit is supposed to make three trees, but they are stubby and strange. You can stack all but five of the leave clusters to make a single tree that looks just fine and will never shed.

A 1/32 scale palm tree can be assembled from a single tuft of plastic air fern and a length of bamboo. Craft stores that sell plastic flowers usually carry both the air fern and the bamboo. They may also have some 3-inch plastic suction cups that you can use for the base of each palm tree. Cut the bamboo into 6- to 12-inch pieces with a razor saw. Use diagonal cutters to trim the

Craft stores usually carry plastic air ferns, bamboo sticks, and plastic suction cups.

Use the bamboo for the trunk and the suction cup for the base of the palm tree.

edges of the top of the suction cup so it will fit inside the bamboo. Finally, spread the air fern leaves to match the appearance of a real palm tree. I found the air fern looked more like a palm if painted a darker green with a misted-on coat of medium green. Paint the suction cup an earth brown. The suction cup does not need to function, it simply serves as a stand for the tree.

Racing Pits, Grandstands, and Towers

Buildings imply life beyond the cockpit of the race car. On a race track, buildings are usually the sign of rather frantic life, with harried pit crews and excited spectators.

Scalextric has a range of plastic buildings that includes the C639 Pit Stop buildings with tools, C642 Control Tower, C636 Grandstand,

Assemble four of MRRC Pit Buildings side by side and wear a rubber glove while you spray paint them

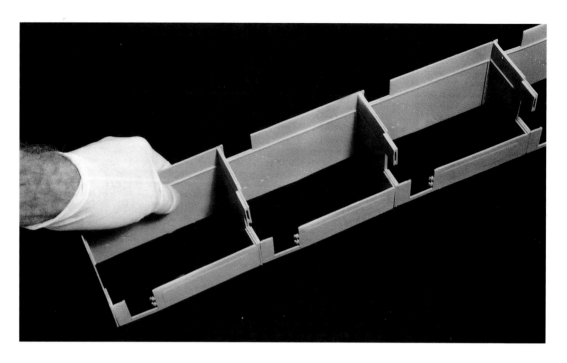

and the famous C641 Goodyear Bridge. Scalextric also has three modern card buildings: the C8151 Control Tower, C8150 Pit Stop, and C8152 Grandstand with photo mural spectators. SCX's 88260 Pit Building has a grandstand on top.

MRRC still offers the Airfix Pit Stop, Press Box, and Timekeeper's Hut as plastic kits. Four or more of the MRRC pit buildings can be assembled into a single unit. First, paint the whole unit. To paint the details, make a holder from a scrap of wood. Make loops of masking tape (sticky side out) and press them onto the board. Press the loose parts onto the tape. Hold the board as a handle while you spray the parts. Touch up the smaller parts with a number 00

Above: Use a board and masking tape to make a holder to spray the roofs and stairs of the pit buildings.

The tools and fuel hoses are from the Scalextric C639 Pit Stops. The signs are copied from old magazines.

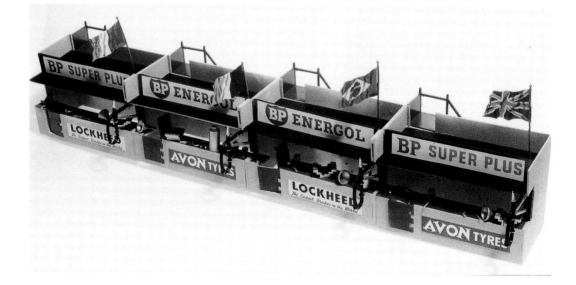

These MRRC Press Boxes have been detailed with color copies of period advertisements.

paintbrush. Preiser makes a very realistic set of welding tanks and tools (Number 45211 Track Tools) that will add super detail to any pit scene.

Riggen (from REH) produces the Pit Garage (but alas, not the grandstand) from the original Strombecker molds. The Bachmann O scale Plasticville Number 45985 Airport Terminal has a control tower that is very similar to towers at many race tracks and is close enough to 1/32 scale. Additionally, the Plasticville 45606 Frosty Bar is a reasonable stand-in for a refreshment stand like those seen at some race tracks.

Grandstands and pits are often decorated with the national flags of all the drivers. Scalextric includes a few with their plastic grandstands and pits. I copied a set from a race calendar and had the photocopy shop reverse or mirror one copy. I then cemented the two copies

MRRC's Press Box can be placed on top of the pit buildings. Most of the "people" are MRRC figures that I painted.

Make a regular copy and a mirror-image copy of flags from a racing calendar and glue the flags back to back.

back-to-back and cut the flags out with scissors. Stick the flags to Plastruct 1/16-inch ABS rod with Goodyear Pliobond.

Real Life for Race Tracks

You certainly do not need to populate your model race track with a thousand or more spectators and crew. As few as a dozen well-placed figures near the track's highlights can suggest that there are many more spectators than can be seen.

Scalextric and SCX have painted 1/32 figures, and MRRC has a wonderful range of unpainted figures that includes some from the Airfix and Monogram ranges of the 1960s. Preiser offers more than 100 very realistic painted figures. And don't forget to include a half-dozen or more street vehicles, the visible means those spectators and crew used to get to the track. Toy departments are the best sources for 1/32 scale diecast cars and trucks.

Preiser offers nearly a hundred different painted 1/32 scale figures.

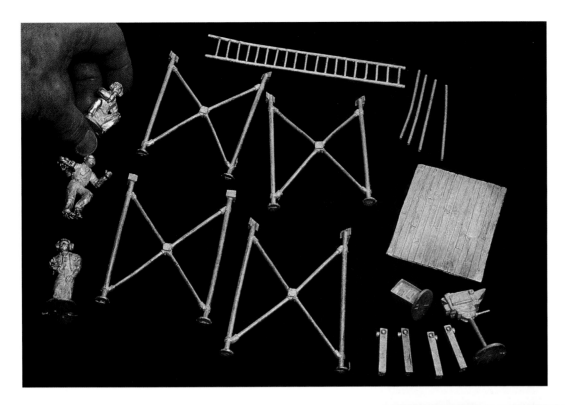

Left: SRA (Slot Racing Accessories) has a range of cast-metal figures, including this TV crew with an elevated stand.

Below: Use a saber saw to cut the foamboard building flats.

Bottom: Color the edges of the flats with a felt-tip pen.

Zero-Space Buildings

There is never enough room for the race track you want, let alone extra space for buildings. The re-creation of the Monaco Grand Prix circuit in chapter 5 effectively simulates the hundreds of buildings that surround that street course with photos of the actual structures at Monaco. Theater stage props like these are called "flats."

Use a color photocopy machine to enlarge a photograph from any book up to 11x14 inches. You can make even longer enlargements by piecing two or more 11x14 copies together. There are dozens of books with color photos of Monaco and the other famous racing circuits. You could just as easily create flats of the grandstands and judges' buildings at Daytona or Indianapolis. Use 3M Sprayment to mount the color copies on 1/8-inch foam-filled posterboard like Gator-foam. The shops that specialize in mounting and framing posters will carry the board and you can often buy 1- or 2-foot wide scraps for a few dollars. You can use a craft or box knife to cut the photo and the foamboard at the same time, but it's easier to use a knife blade in a saber saw. Sears sells a saber saw blade assortment that includes a knife.

Try to find black foamboard. If you cannot, use a wide felt-tip pen to "kill" the edges of the white board. In fact, use a felt-tip pen to color the cut edges even if you use black foamboard.

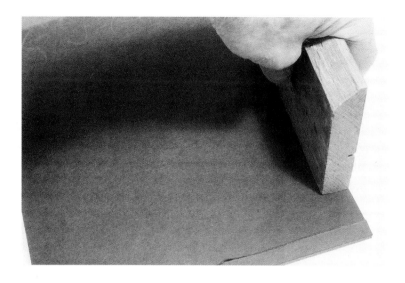

Use a 2x2 or 1x4 to support the building flats so they will be free-standing.

Mount the flats on the wall with foam poster stickers. If the buildings need to stand on their own, glue them to chunks of 2x2 and paint the 2x2s to match the track surface.

Racing Uphill and Down

Few model car racers assemble tracks that recreate the hills common to most real road courses. The overpass for a figure-eight-style track is about as far as most of us go with uphills and downhills. The 9x16-foot Monaco Grand Prix track assembled with Carrera track sections in chapter 5 has an 8 percent uphill grade with the downhill a combination of two of Carrera's Number 20545 Crossing Bridges arranged to go down and down, rather than up and down.

Make two flexible pieces of track to install at the bottom and the top of the grade on the straightaway so the cars will not de-slot. Join four pieces of 1/4-straight for each piece of "flex" track, and the joints will provide all the flex the track needs for the vertical curve at the bottom of the hill and at the hump at the top. I did not want to cut borders for the Carrera track so I joined eight of the 1/4-length sections in four

The Monaco Grand Prix circuit assembled with Carrera track as shown in chapter 5 with the uphill section shown in this chapter. The buildings are located in about the same places they would be on the full-size Monaco circuit.

Above: The Monaco Grand Prix circuit is not as realistic when viewed on end, where you can see the two-dimensional nature of most of the buildings.

Left: Mask the outer lanes on the four 1/4-section "flex" tracks and paint them to match the other borders on the Carrera track.

Use a white-out tape dispenser to roll on the white curb lines.

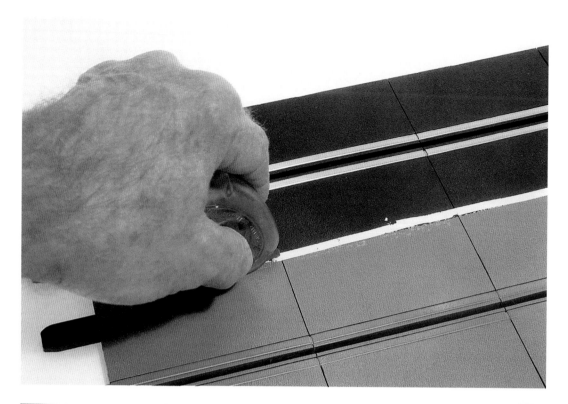

The joints between the four 1/4-straight pieces are just loose enough to allow the track to flex for the beginning of the uphill section and to bow downward for the top of the uphill section.

pairs, side by side. The two outer lanes are not used, of course, so I painted them grass green.

Painting Grass Borders

I painted all the Carrera borders except those on the outside of the outer banked curves. First, paint the entire border with a white primer and let it dry. Next, mask the edge of the border near the track with 1/8-inch Scotch Automotive Masking Tape (paint stores sell it), then spray the border grass green or sand beige. Remove the tape when the paint is dry.

I skipped the masking on these flex track sections and just masked off the center of the track with masking tape and sprayed the green paint. When the paint dries remove the tape. The white curb can also be simulated using one of the tape-style type or ink eradicator ribbons sold by office supply stores. These devices lay down a 5/32-inch white strip of white that looks like dry transfer or rub-on material. Use a ruler to guide the device so it lays a straight white line.

Track Elevation Supports

Woodland Scenics makes a simple system of white expanded Styrofoam blocks called Risers that are available at any hobby shop. Several sizes of Risers are available, but the one that works for most model car racing tracks is Number ST1409 that is 2-1/2 inches wide and 4 inches tall. They are sold in 2-foot lengths and are a zig-zag pat-

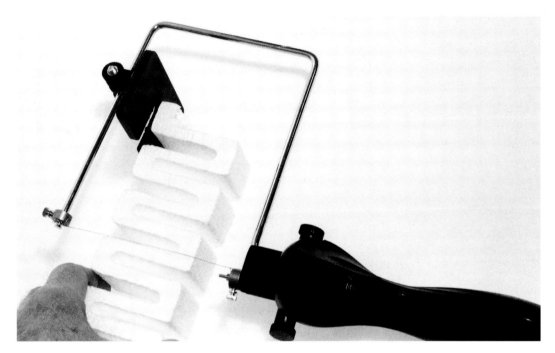

Use a Woodland Scenics ST1437 Foam Cutter Bow and Guide to cut an 8 percent grade into the Riser.

Use the Woodland Scenics ST1445 Low Temp Foam Glue Gun and ST1446 Glue Sticks to attach the 8 percent Risers to each side of 1x2-foot sheet of ST1423 foam.

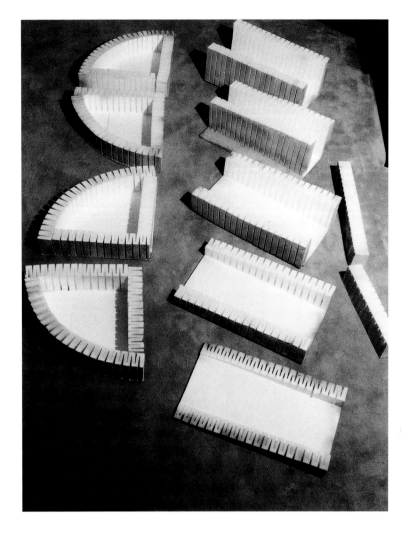

tern when viewed from the top so they can flex to form curves. Woodland Scenics also has ST1423, 1x2-foot sheets of 1/2-inch white expanded Styrofoam that is a bit stronger than most white Styrofoam. All the supports for the Monaco track were made from a combination of these two products.

Woodland Scenics sells Number ST1437 Foam Cutter Bow and Guide which is, effectively, a hot wire coping saw used to cut the foam. With a yardstick, mark the 4-inch Risers to cut them for an 8 percent upgrade—in the middle of one of the 4-inch sides at 2 inches. Hold the yardstick over that mark and connect it to the opposite corner and draw a line. When you cut along that line, you will get a tapered piece of Riser that starts at zero and angles upward over 2 feet to 2 inches. That single cut through the Riser will also yield a second piece of Riser that starts at 2 inches and tapers up to 4 inches.

To make supports for the upgrade, cement two of the 0-to-2-inch cut Risers on each side of one of the 1x2-foot pieces of 1/2-inch foam. Cement two more of the 2-to-4-inch cut Risers to a second piece of 1x2-foot 1/2-inch foam and you will have support for 4 feet of any brand of model car race track to rise 4 inches from the tabletop. I used various combinations of these pieces to gain a full 8 inches. Assemble the pieces with the Woodland Scenics ST1445 Low Temp Foam Glue Gun and ST1446 Glue Sticks.

The modules used to support the 8-foot uphill so the track could rise to an 8-inch-high, 180-degree turn on the Monaco Grand Prix track.

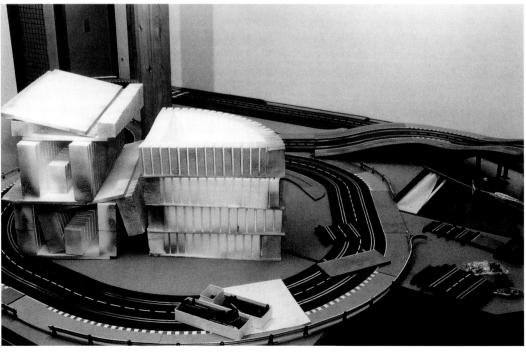

The elevation modules stacked for storage. The pair of Carrera 20545 Crossings are already in place in the upper right.

Curves can be supported with the same system except that the shape of the curved track must be traced onto two or more of the 1/2-inch sheets of the 1x2-foot foam. I made four 90-degree supports so I could stack them to support 180 degrees of track 8 inches above the tabletop. The modular nature of all these components allows you to use them with a variety of different track combinations. You might also want to assemble an 8 percent upgrade on a curve. Each half of that Carrera Number 20545 Crossing rises 4 inches, so linking two of them together produces the same 8 inches of rise created by the Woodland Scenics supports.

The hillclimb portion of the Monaco track adds a new dimension to tabletop racing—now, the track looks and drives even more like the real Monaco Grand Prix circuit.

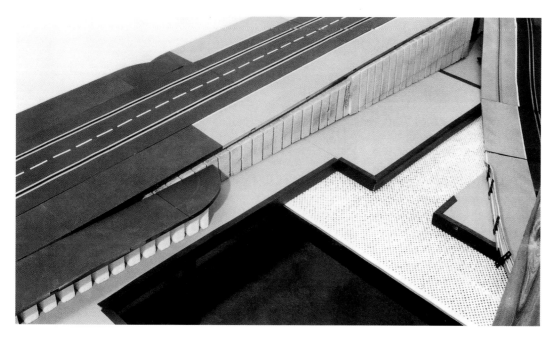

The uphill is supported by the 8 percent grade Risers. Extra Risers support the border for the pit apron at the lower left.

The 90-degree segments of 4-inch curve supports are at the far right. The last 2 feet of the straight are level, 8 inches above the tabletop.

The Scalextric version of Monaco with the Gasworks (now La Rascasse) turn in the lower foreground. The trees and building flats used on these re-creations of the Monaco course are shown in chapter 4.

The 9x14-foot version of Monaco for Scalextric track with the building flats of the real structures in Monaco. The curve at Station (later Loews) Hairpin uses the R2-size Scalextric standard curves. The alternate plan illustrates how to build the track with the R1 chicaned inner curve.

Monaco for Scalextric, SCX, and Ninco Track

The model track is a much shorter version of the nearly 2-mile-long Monaco course, reduced to fit a reasonable 9x14-foot area. The right-angle bend in the course at St. Devote is eliminated, as is the curve in front of the Hôtel de Paris. I numbered the turns on the plans T1 through T7: T1 is Mirabeau, T2 is Station (today called "Loews"), T3 is the turn just past Station, T4 and T5 are the sweeping turns through the tunnel, T6 is Tabac, and T7 is Gasworks (now known as La Rascasse). I have, incidentally, indicated two terminal tracks (A) so you can have driving positions at two different places—just be sure to tape over the unused controller socket on each terminal so you do not create a short circuit by plugging two controllers into the same lane.

The first plan shows Station Hairpin assembled with standard Scalextric Sport or Scalextric Classic R2 curves, while the second shows the Station Hairpin assembled with two of the new Sport R1 (number C8201) hairpin curves and a pair of C8246 Side Swipe Straights. These four track sections, assembled as shown in the plan, produce a chicaned 180-degree turn that looks like the custom-made Carrera chicaned turn shown in the first photo of this chapter.

This second plan takes full advantage of the option of having eight lanes of racing with

Scalextric Sport track sections. To the home racer, that doesn't mean eight lanes side-by-side, but the option of eight different curve radii (actually, four pairs of curve radii). Ninco also offers a similar choice of four different curved track radii. The plan can be assembled from Ninco track but because Ninco is a bit wider, it will probably require another foot or so of length and width, a custom-cut half-length standard curve (as shown in chapter 3, page 26), and a few additional short pieces of track to get the final joints to align properly.

The straight can be elevated as it was for the Carrera version of Monaco using supports cut from Woodland Scenics Risers as shown in chapter 4 so that Mirabeau is 8 inches above the tabletop, with the track descending (on similar supports) down to Station Hairpin. The Scalextric or SCX re-creation of the Monaco Grand Prix Circuit has a 49-1/2-foot length on the inner lane and a 52-foot length on the outer lane. In actual racing, there's really no clear advantage to either lane.

Hairpin Turns

Scalextric offers an inner turn in both the Classic (C8029) and Sport lines (C8202). The inner lane of this curve is really a bit too tight for most 1/32 cars to negotiate. You will not see these inner-inner curves (Scalextric Classic and Sport call the size an "R1") on any plans in this book or in *Racing and Collecting Slot Cars*. Scalextric redesigned

the inner turn for the Sport line of track, with the inside lane of the C8202 moved out to be closer to the outside lane to create the C8201 Hairpin Turn. The chicane for Sport track (C8246) is designed so only one lane moves closer to the next. When you connect the two halves of this Sport chicane to one or more sections of

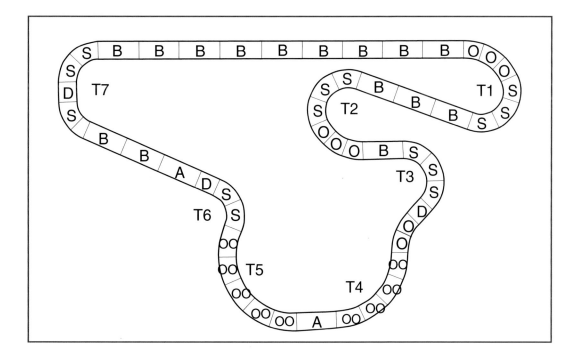

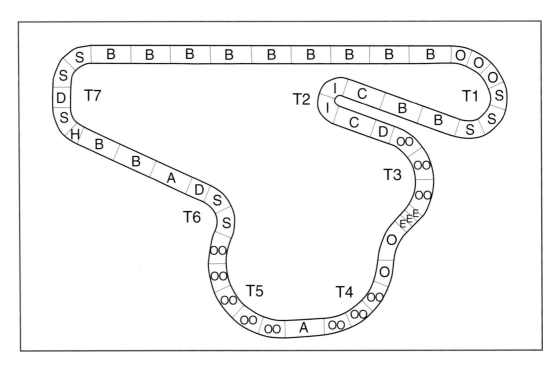

curves on alternate versions of both the Scalextric/Ninco and the Carrera re-creations of Monaco. There are also plans using the standard Scalextric/Ninco curves if you would rather not use such tight curves.

Two of the three versions of Monaco for Carrera track also utilize an inner-inner hairpin turn. Carrera does not offer this curve but it is available as a custom-built section from Brad's Tracks. Since it is a handmade section, it's almost as expensive as a basic race set. The section is only offered in one size, a 180-degree curve with a built-in length of full straight. It duplicates the effect of the chicaned 180-degree hairpin curve.

These hairpin turns can make a much more interesting plan and are a thrill to drive because they force the cars to perform almost like a real car's brake-slide turn. Today, Formula 1 cars power gently around Loews Hairpin at Monaco but, in the 1950s and 1960s, it was a power-slide turn. The hairpin curve can also be useful if you want to make an extension off one corner of a slot car table to make an L-shape table. The extension can be as little as a foot wide for a two-lane track with a hairpin turn at the end. If you are cramped for space, this might be a way to create an extra 10 to 15 feet of straight.

Monaco for Carrera Track

There are three different versions of Monaco for Carrera track. You can mix or match major

C8201 Sport curved track sections you produce a curve very similar to the custom-made Carrera curve shown later in this chapter and in chapter 2. The Ninco number 10106 inner-inner curve has an inner lane with a radius that is about the same as that on the inner lane of the new Sport inner-inner curve. I have used these inner-inner

This version of Monaco assembled from Carrera track has the uphill on the straight supported by Woodland Scenics Risers and the photo flats of the buildings at Monaco as described in chapter 4. This track was also assembled with the custom-made 1/4-straight terminal track sections described in chapter 14.

The action of the cars brings racing to this scene. The uphill and the photo murals make it seem even more like this really is Monaco—it's just a bit smaller than the real place.

sections of each to suit your space or desires. Any of the three can be extended as far as you wish merely by adding pairs of straight track sections at the places marked "L" on the plans, but I do not recommend that you try to make them any wider. The first two utilize a custom-made inner-inner curve produced by Brad's Tracks and the third uses standard Number 1 Carrera curves for Station Hairpin (T2).

The track in the first picture in this chapter and the one illustrating the use of photo cutout buildings in chapter 4 is the 9x14-foot version. This track is designed to have an uphill made from Woodland Scenics Risers as shown in chapter 4 with the two pieces of the Carrera number 20545 Crossing Bridge arranged to go down and down rather than up and down. On the plans, these sections are marked with an "R." Look

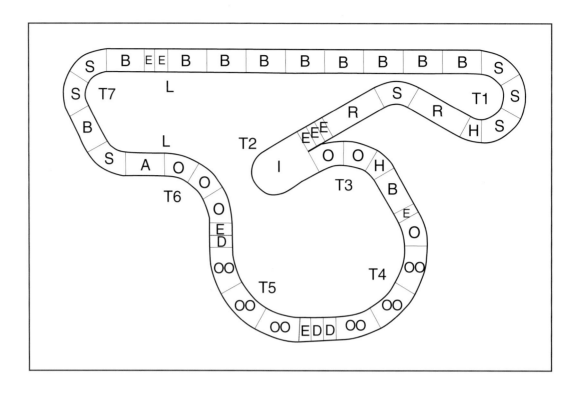

LIST OF CARRERA TRACK REQUIRED FOR 9x14-FOOT MONACO GRAND PRIX TRACK

Chapter 3 includes a list of part numbers for the track sections and borders identified by the key letters in this plan.

Key	Quantity	Description
H	2	1/2 Inner (1) Curve
I	1	Inner-Inner (0) Curve
S	7	Inner (1) Curve
K	0	Banked Inner (1) Curve
O	5	Middle (2) Curve
M	0	Banked Middle (2) Curve
OO	6	Outer (3) Curve
OOO	0	Outer-Outer (4) Curve
N	0	Banked Outer (3) Curve
E	8	1/4-Straight
D	3	1/3-Straight
B	11	Full-Straight
Q	0	Overpass Bridge
R	2	1/2 of Overpass Bridge
A	1	Connector Track
C	0	Chicane
L		Track can be expanded in length by adding matched pairs of straight track sections here
T		Turn numbers (that correspond to real race course)

closely at the uphill portion of the plan. Carrera does not make borders for the crossing track sections, but they are necessary if the crossings are placed near turns as they are on these tracks. To create borders for the Carrera 20545 Crossing, simply use two of the track sections side by side. The geometry of Carrera's track allows you to offset any section by half a section, so the side-by-side tracks work quite well. A similar set of eight Carrera 20612 straight track sections were placed side by side to make flexible track sections for the bottom and top of the uphill on the Monaco plan as shown in chapter 4. These sections, however, are indicated as full-length straights (B) on the plan and the chart of track required. You will need at least eight more Carrera 20612 1/4-length straights (and two less full-length straights) if you want to assemble these flex tracks.

If you want to build the track on a flat area, you can substitute a full-length straight combined with two 1/4-length straights for each half of the overpass as shown on the third version of Monaco for Carrera. The lane length in the first version measures 43 feet, 9 inches and 46 feet per lap. Again, as with the Scalextric Classic and Sport versions, there's little difference in lap times. The laps are a bit shorter than with the Scalextric/SCX version because Carrera track is wider and takes up a bit more space. The Carrera

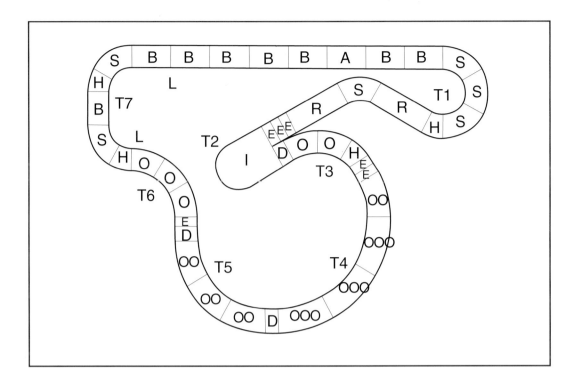

version, however, is just a bit smoother to drive on with less abrupt changes in direction.

Ten Lanes of Racing on Carrera Track

Yes, you can combine all the Carrera track sections, including the custom-made "0" size inner hairpin curve, to make a 10-lane track. This plan uses this entire track, including the Carrera outer-outer-outer curve (they call it a "4"), as well as the custom-made Brad's Tracks inner-inner curve (that I call a "number 0"). You could assemble these five curves into a 10-lane oval or figure eight, but I definitely do not recommend it because there is too much variation in lane length.

When you have the option of five different curves you can create a plan like this version of Monaco. The sweeping curve through the tunnel area has a radius decreasing from huge (at T4) to merely massive (at Turn 5), while the downhill from Mirabeau (T1) to Station (T2) goes from tight to tighter. And there's a nice 90-degree conventional curve at Tabac (T6) with a right turn into Gasworks (T7), as well as a nice long straight that can be, like the real track, on an uphill if you use Woodland Scenics Risers to elevate the track as shown in chapter 4. If you want to assemble the track for this plan without an uphill, replace each of the two "R" number 20545 crossing sections with a standard straight 20609 and two 20612 1/4-length straight track sections.

LIST OF CARRERA TRACK REQUIRED FOR 9x12-FOOT MONACO GRAND PRIX TRACK

Chapter 3 includes a list of part numbers for the track sections and borders identified by the key letters in this plan.

Key	Quantity	Description
H	4	1/2 Inner (1) Curve
I	1	Inner-Inner (0) Curve
S	5	Inner (1) Curve
K	0	Banked Inner (1) Curve
O	5	Middle (2) Curve
M	0	Banked Middle (2) Curve
OO	4	Outer (3) Curve
OOO	3	Outer-Outer (4) Curve
N	0	Banked Outer (3) Curve
E	6	1/4-Straight
D	3	1/3-Straight
B	8	Full-Straight
Q	0	Overpass Bridge
R	2	1/2 of Overpass Bridge
A	1	Connector Track
C	0	Chicane
L		Track can be expanded in length by adding matched pairs of straight track sections here
T		Turn numbers (that correspond to real race course)

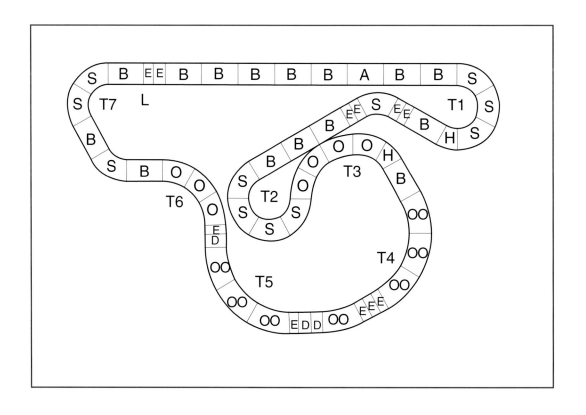

LIST OF CARRERA TRACK REQUIRED FOR 9x14-FOOT MONACO GRAND PRIX TRACK

Chapter 3 includes a list of part numbers for the track sections and borders identified by the key letters in this plan.

Key	Quantity	Description
H	2	1/2 Inner (1) Curve
I	0	Inner-Inner (0) Curve
S	11	Inner (1) Curve
K	0	Banked Inner (1) Curve
O	7	Middle (2) Curve
M	0	Banked Middle (2) Curve
OO	7	Outer (3) Curve
OOO	0	Outer-Outer (4) Curve
N	0	Banked Outer (3) Curve
E	11	1/4-Straight
D	3	1/3-Straight
B	15	Full-Straight
Q	0	Overpass Bridge
R	0	1/2 of Overpass Bridge
A	1	Connector Track
C	0	Chicane
L		Track can be expanded in length by adding matched pairs of straight track sections here
T		Turn numbers (that correspond to real race course)

The Flat Version of Monaco for Carrera

If you want to avoid custom-made track sections, you can assemble a 9x14-foot version of Monaco with only standard Carrera track sections. The Brad's Tracks custom-made hairpin turn (T2) is replaced with the smallest out-of-the-box Carrera 20571 curves. Also on this plan, the two "R" number 20545 crossing sections are replaced with a standard straight 20609 and two 20612 1/4-length straight track sections. You can make this substitution on the previous two plans if you wish.

12x16 Monaco for Revell, Monogram, and Strombecker

The plastic track sections originally made by Revell are now available to hobby dealers from REH, which also offers Strombecker track. Only standard curve track sections and full-length straights are available for either brand. The outer curves, half-straights, and borders are no longer produced. You can modify this four-lane plan, however, to assemble a two-lane version. This plan was originally published in the October 1964 issue of the now-defunct *Model Car & Track* magazine as part of series of plans reprinted in *Model Car Racing* magazine.

Paramount Ranch Raceway in 1/32 Scale

Only two significant real race tracks are laid out in a figure eight: Paramount Ranch in Southern California and Suzuka in Japan. Model car racers like the figure eight because it provides a better chance for equal lane lengths and thus, more competitive racing. In reality, there's usually not much difference in lap times on road racing courses regardless of whether the track has a theoretical lane-matching

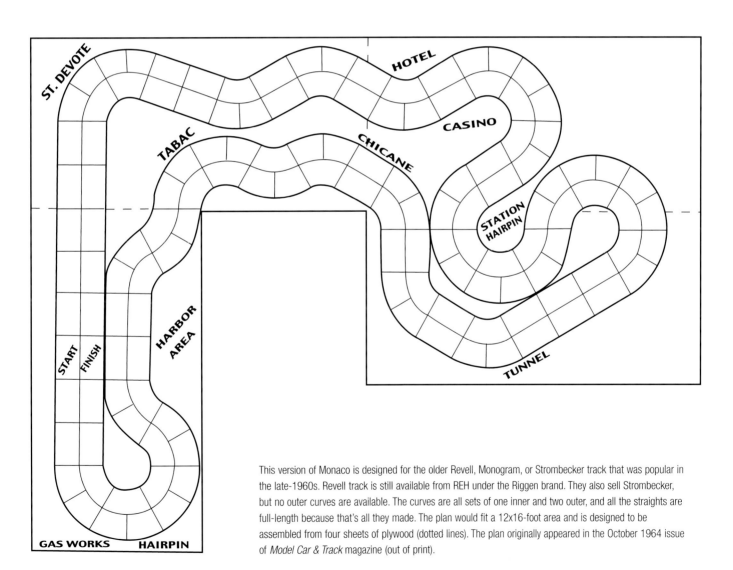

This version of Monaco is designed for the older Revell, Monogram, or Strombecker track that was popular in the late-1960s. Revell track is still available from REH under the Riggen brand. They also sell Strombecker, but no outer curves are available. The curves are all sets of one inner and two outer, and all the straights are full-length because that's all they made. The plan would fit a 12x16-foot area and is designed to be assembled from four sheets of plywood (dotted lines). The plan originally appeared in the October 1964 issue of *Model Car & Track* magazine (out of print).

The plan for this two-lane, 9x12-foot version of Paramount Ranch appeared in *Racing and Collecting Slot Cars*. All the Carrera two- and four-lane re-creations of Paramount Ranch have the corkscrew downhill ess bend that was illustrated in that book as well. Note that there are two pieces of banked turn incorporated into the turn on the "List of Track Required" to create the corkscrew for all these Carrera versions of Paramount Ranch. To assemble this track as a two-lane, merely ignore the lane that includes the outer ("O") curves in the upper left of the plan for the four-lane version.

figure-eight design. In fact, you will be surprised at how equal a four-lane oval can be, especially if you use the largest curves for the corners. What you will discover is that on a four-lane road racing course it is usually the two middle lanes that provide the best lap times, while the two outer lanes, especially on figure eights, are usually the slowest. My advice? Don't worry about it. Set up the track that you want and adjust the racing lane differences by making everyone race on every lane as described in chapter 14.

The real Paramount Ranch had a short life, indeed. It opened on August 18, 1956, and hosted its final race on December 8, 1957. Except for Riverside, it was the only road racing course in Southern California. Dan Gurney, Richie Ginther, and Ken Miles ran at Paramount, and there was even a United States Auto Club (USAC)—pre-NASCAR—sedan race featuring Sam Hanks, Troy Ruttman, and Jimmy Bryan.

Model car racers knew all about Paramount, in part because I prepared a lengthy series of articles in the late-1960s for the now defunct *Car Model* magazine on how to re-create the circuit in 1/32 scale as a four-lane track routed

from particleboard. (Examples of that track and a routed version of Suzuka are included in chapter 6.) Additional two-lane versions of Paramount Ranch for Scalextric/SCX/Ninco/Carrera track are illustrated in *Racing and Collecting Slot Cars*.

Paramount Ranch for Carrera Track

This track plan for a 9x12-foot version of Paramount Ranch illustrates the four-lane version of the track. There are photos of both two-lane (the plan is in *Racing and Collecting Slot Cars*) and four-lane versions of the track in this chapter. These plans are really mirror images of Paramount because that's the shape that was needed to fill the space. Also, the overpass should be beneath the straight, not above it. To get the plastic track version to capture as much of the character of Paramount Ranch as the routed version in chapter 6, you can use Woodland Scenics Risers to elevate the full length of the straight four inches, as shown in chapter 4. When built with Carrera track, all these plans do include the downhill corkscrew ess bends through Turns 6 and 7. You sacrifice that if you elevate the straight. The uphill for the corkscrew is simply a section of Carrera's Number

The four-lane version of the 9x12-foot Paramount Ranch track also has the corkscrew downhill ess bends. The Mercedes and Maserati are drifting through the banked turn sections of the corkscrew—all the other track sections are flat curves.

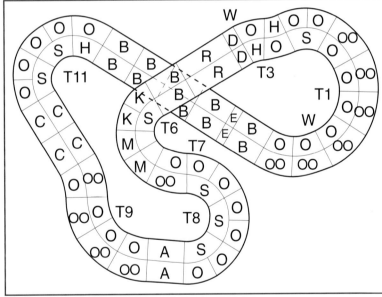

LIST OF CARRERA TRACK REQUIRED FOR 9x12-FOOT PARAMOUNT RANCH FOUR-LANE TRACK

Chapter 3 includes a list of part numbers for the track sections and borders identified by the key letters in this plan.

Key	Quantity	Description
H	3	1/2 Inner (1) Curve
I	0	Inner-Inner (0) Curve
S	7	Inner (1) Curve
K	2	Banked Inner (1) Curve
O	28	Middle (2) Curve
M	2	Banked Middle (2) Curve
OO	9	Outer (3) Curve
OOO	0	Outer-Outer (4) Curve
N	0	Banked Outer (3) Curve
E	2	1/4-Straight
D	2	1/3-Straight
B	12	Full-Straight
Q	0	Overpass Bridge
R	2	1/2 of Overpass Bridge
A	2	Connector Track
C	4	Chicane
L		Track can be expanded in length by adding matched pairs of straight track sections here
T		Turn numbers (that correspond to real race course)

20545 Crossing, marked "R" on the plan. You will see in the photos, however, that "R" is actually three sections of 25045 placed side by side to provide both inside and outside borders at this turn. There are photos of these side-by-side crossings as they are used on the Suzuka track for Carrera on page 91. The track has a chicane along the far left.

The 9x14-foot version of Paramount Ranch for Carrera track is illustrated with plans for both the two- and four-lane versions. You can see from the plans how the two-lane track can be

The four-lane Paramount Ranch enlarged to 9x14 feet, without the chicanes. The plans here illustrate both the two-lane and this four-lane version. The chicanes have been eliminated from this version because the modification made racing more interesting and exciting. This track also has the corkscrew (the four cars are all negotiating various stages of it).

LIST OF CARRERA TRACK REQUIRED FOR 9x14-FOOT PARAMOUNT RANCH TWO-LANE TRACK
(PAGE 73, TOP)

Chapter 3 includes a list of part numbers for the track sections and borders identified by the key letters in this plan.

Key	Quantity	Description
H	1	1/2 Inner (1) Curve
I	0	Inner-Inner (0) Curve
S	2	Inner (1) Curve
K	2	Banked Inner (1) Curve
O	22	Middle (2) Curve
M	0	Banked Middle (2) Curve
OO	3	Outer (3) Curve
OOO	0	Outer-Outer (4) Curve
N	0	Banked Outer (3) Curve
E	1	1/4-Straight
D	1	1/3-Straight
B	10	Full-Straight
Q	0	Overpass Bridge
R	1	1/2 of Overpass Bridge
A	1	Connector Track
C	0	Chicane
L		Track can be expanded in length by adding matched pairs of straight track sections here
T		Turn numbers (that correspond to real race course)
W		Track can be expanded in width by adding matched pairs of straight track sections here

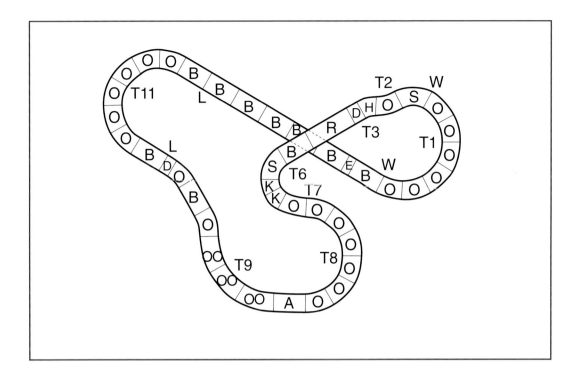

expanded into a four-lane without relocating any track. The extra 2 feet of space allows a bit more than 2 extra feet of straight. The chicanes are eliminated because the two curves and straight provide what amounts to a giant sweeping turn that is much more enjoyable to drive than the chicane area on the 9x12-foot version. The Carrera Number 4 outer-outer-outer curves were not available when this track was assembled, but I would certainly try to include two of them (with outer-outer curves beside them) on the far right. You will need some 1/4-length straight-track sections to fill in the gaps if you do opt for the larger radius turns. This track is actually far more interesting to drive than the 9x12 version, in spite of loosing the chicanes.

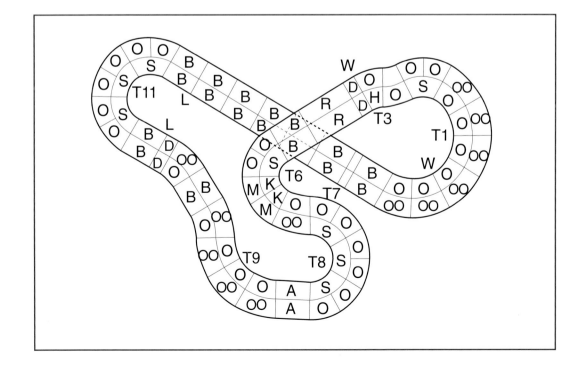

LIST OF CARRERA TRACK REQUIRED FOR 9x14-FOOT PARAMOUNT RANCH FOUR-LANE TRACK
(PAGE 73, BOTTOM)

Chapter 3 includes a list of part numbers for the track sections and borders identified by the key letters in this plan.

Key	Quantity	Description
H	2	1/2 Inner (1) Curve
I	0	Inner-Inner (0) Curve
S	8	Inner (1) Curve
K	2	Banked Inner (1) Curve
O	30	Middle (2) Curve
M	2	Banked Middle (2) Curve
OO	11	Outer (3) Curve
OOO	0	Outer-Outer (4) Curve
N	0	Banked Outer (3) Curve
E	2	1/4-Straight
D	2	1/3-Straight
B	20	Full-Straight
Q	0	Overpass Bridge
R	2	1/2 of Overpass Bridge
A	2	Connector Track
C	0	Chicane
L		Track can be expanded in length by adding matched pairs of straight track sections here
T		Turn numbers (that correspond to real race course)
W		Track can be expanded in width by adding matched pairs of straight track sections here

The Paramount Ranch track assembled from two lanes of Scalextric and SCX track for a 9x14-foot space. A plan for this track appeared in *Racing and Collecting Slot Cars*. The plan in this book is the four-lane version created by merely adding a second lane to this track.

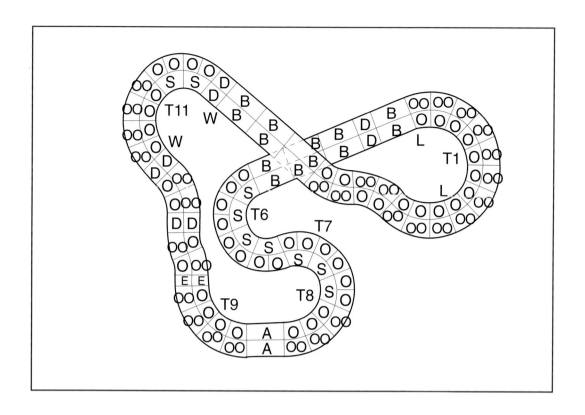

Paramount Ranch for Scalextric, SCX, and Ninco Track

The plan for the Scalextric/SCX/Ninco version of Paramount Ranch illustrates the four-lane version of the track that can be expanded from the two-lane version in the photograph. A plan for this two-lane version appears in *Racing and Collecting Slot Cars*. The track is assembled with a combination of Scalextric and SCX track sections but the plan works just as well for a completely Scalextric Sport, Scalextric Classic, or SCX track. It can also be assembled with Ninco track, but it will require a bit larger space and you will have to use some short pieces of straight track to fill in some gaps.

Indy F1 U. S. Grand Prix Track

The Indianapolis Formula 1 track uses abut half of the Indianapolis 500 oval's surface, including the main start-finish straight and Turn 1. The Formula 1 cars, however, run in the opposite direction on this track, so Turn 1 becomes Turn 13 on the F1 track. The cars make a tight right turn into the infield where the course makes 11 turns before re-entering the older course through Turn 12. The F1 Grand Prix course is approximately the same length as the 2.6-mile course used by Indy cars on Memorial Day and by NASCAR sedans in the Brickyard 400.

LIST OF SCALEXTRIC SPORT, SCALEXTRIC CLASSIC, OR SCX TRACK REQUIRED FOR 9x14-FOOT PARAMOUNT RANCH TRACK

Chapter 3 includes a list of part numbers for the track sections and borders identified by the key letters in this plan.

Key	Quantity	Description
H	0	1/2 Standard (R2) Curve
I	0	Inner-Inner (R1) Curve
S	9	Standard (R2) Curve
O	48	Outer (R3) Curve
OO	30	Outer-Outer (R4) Curve
E	2	1/4-Straight
D	8	1/2-Straight
B	14	Full-Straight
V	0	Crossover Track
A	2	Connector Track
C	0	Chicane
L		Track can be expanded in length by adding matched pairs of straight track sections here
T		Turn numbers (that correspond to real race course)
W		Track can be expanded in width by adding matched pairs of straight track sections here

9x12 Indy F1 U. S. Grand Prix Track for Carrera

The Carrera version of the Indy F1 track appears as a two-lane track in *Racing and Collecting Slot Cars*. The plan for the four-lane version of that track is shown here. The Carrera version re-creates the more significant turns, including having a banked Turn 13 with a flat entrance through Turn 12. In effect, the banking makes Turns 12 and 13 a single increasing radius turn that leads onto the main straight. This track, like most of the tracks in this chapter, could be extended indefinitely by adding pairs of straight track sections at the locations marked "L" on the plan.

The Indianapolis Formula 1 track can begin as a two-lane track. The plan for this track is in *Racing and Collecting Slot Cars*.

The two-lane 9x12-foot Indy F1 Grand Prix track expanded to four lanes. Note that Turn 13 is banked, leading into a flat Turn 12, just like the real Indy F1 track.

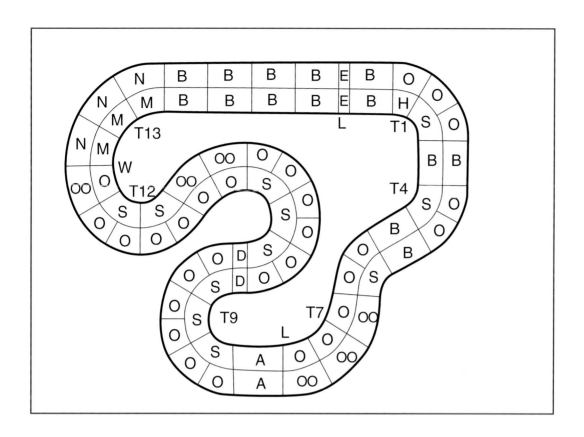

LIST OF CARRERA TRACK REQUIRED FOR 9x14-FOOT PARAMOUNT RANCH FOUR-LANE TRACK

Chapter 3 includes a list of part numbers for the track sections and borders identified by the key letters in this plan.

Key	Quantity	Description
H	1	1/2 Inner (1) Curve
I	0	Inner-Inner (0) Curve
S	11	Inner (1) Curve
K	0	Banked Inner (1) Curve
O	29	Middle (2) Curve
M	3	Banked Middle (2) Curve
OO	6	Outer (3) Curve
OOO	0	Outer-Outer (4) Curve
N	3	Banked Outer (3) Curve
E	2	1/4-Straight
D	2	1/3-Straight
B	14	Full-Straight
Q	0	Overpass Bridge
R	0	1/2 of Overpass Bridge
A	2	Connector Track
C	0	Chicane
L		Track can be expanded in length by adding matched pairs of straight track sections here
T		Turn numbers (that correspond to real race course)

The two-lane, 9x12-foot Indy F1 Grand Prix track for Scalextric and SCX track can be expanded into the four-lane track in this book. Plans for the two-lane version shown are in *Racing and Collecting Slot Cars*.

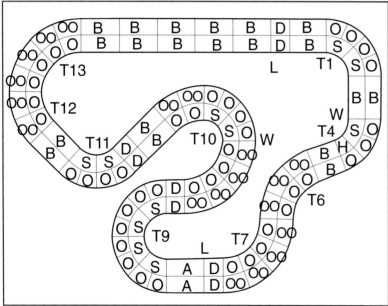

9x12 Indy F1 U. S. Grand Prix Track for Scalextric and SCX

The somewhat tighter turns of Scalextric and SCX track make it possible to more closely match the footprint of the Indy F1 Grand Prix track. Still, there is only room in 9x12 feet for 8 of the 13 turns. The most significant turns are, however, duplicated in the plan. The plan for the two-lane version appears in *Racing and Collecting Slot Cars*. The four-lane version shown in the plan in this chapter merely has a second pair of lanes around the outside of the two-lane track.

LIST OF SCALEXTRIC SPORT, SCALEXTRIC CLASSIC, OR SCX TRACK REQUIRED FOR 9x14-FOOT INDY F1 GRAND PRIX TRACK

Chapter 3 includes a list of part numbers for the track sections and borders identified by the key letters in this plan.

Key	Quantity	Description
H	1	1/2 Standard (R2) Curve
I	0	Inner-Inner (R1) Curve
S	11	Standard (R2) Curve
O	43	Outer (R3) Curve
OO	19	Outer-Outer (R4) Curve
E	0	1/4-Straight
D	6	1/2-Straight
B	18	Full-Straight
V	0	Crossover Track
A	2	Connector Track
C	0	Chicane
L		Track can be expanded in length by adding matched pairs of straight track sections here
T		Turn numbers (that correspond to real race course)
W		Track can be expanded in width by adding matched pairs of straight track sections here

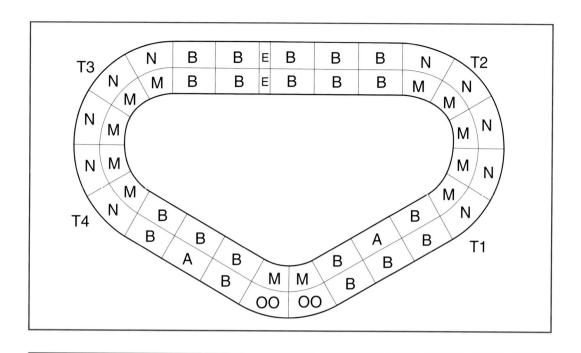

LIST OF CARRERA TRACK REQUIRED FOR 9x12-FOOT DAYTONA INTERNATIONAL RACEWAY

Chapter 3 includes a list of part numbers for the track sections and borders identified by the key letters in this plan.

Key	Quantity	Description
H	0	1/2 Inner (1) Curve
I	0	Inner-Inner (0) Curve
S	0	Inner (1) Curve
K	0	Banked Inner (1) Curve
O	2	Middle (2) Curve
M	10	Banked Middle (2) Curve
OO	2	Outer (3) Curve
OOO	0	Outer-Outer (4) Curve
N	10	Banked Outer (3) Curve
E	2	1/4-Straight
D	0	1/3-Straight
B	20	Full-Straight
Q	0	Overpass Bridge
R	0	1/2 of Overpass Bridge
A	2	Connector Track
C	0	Chicane
T		Turn numbers (that correspond to real race course)

Daytona International Speedway

Built in 1959, Daytona International Speedway is the most famous track in America, next to Indy. The track is a 3.56-mile tri-oval with banked turns at each end. The two banked turns are numbered 1 and 2, and 3 and 4, in accordance with the Indy and NASCAR convention of identifying a turn of more than approximately 120 degrees as two turns. The track was built in 1959 and was originally host to NASCAR sedans; today, two NASCAR events are staged there each year. The 3.81-mile road course was built in 1966 and although not shown on the plan, a chicane was inserted in the main straight just before Turn 3.

The two-lane version of the 9x12-foot Daytona International Speedway for Carrera, assembled with flat, rather than banked, curves at Turns 1/2 and 3/4.

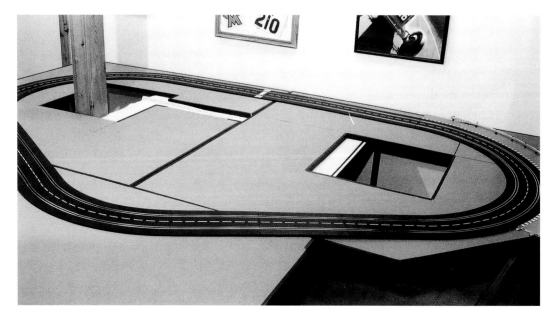

By adding the ess bend through the infield of the 9x12-foot plan, the two-lane road course version of Daytona International Speedway for Carrera track was far more exciting to drive. The final change was to substitute banked turns at both ends for the flat turns.

The road course at the Daytona International Speedway sweeps into the infield from the tri-oval used by the NASCAR sedans.

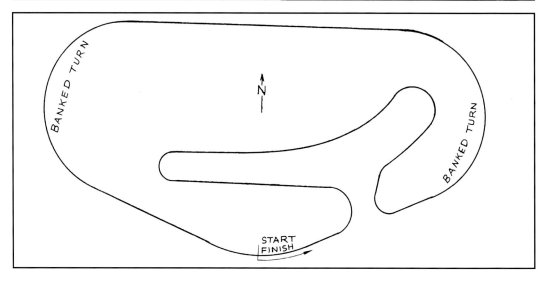

9x12 Daytona International Speedway for Carrera

There's a 5x9-foot two-lane version of Daytona for Carrera in chapter 3. If you have 9x12 feet you can make an incredibly realistic version of the tri-oval thanks to the availability of banked turns from Carrera. I tried the track as a two-lane course with flat outer-outer curves at Turns 1/2 and 3/4, but the track really did not come alive until these turns were replaced with the banked turns that Carrera offers. Turns 1/2 and 3/4 are all banked with Carrera's outer-outer on the outside and their outer on the inside of each turn. There's really no difference in the plans of a track made with flat versus banked turns. When adding banks, however, you need enough area for the turn to flatten out before the cars turn in the opposite direction. Therefore, it is not wise to insert banked turns in half of an ess turn (except through the unusual corkscrew ess used on the Paramount Ranch tracks in this chapter). The flat turn at the start-finish area in the bottom of the plan is assembled from Carrera flat outer and outer-outer turns. The two middle lanes are the quickest, while the inner and outer lanes are nearly equal, albeit a bit slower, than the two middle lanes. There is not a lot of difference—maybe a car length or two per lap. Run races on this track in four heats, with drivers taking their turns on each of the four lanes, and any differences in lane speeds will be negated.

The road racing version of Daytona for Carrera track is even more exciting. I developed this plan, as you could with any race track, by starting with the simple road course with a 180-degree turn in the center. The track was far more exciting to drive, however, when the 180-degree turn was extended to the 210-degree turn shown on the final plans. The flat corners at each end were also replaced with banked turns, even on the two-lane version. Those ess bends that begin at Turn 1 and end at Turn 4 are shown in chapter 1 from a grandstand view. Cars fly through the broad curves and retain their speed around the banking at Turns 2 and 3. The course can be run in either direction for variety. Incidentally, I did try placing a string of chicanes down the long straight so the cars could simulate the drafting movements of real racers tucking in behind one another for greater speeds. It did not work on the banked track because the straight never had enough room to completely flatten between the two banked turns, and the cars tended to slide sideways off the straight.

9x16 Daytona Road Course for Carrera

The 9x16-foot version of Daytona for Carrera track is a bit more than an enlarged version of the 9x12 plan. Again, I tried the track as a flat two-lane, but it was nowhere near as exciting to drive as it was when banked turns were substituted for the flat Turns 1/2 and 3/4. The 9x16 version allows you to bring the banked Turns 1/2 and 3/4 around one more track section to more closely match the shape of the real track. Speeds on this larger version are much higher because the cars have a decently long pair of straights in addition to the main straight.

The sweeping ess bends of the infield area of the Carrera version of Daytona. Here, the cars are running in the reverse of the direction they usually run on the real track.

The four-lane
9x12-foot Daytona
International Speedway
road course for
Carrera track.

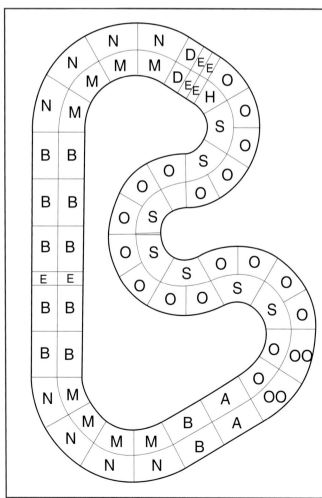

LIST OF CARRERA TRACK REQUIRED FOR 9x12-FOOT DAYTONA INTERNATIONAL RACEWAY

Chapter 3 includes a list of part numbers for the track sections and borders identified by the key letters in this plan.

Key	Quantity	Description
H	2	1/2 Inner (1) Curve
I	0	Inner-Inner (0) Curve
S	7	Inner (1) Curve
K	0	Banked Inner (1) Curve
O	11	Middle (2) Curve
M	8	Banked Middle (2) Curve
OO	2	Outer (3) Curve
OOO	0	Outer-Outer (4) Curve
N	8	Banked Outer (3) Curve
E	6	1/4-Straight
D	2	1/3-Straight
B	12	Full-Straight
Q	0	Overpass Bridge
R	0	1/2 of Overpass Bridge
A	2	Connector Track
C	0	Chicane
T		Turn numbers (that correspond to real race course)

9x12 Daytona International Speedway for Scalextric and SCX

The 9x12-foot Daytona road course for Scalextric and SCX track utilizes the largest curves available for these brands. No banked turns are available but you can achieve some of the effect by simply propping up the ends of the track at Turns 1/2 and 3/4. You may also be able to force a bank into the turns by removing the 1/4-length straight track sections (E) on the main straight. You will need to support the curves with a thin sheet of 1/16-inch plywood to keep a smooth joint between the side-by-side tracks and the borders around the outside of the turns.

8x12 Daytona International Speedway for Revell, Monogram, and Strombecker

Some model car collectors still prefer the plastic track sections produced by Revell, Monogram, and Strombecker in the 1960s. Although Monogram track is no longer available, REH does offer Revell track under the Riggen label. They also have a stock of Strombecker track. Unfortunately, only standard curves and full-length straights are available, so you would have to create a two-lane version of this plan. The plan shown here originally appeared in *Model Road Racing Handbook*,

LIST OF CARRERA TRACK REQUIRED FOR 9x16-FOOT DAYTONA INTERNATIONAL RACEWAY

Chapter 3 includes a list of part numbers for the track sections and borders identified by the key letters in this plan.

Key	Quantity	Description
H	2	1/2 Inner (1) Curve
I	0	Inner-Inner (0) Curve
S	7	Inner (1) Curve
K	0	Banked Inner (1) Curve
O	16	Middle (2) Curve
M	10	Banked Middle (2) Curve
OO	0	Outer (3) Curve
OOO	0	Outer-Outer (4) Curve
N	10	Banked Outer (3) Curve
E	4	1/4-Straight
D	0	1/3-Straight
B	28	Full-Straight
Q	0	Overpass Bridge
R	0	1/2 of Overpass Bridge
A	2	Connector Track
C	0	Chicane
T		Turn numbers (that correspond to real race course)

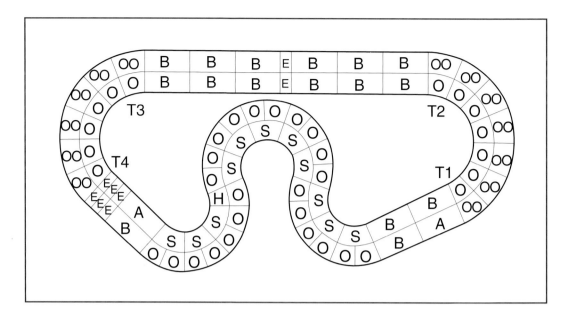

published by Van Nostrand in 1967 (and now long out of print). The 8x12-foot area can be created with three portable 4x8-foot tabletops placed side by side.

Suzuka Grand Prix Raceway

Suzuka has long been a favorite among model car racers because it is a real race track that offers the figure-eight configuration that some modelers prefer to help equalize lane lengths. The real race track is located in a park-like, hilly area, so there are elevation changes that are similar to those at Monaco (but not as steep). The 3.6-mile track was built by Honda in 1962, but the first Formula 1 Grand Prix was not held there until 1987. The track is host to a number of Japanese races, so virtually every type of car has appeared on the real circuit. Because it's a classic track for model car racers, I have designed and race-tested Suzuka for Scalextric, SCX, and Carrera track sections in order to assemble the tracks in this chapter.

LIST OF SCALEXTRIC SPORT, SCALEXTRIC CLASSIC, OR SCX TRACK REQUIRED FOR 9x12-FOOT DAYTONA INTERNATIONAL RACEWAY

Chapter 3 includes a list of part numbers for the track sections and borders identified by the key letters in this plan.

Key	Quantity	Description
H	1	1/2 Standard (R2) Curve
I	0	Inner-Inner (R1) Curve
S	11	Standard (R2) Curve
O	36	Outer (R3) Curve
OO	13	Outer-Outer (R4) Curve
E	8	1/4-Straight
D	0	1/2-Straight
B	16	Full-Straight
V	0	Crossover Track
A	2	Connector Track
C	0	Chicane
T		Turn numbers (that correspond to real race course)

All these 1/32 scale plans illustrate the circuit upside down from the drawing of the real race track. Also, the plans for the Scalextric, SCX, and the Carrera versions have the straight going beneath the bridge, while on the real track, the straight is above the curve at Turn 5. On a model raceway, it is more important to be able to see the curves through Turns 3 and 5 than the straight. Also, there is no Turn 4 on the model, and Turn 6 has been designed with a larger radius than the hairpin on the real track.

9x14 Suzuka Grand Prix Raceway for Scalextric and SCX

Like all the four-lane tracks in this book and those in *Racing and Collecting Slot Cars*, the track can be assembled as just a two-lane track as shown in the photo and the plan. Note that the two-lane plan includes the lanes with the largest-radius turns (the outer two lanes on the right side of the overpass). You can add the second two lanes at a later time. The kink in the straight at Turn 8 is not as damaging to the speed of the cars as you might expect because they are still accelerating out of the sweeping Turn 7. The chi-

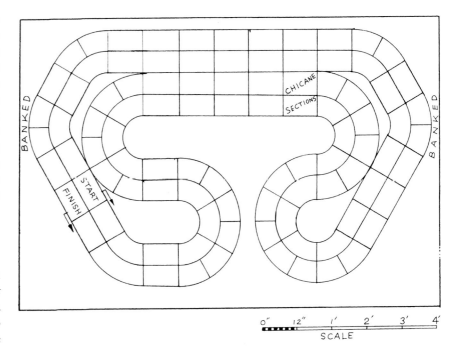

cane simulates the effect of one car tucking in behind the other during a race, so both cars get an aerodynamic tow that increases the top speed of both cars. The uphill and downhill portions of the track are supported on the posts Scalextric supplies with their sets.

The Daytona road course can also be assembled from collector track pieces originally made by Revell, Monogram, or Strombecker. The curves are all sets of one inner and two outer, and all the straights are full-length because that's all they made. The plan would fit an 8x12-foot area.

The ess bends through the infield area of the 9x12-foot Scalextric/SCX version of the Suzuka Grand Prix track are as exciting to drive as they are to see.

The Suzuka track in Japan is one of the only remaining road racing tracks in the world that has an overpass for a convoluted figure-eight configuration.

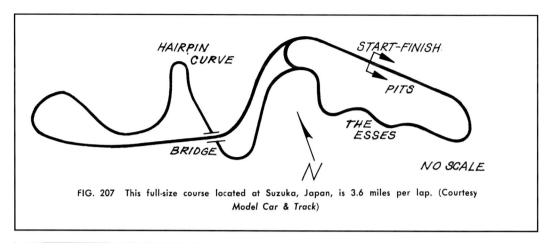

FIG. 207 This full-size course located at Suzuka, Japan, is 3.6 miles per lap. (Courtesy Model Car & Track)

The two-lane version of Suzuka, assembled from Scalextric and SCX track sections, in a 9x14-foot area.

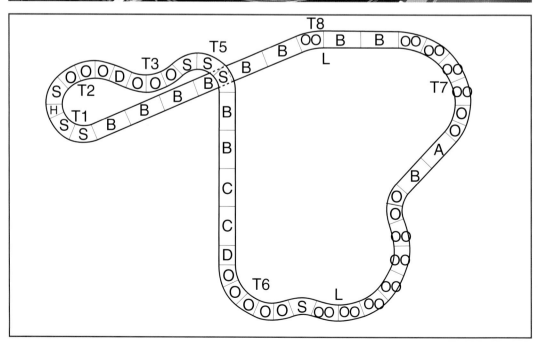

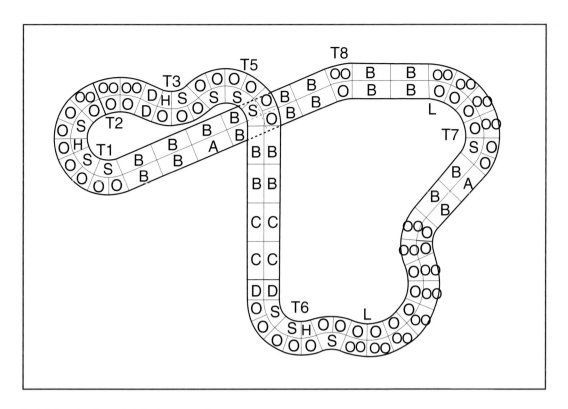

9x14 Suzuka Grand Prix Raceway for Carrera

There are three versions of the Suzuka Grand Prix circuit for Carrera track. The first illustrates both a two-lane and four-lane version of the same plan. Again, the two-lane version utilizes the outside lanes from the four-lane, so the additional two lanes for the four-lane version mostly tuck inside the two-lane version. The two-lane track looks more like the real course because the proportions are closer to the real track. The curves are broad enough, however, so that all the lanes on the four-lane version are very near equal. These two tracks also have chicanes along the short straight.

The track runs uphill on supports made from small boxes (although Woodland Scenics Risers cut as shown in chapter 4 would be a more elegant approach) and descends on half of a Carrera Number 20545 Crossing. Since there are no Carrera borders for the crossing, I joined two of the crossings side by side to provide a border on each side of the track for the two-lane version. For the four-lane version, I joined three 20545 Crossings side by side as shown in the photo. Both versions use a few too many standard/outer (S/O) pairs of curves that make it a bit dull to drive on after a few dozen races.

The third version has much more severe ess curves between Turns 6 and 7, so it does not match the appearance of the real Suzuka Grand

LIST OF SCALEXTRIC SPORT, SCALEXTRIC CLASSIC, OR SCX TRACK REQUIRED FOR 9x14-FOOT SUZUKA GRAND PRIX

Chapter 3 includes a list of part numbers for the track sections and borders identified by the key letters in this plan.

Key	Quantity		Description
	2-Lane	**4-Lane**	
H	1	3	1/2 Standard (R2) Curve
I	0	0	Inner-Inner (R1) Curve
S	6	11	Standard (R2) Curve
O	15	40	Outer (R3) Curve
OO	10	16	Outer-Outer (R4) Curve
E	0	0	1/4-Straight
D	2	4	1/2-Straight
B	11	22	Full-Straight
V	0	0	Crossover Track
A	1	2	Connector Track
C	1	2	Chicane
L	Track can be expanded in length by adding matched pairs of straight track sections here		
T	Turn numbers (that correspond to real race course)		
W	Track can be expanded in width by adding matched pairs of straight track sections here		

Above: A Carrera Corvette and Mustang leap down the crossing incline on the Suzuka track. This is really two of the Carrera 20545 crossing sections placed side-by-side (rather than end-to-end) to provide a border on both sides of the track.

Turns 1, 2, and 3 of the two-lane Carrera re-creation of the Suzuka Grand Prix circuit.

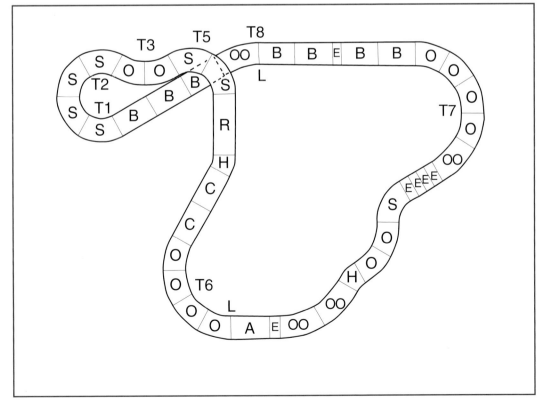

The chicane and Turns 6 and 7 (upper center) with a row of SCX 88100 Barrels with Banners (the banners are not attached in the photo) around the outside of Turn 7.

LIST OF CARRERA TRACK REQUIRED FOR 9x14-FOOT TWO-LANE SUZUKA GRAND PRIX TRACK (PAGE 89, BOTTOM)

Chapter 3 includes a list of part numbers for the track sections and borders identified by the key letters in this plan.

Key	Quantity	Description
H	2	1/2 Inner (1) Curve
I	0	Inner-Inner (0) Curve
S	7	Inner (1) Curve
K	0	Banked Inner (1) Curve
O	12	Middle (2) Curve
M	0	Banked Middle (2) Curve
OO	4	Outer (3) Curve
OOO	0	Outer-Outer (4) Curve
N	0	Banked Outer (3) Curve
E	6	1/4-Straight
D	0	1/3-Straight
B	7	Full-Straight
Q	0	Overpass Bridge
R	1	1/2 of Overpass Bridge
A	1	Connector Track
C	2	Chicane
L		Track can be expanded in length by adding matched pairs of straight track sections here
T		Turn numbers (that correspond to real race course)

LIST OF CARRERA TRACK REQUIRED FOR 9x14-FOOT FOUR-LANE SUZUKA GRAND PRIX TRACK (BELOW)

Chapter 3 includes a list of part numbers for the track sections and borders identified by the key letters in this plan.

Key	Quantity	Description
H	2	1/2 Inner (1) Curve
I	0	Inner-Inner (0) Curve
S	13	Inner (1) Curve
K	0	Banked Inner (1) Curve
O	32	Middle (2) Curve
M	0	Banked Middle (2) Curve
OO	4	Outer (3) Curve
OOO	0	Outer-Outer (4) Curve
N	0	Banked Outer (3) Curve
E	12	1/4-Straight
D	0	1/3-Straight
B	14	Full-Straight
Q	0	Overpass Bridge
R	2	1/2 of Overpass Bridge
A	2	Connector Track
C	4	Chicane
L		Track can be expanded in length by adding matched pairs of straight track sections here
T		Turn numbers (that correspond to real race course)

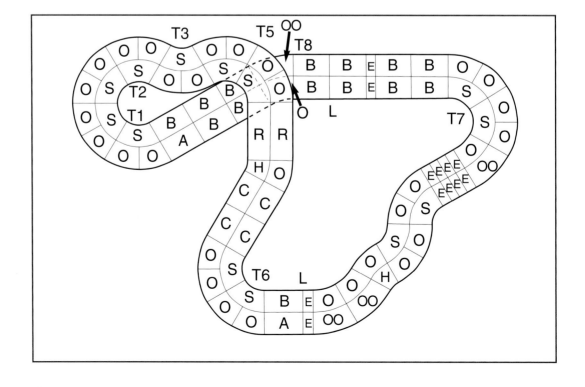

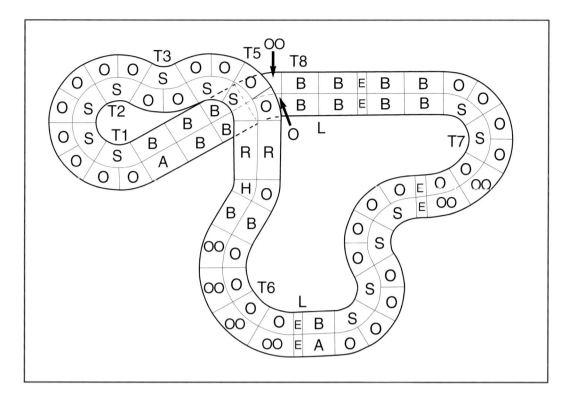

Prix track as closely as the first two versions. These ess bends, however, are incredibly fun to drive and there is a broader-radius curve at Turn 6. Carrera now has Number 4 outer-outer-outer (OOO on the plans) curves that I would substitute for the four pairs of outer and outer-outer curves at Turn 6, with a few 1/4-length straights to fill in the gaps. The lap length on this track is about 41 feet. As it is, this is one of the most enjoyable tracks to drive in this chapter.

LIST OF CARRERA TRACK REQUIRED FOR 9x14-FOOT FOUR-LANE SUZUKA GRAND PRIX TRACK

Chapter 3 includes a list of part numbers for the track sections and borders identified by the key letters in this plan.

Key	Quantity	Description
H	1	1/2 Inner (1) Curve
I	0	Inner-Inner (0) Curve
S	13	Inner (1) Curve
K	0	Banked Inner (1) Curve
O	34	Middle (2) Curve
M	0	Banked Middle (2) Curve
OO	7	Outer (3) Curve
OOO	0	Outer-Outer (4) Curve
N	0	Banked Outer (3) Curve
E	6	1/4-Straight
D	0	1/3-Straight
B	16	Full-Straight
Q	0	Overpass Bridge
R	2	1/2 of Overpass Bridge
A	2	Connector Track
C	0	Chicane
L		Track can be expanded in length by adding matched pairs of straight track sections here
T		Turn numbers (that correspond to real race course)

The two-lane version of Suzuka expanded to four lanes with Carrera track, but modified with longer ess turns between Turns 6 and 7 and a broader radius for Turn 6. There's another view of this track and a photo of the two-lane version in chapter 1. The four 1/4-length straights near Turn 7 are used so the custom-made controller plug-in track section shown in chapter 14 can be used, with another controller location near Turn 6.

10x20 Suzuka Grand Prix Raceway for Revell/Monogram/Strombecker

The track plan for the four-lane Revell/Monogram/Strombecker version of Suzuka can only be assembled with out-of-production track sections. REH still offers Revell track under the Riggen label and sells Strombecker track, but only standard curves and full-length straights are available. You can easily assemble a two-plan version Suzuka with these track sections.

The plan includes small arrows marks and "4" markings to indicate track elevation above the tabletop—arrows indicate up and down grades. A model of Suzuka assembled from collector track pieces or from currently available track sections would be most realistic if the main straight was supported 4 inches above the tabletop—that's easy enough to accomplish using Woodland Scenics 4-inch Risers as shown in chapter 4.

Perhaps the most interesting aspect of this plan is that it is assembled on four 4x8-foot tables arranged in a stair-step pattern. A similar version could be assembled with Scalextric, SCX, Ninco, or Carrera track on four 4x8 tables.

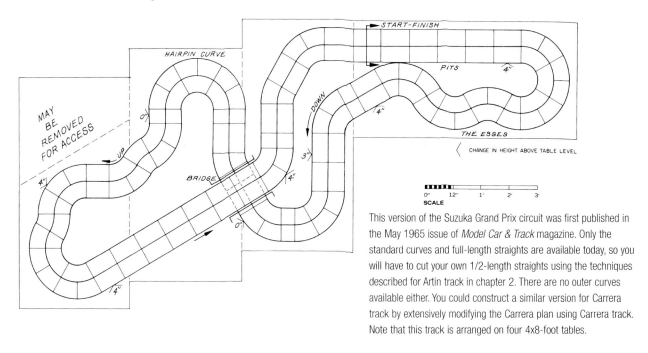

This version of the Suzuka Grand Prix circuit was first published in the May 1965 issue of *Model Car & Track* magazine. Only the standard curves and full-length straights are available today, so you will have to cut your own 1/2-length straights using the techniques described for Artin track in chapter 2. There are no outer curves available either. You could construct a similar version for Carrera track by extensively modifying the Carrera plan using Carrera track. Note that this track is arranged on four 4x8-foot tables.

Chapter Six

CUSTOM-BUILT 1/32 TRACKS

Paramount Ranch is one of two tracks that have an overpass for a figure-eight configuration, the other being Suzuka.

You can design and build your own 1/32 scale race track, routing the circuit exactly where you want it with no compromises. The first model racing tracks were, in fact, cut from wood by hand.

All the massive commercial race tracks for 1/24 scale cars are made like the tracks in this chapter. In 1970 there were over 6,000 of them in operation. Today there are less than 200. Model car racers refer to these handmade tracks as "routed tracks" because the slot is cut into the wood track surface with a power woodworking tool called a router. The router bit is like a tiny

circular saw, with teeth that slice cleanly through wood and some plastics.

If you do not want to assemble and route the track yourself, some custom builders can build a track for you. Brad's Tracks and Silky's Custom Slot Car Tracks are two sources, and you may find others through Eagle Distributing.

Finding a Permanent Space to Race
One of the disadvantages of a routed track is that it is heavy and as such, very difficult to consider portable in any way. It's possible to construct a rigging system to hoist a routed track

93

into the ceiling like Fred Martins' Carrera track in chapter 2, but it would be a true theater rigger's engineering task. If you need a portable track, I suggest using plastic track.

There are, however, some rather unusual places you might be able to condemn as a site for your permanent home track. The most obvious are areas where no one else in the house wants to be, like damp basements or attics. If you have enough room you might even consider a separate building. You may also be able to utilize half of a two-car garage.

If you need both stalls of a two-car garage, consider placing the track across the hoods of the cars along the back wall of the garage. You will have to measure the distance from your cars' windshields to the wall, but you can usually fit a 5-foot-wide shelf across the back of most garages and over the hoods of most cars. If you are parking SUVs or pickup trucks, the track will simply have to be higher.

I built a track like this except I could not go all the way across the back wall because there was a door on one corner, the result being a track that was 5x17 feet rather than 5x20. This track however also had a long shelf extending down one of the garage walls. The 24-inch-wide shelf

9x16-foot Paramount Ranch Raceway is routed from 4x8-foot sheets of particleboard. The scenery, colors, track shape, and general driving opportunities of the real track have been re-created on the model.

The real Paramount Ranch Raceway hosted races for only a few years, but it has a place in racing history.

94

was just wide enough to contain a reverse loop with a chicane and 5-, 6-, and 7-inch radius curves with three lanes running down the inside and three back up the outside of the shelf. I was able to add nearly 24 feet of lap length without consuming any usable living area. You might be able to incorporate a similar shelf-style straight from the main track table in a den, running the shelf over a bookcase or, perhaps, behind a couch.

Plans for Routed Tracks

The track plans in this chapter are drawn in the style used by model railroad layout builders. To route a track, you need to know where to locate the curve centers and the diameters of the curves you are cutting and precisely where to start and where to stop cutting each curve. Those marks are all on these plans. The plan must be re-drawn on the actual tabletop for two reasons: 1) You need all those marks, and 2) It's far better to make a mistake with a pencil than with a router. If you design your own track you need to use a similar system. These plans also have small arrows beside the track that indicate elevations above zero for the overpass areas.

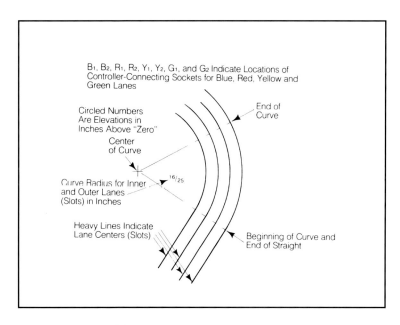

Start Small: So-Cal in 4x8

The So-Cal International Raceway is about 32 feet per lap—as much track distance and racing excitement as you can fit into a 4x8-foot area for 1/32 scale cars. It is also an example of how to have more racing in less space with a routed

Key to markings on the plans for routed tracks.

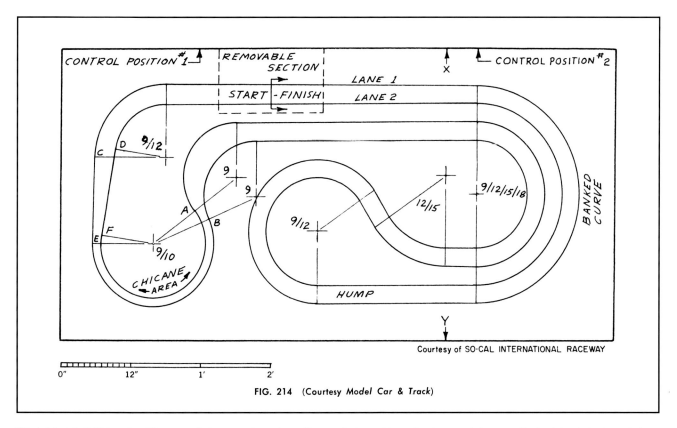

Courtesy of SO-CAL INTERNATIONAL RACEWAY

FIG. 214   (Courtesy Model Car & Track)

This 4x8-foot So-Cal International Raceway will give you a chance to see if you really do want to create a larger routed raceway. The track is only two lanes, but the two share a common road on the right and upper edge of the plan to squeeze a 30-foot lane length into a small space.

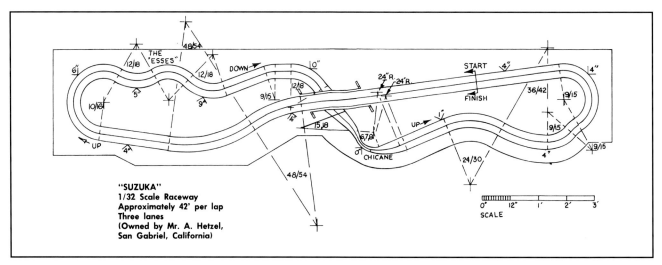

"SUZUKA"
1/32 Scale Raceway
Approximately 42' per lap
Three lanes
(Owned by Mr. A. Hetzel,
San Gabriel, California)

The three-lane version of the Suzuka Grand Prix track will fit in a 4-1/2 x 16–foot space. There are photos of the track under construction later in this chapter.

track: 5x9 feet are needed to assemble a somewhat similar 32-feet-per-lap Indy F1 track from Carrera, Scalextric, or SCX track as shown in *Racing and Collecting Slot Cars*. You might consider building a replica of this 4x8-foot track on a single sheet of 4x8-foot medium-density overlay (MDO) board or medium-density foamboard (MDF) just to see if you can do it. Better to learn on a relatively simple track like this than on an 8x30-foot raceway. The key to the plans indicates what each marking stands for. This removable section is an option that makes it easier to install lap counters.

Three Lanes or Four? The Suzuka Track

This three-lane track is more complex than the plan reveals because the model undulates uphill and downhill very much like on the real track. The track does provide an example of how a routed track can include both the general shape of the real track and provide smooth corners in a smaller space than plastic sectional track. There's a chicane in one corner to match the hairpin Turn 6 on the real track and two 48/54-inch "sweeper" turns off the end of the main straight. In truth, we discovered after it was built

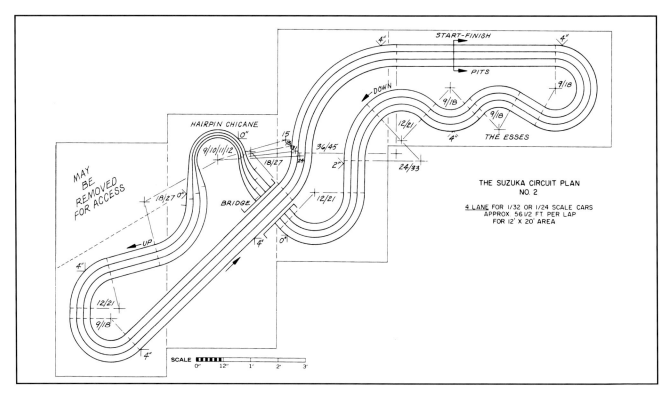

The four-lane 12x20-foot Suzuka Grand Prix track is designed to fit on four sheets of 4x8-foot board.

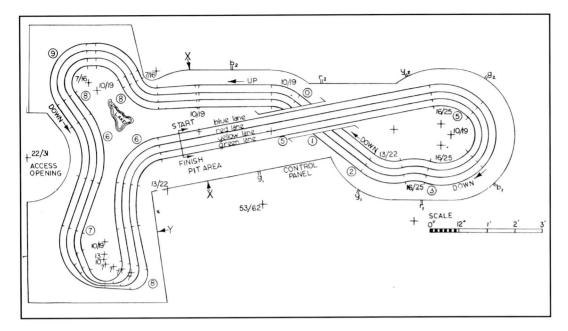

Paramount Ranch in 1/32 scale. The track is but a fraction of the length of an exact-scale replica, but it includes the significant corners and scenic features of the real raceway.

that the track would have been more fun if we'd left out those sweeping ess turns and just ran the straight all the way from one end of the track to the other.

The four-lane version is designed to be routed into four sheets of 4x8-foot MDF or MDO, and is drawn upside down compared to the three-lane version.

Paramount Ranch Raceway

This is the plan for the track that was featured in *Car Model* magazine in the 1960s as part of a multi-issue serial on building a hand-routed track. I built it, so I am prejudiced, but I feel to this day that it was the best home track I ever raced on. I'd have preferred that the straight be another couple of feet longer, but it worked very

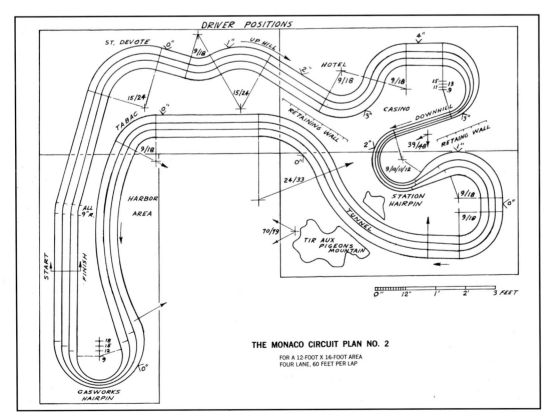

The Monaco Grand Prix circuit fitted on four 4x8-foot panels. There is only a 4-inch elevation change, but it could rise to 8 inches or more like the Carrera version of Monaco in chapter 5.

Daytona International Speedway in 8x12 feet with banked turns and a chicaned turn leading out of the infield.

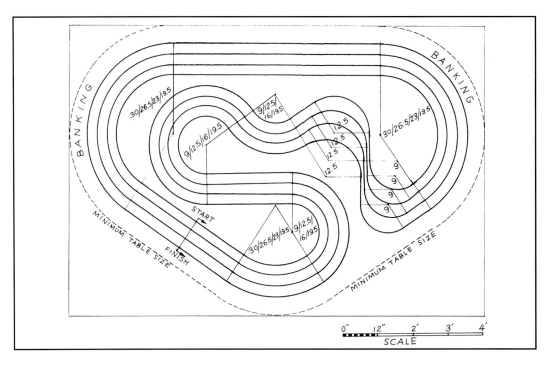

well. The chicane corner is particularly interesting to drive in a close race because the cars tuck in behind one another exactly the way they do on a real track.

Monaco Grand Prix Track
The routed construction of Monaco allows the builder to fit more into the same amount of space as plastic sectional track requires. The turn at the Hôtel de Paris and the single-file chicane

on the downhill leading into Station Hairpin simulate the actual racing paths the cars take on the road at Monaco, as does the chicane at the Gasworks Hairpin and the sweeping 70/79-inch radii turn through the harbor area.

Daytona International Speedway
This is the most difficult track to build of all those in this chapter. If you decide to do it, I suggest you check out the commercial Track

A portion of a garage may provide enough space for a track the size of the Suzuka three-lane raceway, either inside a single stall or positioned above the hoods of the cars in a two-car garage.

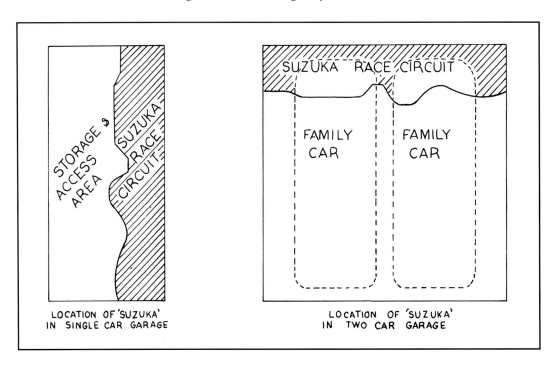

Owner's Association (TOA) Website at www.oldnslo.com/track for more information on constructing banked turns. The chicane is particularly difficult to work out; you may have to settle for just half of the right turn as a bank so it can flatten out in time for the cars to make it through the chicane area.

The track is only 8x12 feet. If it were me, I would forget it and opt for the Carrera 9x12 version, complete with banks that I know work, shown in chapter 5.

The custom-routed version is considerably easier to build if the track is larger, so 3 or 4 feet of straight can be inserted between the banking on the right and the chicane. There is no reason why any track in this chapter, particularly this one, cannot be expanded in any direction—just make the straights longer and/or the curve larger.

How High?

The advantage of the 30-inch-high track (besides being the height of a Ping-Pong or conference table) is that you have better depth perception than if the track and cars are higher. But if you want to see the cars as they would appear in the real world, sit down and race (I can make a strong case for racing on a track placed 48 inches from the floor instead of the usual 30 inches). The height should be the one that you prefer. If you really do prefer the incredible realism of eye-level racing, build the track 48 inches or more and use a bench when you want the better depth perception that this "helicopter" view provides.

Design Your Own Raceway

One of the trickiest aspects of building your own track is designing it. How many lanes? How far apart should the lanes be? Do you want increasing-radius and/or decreasing-radius turns, chicanes, chicanes on straights, or real racing lines through curves? How many chicanes? Most of these answers will depend on how large you want the track to be.

Personally, I feel that three lanes are the best compromise for a home raceway. You cannot buy plastic track with three lanes (although some was made in the 1960s), but it is just about right for most home tracks. As a rough rule, I suggest two lanes for any track smaller than 5x10 feet, three lanes for any track from 5x10 to 9x20 feet, and four lanes for tracks larger than 9x20 feet. Only one of the four plans in this chapter is for a three-lane track, but it's simple enough to eliminate a lane from any of the other three plans if you wish.

I suggest you pick or design a plan that allows the longest possible straight. I also recommend that you have very broad curves on one end of the longest straight, a tight curve at the opposite end, and no chicanes on either end or anywhere along that longest straight. There needs to be someplace on the track where everyone can nail it without fear of banging into something. The remainder of the track is completely up to you.

These four plans were originally published as part of a series in *Model Car & Track* and *Model Car Science* magazines in the 1960s and the remainder of the series is being reprinted in *Model Car Racing* magazine. At the moment I know of no other sources for routed track plans, although I bet you could search some out on the Internet.

Chicanes as Racing Lines

Chicanes along a straight look fascinating because the cars squeeze closer to the middle of the track in order to tuck in and simulate the drafting that real racers use to obtain more speed from both the leading and trailing car. If you have room for another long straight and like the "tow" effect, by all means make most of that straight chicane. A chicane can often be used to build in a larger-radius corner than would normally fit there. I suggest designing the track without chicanes, then look for a corner or two where a chicane might make for a smoother-flowing track. Chicanes on curves should be designed so the slots force the cars to replicate the line that a real car would follow through the corner. Usually, a chicane is a simple curve like those on both the three-lane and four-lane Suzuka Grand Prix tracks and the hairpin turn on the 4x8 So-Cal Raceway, but sometimes the cars can take a slightly different route, like the chicane pattern on the Paramount Ranch Track.

None of these suggestions really makes use of the chicane in the same manner that it is used on a real track: to provide an artificial part of the track to reduce speeds in an area (usually a straight) that is deemed too fast. "Too fast" is not a problem with model car racing tracks because none of us ever has enough space for the track we'd like to have. You can certainly build in a chicane on a short straight to duplicate the action (if not the need) of a chicane on real track. On a real track, a chicane is nearly always a tight right turn followed by an equally tight left turn (or vice versa). The cars are more or less forced to funnel through the two turns on the same racing line. The chicane on the 8x12-foot Daytona International Speedway track is quintessential, especially since the tracks leading into and out of the chicane are straight rather than curved, as they are on the model. In truth, that chicane was meant to be a racing line chicane, but its shape is that of the racing lines that real cars would take through a chicane on a real track.

Track-Building Tools

If you even consider building your own track, I hope you already have your own favorite assortment of woodworking tools. The only special tool you will need is a heavy-duty electric router. Tool supply rental shops usually have routers if you would rather not make the investment. You will also need a piece of 1/8-inch brass or bronze rod that's about 6 inches longer than the largest curve you intend to cut.

I was lucky: I was able to borrow all the tools I needed and the person to operate them. The late Albert Hetzel actually did most of the work, building both the Suzuka three-lane track (which was in his home) and Paramount Ranch (which was in my home). I planned them, helped hold and saw and screw, and took pictures. I could not have done it without him then and I doubt I could do it now.

Buy at least two 1/8-inch router bits to cut the slot because you will likely break at least one. Albert and I discovered that a 1/8-inch bit broke far too easily in particleboard or plywood, so we

eventually went to a 5/32-inch bit. The 1/8-inch bits should work fine for cutting MDF board, MDO, or expanded PVC sheet. Install the router bit so it cuts a 1/4-inch-deep slot. If you wish to use magnetic braid, you will also need a babbiting bit to cut the recesses for the braid on either side of the slot. Braid is available in 1/8-, 3/16-, and 1/4-inch widths, so you will need a babbiting bit that cuts the depression for the braid to cut a recess on both sides of the slot. The braid should not hang over into the slot, so the recess for the braid has to be about 1/16 inch wider than the two widths of braid, plus the 1/8-inch slot. Hence, you'll need a 7/16-inch babbiting bit for a 1/8-inch braid, a 9/16-inch bit for 3/16-inch braid, or an 11/16-inch bit for 1/4-inch braid. The 1/8-inch braid looks the least obtrusive and closely matches the contact strips on plastic track.

Open-Grid Benchwork

The tabletop for a routed track must be supported by a sturdy open-grid benchwork like that used for model railroads. I strongly recommend that you divide the benchwork (and the track surface) into modules no larger than 4x8 feet so you can move them out the door. The benchwork plan for the Paramount Ranch track gives you an idea of how to design open-grid benchwork. If you need more information than you find here, several books on building model railroads are available at large model railroad shops to provide more information, including

The open-grid benchwork for the Paramount Ranch track. All the boards are 1x4s except for the butted-together 1x12s (which could be cut from 3/4-inch plywood) at the center.

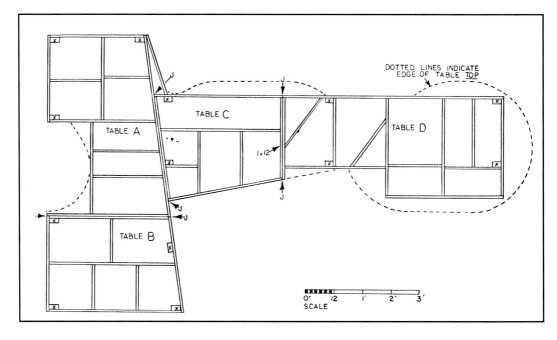

additional methods of making scenery. Make each module a table unto itself (like Tables A through D on the Paramount Ranch track), with removable legs attached with carriage bolts, fender washers, and nuts. Use the same type of bolts to clamp one module to the next. You can cover the entire area with solid sheets of whatever material you choose for the tabletop. The tabletop surface can be cut to the exact size you need after you have securely mounted the track surface and cut all the slots. Remember to disassemble those modules, however, before you install the copper pickup tape or magnetic braid so the tape or braid can wrap over the end of each module. The electrical contact between the modules can simply be the contact of braid touching braid, but you can also solder 6-inch "jumper" wires across each joint if you question the current flow.

Assemble all the joints with 1-1/2-inch flathead number 8 Phillips wood screws, and buy a pilot bit to match the wood screws so you can pre-drill each hole. You can probably use an electric screwdriver, but I prefer a more powerful mechanical "Yankee" screwdriver that drives the screws as you push down on the handle.

Track Surface Materials
The best choices for model racing track surface are, in the order of my preference, expanded PVC black plastic sheet, MDO plywood, MDF, particleboard, and plywood. PVC cuts cleaner that MDO or MDF, but is also much more difficult to fix when you make errors (and you *will* make errors) because the mistakes must be filled with strips of ABS plastic cemented with a nasty solvent like MDK—wear a respirator and work outdoors. In fact, I advise you to wear gloves, goggles, and a respirator when working with any of these materials because you produce a plastic dust even as you cut MDO. Keep a vacuum cleaner with a hose attachment at hand and vacuum frequently. If you have a helper, have him or her keep the vacuum running the whole time you are routing.

MDO offers treated first and second plies that are prepainted for use in sign making. Since the surface is already colored, you may not even need to paint it. MDO is now the first choice for most commercial track builders. MDF is a fine-flake particleboard that looks like powdered wood with a filler, which just about describes what it actually is. It cuts cleanly with a router bit but produces very fine dust. Like conventional particleboard, MDF must be supported every 2 feet or it will sag under its own weight. PVC is a lightweight plastic sheet available from some commercial plastics supply firms. It is only available in 7/32-inch or thinner sheets, so you must laminate it to MDF or plywood with strong contact cement or a similar adhesive before cutting a 1/4-inch deep slot.

Tape or Braid for Pickup Strips
If you use braid, the slot for the braid should be cut and the braid installed before painting. Magnatec offers 1/4-inch, 3/16-inch, and 1/8-inch magnetic braid. The 1/4-inch material is often used on commercial tracks, but, for most home racing, the 1/8-inch braid is the most suitable. The braid must rest as close to level with the track surface as possible. To be safe, cut the recesses so the braid is between .005 inches (about the thickness of this page) above the track and .005 inches below, but try to install the braid perfectly flush with the track surface so the magnets will have an effect similar to that on plastic tracks. Measure the thickness of the braid you are using and adjust the babbiting router bit so it cuts the same depth as the thickness of the braid. Brad's Tracks uses round 12-gauge galvanized stranded wire set in a 3/32-inch square slot on each side of the center slot for the PVC-surfaced Carrera inner-inner curve in chapters 2 and 5.

It is much easier to use self-adhesive copper tape for the pickup strips because you need only cut the single slot (no recesses are needed) and the tape sticks all by itself. You can buy self-adhesive copper tape at craft stores like Hobby Lobby or your hobby dealer can order it through Parma or REH. Just press it in place on the painted track surface.

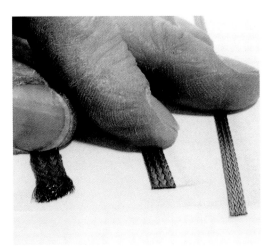

The three sizes of magnetic braid from Magnatec: 1/4, 3/16, and 1/8 inch wide.

Use number 8x1-1/2-inch Phillips flathead screws to assemble the open grid benchwork and the tabletop. Drill a pilot hole for each screw and install the screws with a Yankee screwdriver (shown) or an electric screwdriver.

The legs can be 1x4s, attached to the benchwork with 1/4-inch carriage bolts, fender washers, and nuts so they can be removed, raised, and/or lowered.

"Paving" the Track Surface

Draw the layout of all the slots on the bare track surface with a pencil, using a trammel to draw all the curves first. (To make a trammel, simply drill a pencil-size hole in the end of a board or yard-stick, then drill 1/16-inch holes the appropriate distance from the pencil to match each of the different curve radii you will be using.) Next, connect the curves with a pencil guided by a straight piece of wood. Make a dark, clear pencil mark at the point where the straight intersects with the curve because those are the points where you will begin and stop the actual routing of each curve.

Assemble the complete track with all the slots marked on the track surface. Erase or paint over any errors made with the pencil marks. In general take a close look at every inch of the tabletop so you know this really is where you want the track to be located—it's relatively simple to change a pencil line, but a lot harder to fill in a slot and start again. You might want to mark the outside border or skid area of every curve if you want to elevate the track. Accurate borders will be necessary if you opt for the commercial track routing system described later in this chapter. Remember to make a second layer if your track has an overpass like Paramount Ranch or Suzuka.

When the track satisfies your critical eye, re-move all the track surface so you can route the slots on the floor, where it is much easier to swing the router and move the wooden straight edges that guide it. You can also bend the track surface into banked turns or uphills and down-hills while it is secured to the open-grid bench-work. Those areas will be routed as precisely as the flat areas if you remove the track surface. When you reinstall the track surface, insert the screws in the same holes and everything should align nicely, ready for painting and installing the copper tape or steel braid.

Routing the Curved Slots

For the trammel that will guide the router, use a 1/8-inch diameter brass or bronze rod that's 6 inches longer than the widest curve. Use a file or grinder to make a point on one end of the rod, and bend about 2 inches of that end of the rod 90 degrees. The point will be the center of the curve and will rest in a 1/16-inch hole you drill to locate the center of every curve. Clamp the free end of the rod in two of the pockets in the side of the router. Adjust the router back and

The open-grid benchwork for the Suzuka track is higher along the far end and at the rear of the track to support the elevated main straightaway.

Draw the entire track plan on the tabletop, just as you see it in the plans. Attach the tabletop and cut all the outer edges and realign any marks for the slots so they will flow smoothly.

forth on the rod so the distance between the point of the trammel and the center of the router bit matches the diameter of the curve you wish to cut.

To cut the slot, position the pointed tip of the trammel over the hole at the center of the circle and start the router while it is tilted up enough so the bit does not touch the track. Using the trammel as a pivot, keep the router running while gently swinging it over to drill a starter hole with the router bit. Hold the trammel firmly into the center hole while you apply a steady pressure on the router to cut the slot. Always work only in one direction—do not back up or the slot will be wider than you want. When you are finished with that curve, gently tilt the router out of the slot, then turn it off. If you try to turn the router on or off while it is in the slot, the bit is likely to catch on the edge and break. Rout all the curves first. Then install the babbiting bit if you are going to cut recesses for magnetic braid on both sides of the slot. When they are done, remove the trammel.

Use a trammel to draw every curve and a straight piece of wood to guide your pencil when you draw the straights. This track was routed in particleboard—today I recommend MDO, MDF, or PVC plastic.

Ruting the Straight Slots

With the router off, set it in the slot at the end of one curve and rest a straight board against its side. Hold the board in place while you move the router (still turned off) to the beginning of the curve (which you have already routed) at the other end of the straight. Press the board firmly against the router at that end, then go back and be sure the board is positioned to guide the router from the first curve to the sec-

ond. Again, start the router just above the track and tilt the spinning bit into the slot. Push the router along, applying pressure against the guide board, until the slot is cut all the way from the end of the first curve to the beginning of the next curve. Tilt the router gently to one side to lift the bit from the slot and turn it off. Repeat the process to rout all the straights. It works best if you have a helper to clamp the

Drill a 1/16-inch hole at the "X" indicated for the center of the curve. Push the tip of the 1/8-inch trammel rod for the router into the hole. Hold the tip in the hole while you swing the router to cut the slot. This really works best with two people: one to hold the trammel and one to move the router.

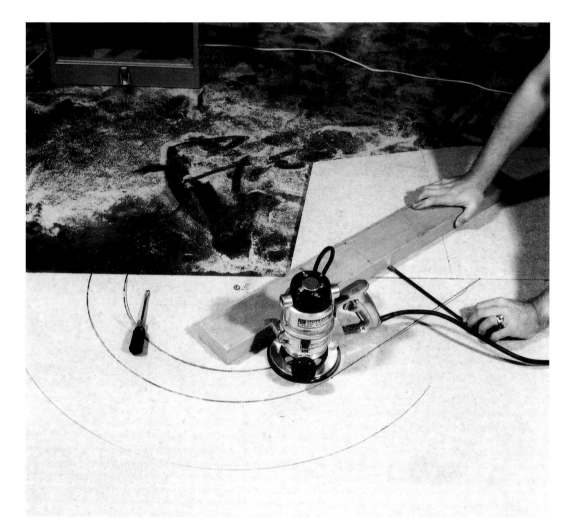

Use a solid 2x4 that is perfectly straight to guide the router as it cuts the straights from the end of one curve to the beginning of the next curve.

If you cut the slot too wide in places, jam a 1/8-inch-thick piece of plastic or Masonite wrapped with wax paper into the slot. Push putty between the waxed paper and the track to fill in the slot.

board for the straight. If you are working alone, you may have to nail the board to the track for each straight. If you are routing recesses for magnetic braid, install the babbiting bit and route all the straight recesses last.

Fixing Routing Mistakes

You *will* make mistakes cutting the slot. Usually, you will run a curve a bit too far or you will let the router bounce off the board on a straight. The result of nearly every routing mistake is a slot that's too wide. If you use MDO or MDF wood panels, fill in the slot with the strongest wood-filler putty you can buy. Use a piece of 1/8-inch styrene sheet or Masonite cut into a 1x4-inch strip. Wrap waxed paper over one edge and push the strip into the slot at the area that's too wide. Fill in the area with the wood filler and let it dry overnight. If you've made a dozen mistakes, for example, make a dozen 1x4-inch pieces of 1/8-inch styrene or Masonite and fill all the error areas once.

Use putty to fill in any gaps between the panels. Use a block of wood (or an electric sander) to be sure the joints between the panels are perfectly smooth.

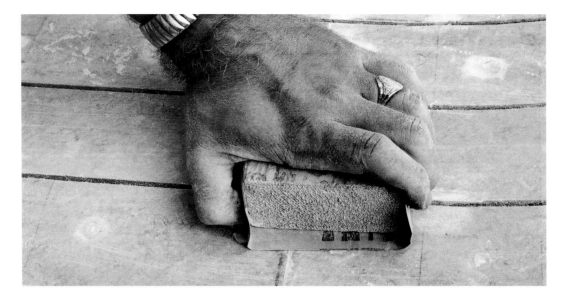

If the slot is too shallow, you can cut it deeper for short distances with a 3/32-inch straight router bit in a Dremel motor tool.

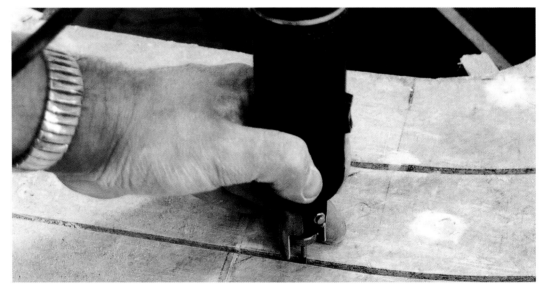

Sand the inside edges of the slot with sandpaper wrapped around a 3/32-inch-thick piece of plastic or hardboard.

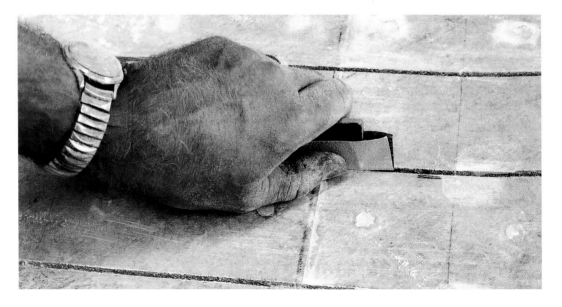

Run a spare guide flag from one of the cars through every inch of the slot to be sure the slot is smooth and deep enough. You will be able to feel any rough or shallow spots. If the slot is too shallow, it is possible to set up the trammel or straight guide board and re-cut it, but you will almost always make the slot wider. If the slot is only shallow for a few inches, you can deepen it with a motor tool like a Dremel, using a 3/32-inch straight router bit to shave away the bottom of the slot to the proper depth. Get the slot absolutely perfect because any slot-created wrecks will later drive you nuts. Also, if you are installing braid, use the guide to check the smoothness of the recesses.

Installing Tape or Braid

To install 1/8-inch braid or copper tape, drill a 3/16-inch hole directly beside the slot and countersink it about 1/16-inch. If you are using tape, install a 1-inch-long flathead 6-32 or 1/8-inch brass screw in the hole to clamp the tape. If you are using braid, use a smaller 1-inch flathead 4-40 screw. Use a brass washer beneath the track surface to clamp the tape or braid and install a nut to fit the screw and turn it tightly against the tape. The head of the screw must be just below the level of the tape or braid.

Push the first free end of the tape or braid into the hole beside the slot so at least 2 inches of tape or braid protrude below the track surface. The end of the next piece of tape or braid goes into the same hole. The process of installing tape or braid begins with tucking the ends of the first and last sections of braid into the starter hole. If you are building a track that can be easily disassembled, simply separate the surfaces and wrap the braid or tape around the exposed ends of the track and anchor the braid to the bottom of the track with a staple.

To install the copper pickup tape, unroll it and press it firmly onto the track as you go. Paint stores sell small rubber rollers that can be helpful, or you can use a thick glove and push the tape in place with your fingers. Try to keep the tape precisely 1/32 inch from the edge of the slot. When you come to a curve, push the outer edge of the tape down first, then the inner, because the inner will wrinkle just slightly. You can minimize the wrinkles by working slowly and using as much force as possible to push the tape into place.

To install magnetic braid, coat the recesses for the braid and the one side of the braid with contact cement. You can use a squeeze-type

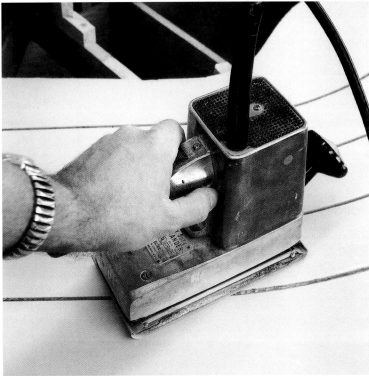

Top: This track surface for the Suzuka Grand Prix track has been routed on the floor and reinstalled on the tabletop, then sanded perfectly flat at each joint.

Above: Paint the track and let it dry, then sand it at least once to get the surface perfectly smooth and flat.

Chapter Seven

REAL RACE CARS IN 1/32

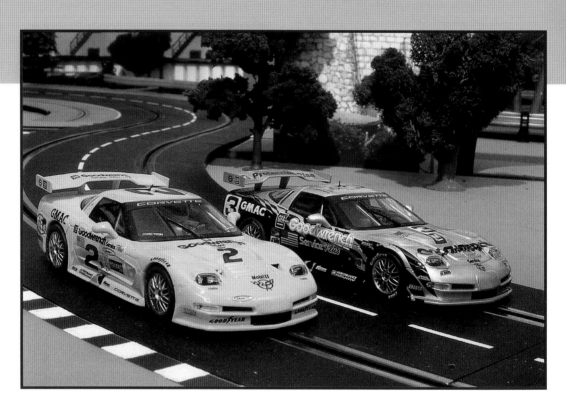

The Fly Corvette C5R has been offered in both the silver and yellow paint schemes. The model has a full interior, including the rear suspension parts visible through the rear window.

Below: The Audi R8 (from SCX) and Bentley Speed 8 GTP (from Carrera) cars both ran at the 2001 Le Mans endurance race.

Today is the golden age of model car racing. You can buy a replica of nearly any full-size race car that has been built since 1955. More models appear every week, so if you find only 6 of your 24 favorite real racing cars, just wait awhile. If you don't want to wait, chances are you can assemble 20 of your 24 missing favorites from aftermarket chassis, wheels, tires, gears, bodies, and decals.

Reach for Ready-to-Run

It is much quicker and easier to reach for a ready-to-run car than it is to build your own. All you need to do in order to have a race-ready model car is to open the box and perhaps adjust the pickup braid as shown later in this chapter. All the 1/32 scale cars currently

on the market run on any of the 1/32 scale track currently sold. There are some older tracks on which the slot might be too shallow, but you can solve that problem by trimming the car's guide shoe. Some collector cars from the 1960s have motors that require more power than you can squeeze from a race set power pack but, as you'll see in chapter 14, that problem can also be remedied.

Picking the Best Race Car

Go for what you like. Understand, however, that while some brands are designed for the mass market and will almost always work well right out of the box, others are serious race cars intended for adults and may need minor adjustments as described in chapter 9.

Sorting Cars by Racing Classes

Since there is a choice of just about any kind of race car from any class in the world from 1951 to the present, you may decide to divide your racing into classes that represent real-world competition. It can be a kind of time warp, because you can re-create specific years and even specific racing grids or groups of cars—or not. Consider your track open to vintage racing and run anything from any time period.

Top: Eight different makes of current Formula 1 cars are available, including Pro Slot's Ferrari, Ninco's Jordan, Carrera's McLaren, and SCX's Arrows. The grandstand is Scalextric.

Above: Four Scalextric NASCAR Ford Tauruses thunder around the high banks of the Carrera Daytona track from chapter 6.

Every popular type of world-class racing cars is available as ready-to-run 1/32 scale models. These are the Mercedes CLK DTM cars from the German Touring Car Championship.

European Truck Champion semi-trucks are available from Fly, including Sisu (shown) and Mercedes trucks.

These 1/32 scale replicas of the Porsche 911 GT3 are from (left to right) Ninco, Scalextric, and Artin.

All three of these are 1/32 scale NASCAR cars (left to right): the older SCX Chevrolet with steering chassis, a Scalextric Pontiac with an inline motor, and the newest Scalextric Ford Taurus with a sidewinder motor and fully detailed interior.

Currently, there's a choice of about 10 or more different cars in each of several major racing classes—Grand Touring (GT) cars, modern Formula 1 cars, vintage Grand Prix cars, NASCAR sedans, CART and Indy Racing League (IRL) open-wheel cars, Trans Am cars, Rally cars, and racing trucks—in addition to a choice of several paint schemes for each car. Model car makers also offer a variety of touring cars and mass-produced, limited-production, and prototype sports cars.

Race Car Maintenance

The only components you are likely to wear out on any of these cars are the braided-wire pickup brushes and the tires. Your hobby dealer can order new braid for the pickup and replacement tires or alternate silicone tires from firms like

Indy Grips. Each of the four axle bearings and the two motor bearings should receive a drop of oil after about every 50 hours of running. Use the oils that are sold by hobby shops and compatible with plastic. There is information on optimizing the performance of any 1/32 scale car in chapter 9.

Troubleshooting Cars

If a car runs erratically, stalling on some part of the track but not others, the problem is nearly always with the pickup brushes that contact the track rails. There's really nothing magical about it: at least three or four of those tiny metal fibers must always be in contact with the metal pickup rails. It is, however, far too easy to adjust the pickup brushes so their outer edges contact the plastic on either side of the track, forcing the brushes directly over the metal to be too high to make contact.

Use a spare piece of track as a gauge to see if the brushes really are making contact. Push the car sideways to see if the brushes continue to reach the pickup strips regardless of the position of the car. The metal strands have the best chance of touching if they are bent so they literally sweep rather than drag over the track surface. Bend the brushes into a slight ess pattern

Top: If the car stalls or runs erratically, the fault is nearly always with the pickup brushes on either side of the pickup shoe. Bend the brushes so the ends curve down to about a 45-degree angle.

Above: Hold the car in the slot on a spare piece of track and look to see exactly how the pickup braid contacts the track. If the front of the braid touches, but not the rear, you may need to install slightly larger front tires to raise the front, or find a thinner guide shoe. The tiny strands that trail behind the braid are where most of the contact is made between the braid and the pickup rails.

The Slot Classic 1/32 scale Morgan 4/4 and Alfa Romeo Spider are limited-production, cast-resin models that were offered both as kits and ready to run.

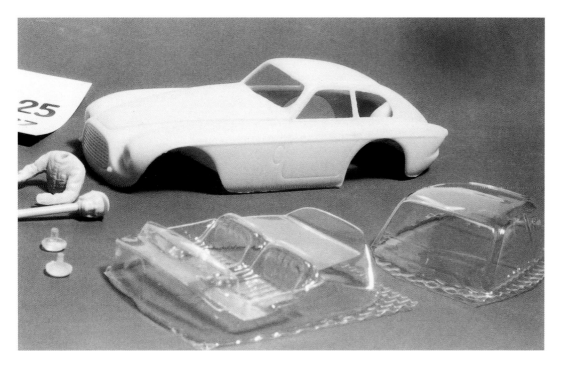

when viewed from the side so the strands at the tips of the brushes lay on the track at about a 15-degree angle. Push the car into the slot and look at the pickup from the end to be sure that it is really these stranded tail ends of the brushes that contact the track.

If the brushes are adjusted properly and the car still does not run, try another car. If neither car runs, try another controller. Try the faulty car on another part of the track. If it's really the car and the brushes look okay, remove the car's body and check that the flexible wires that lead from the motor to the pickup shoe and brushes are firmly attached to both the brushes and the motor. If it looks good, remove the motor and unplug the wires to test the motor alone by pressing one of the wires on one pickup rail and the other on the other pickup rail while you depress the controller trigger. If the motor still does not run, you will likely have to replace it. If the motor is in the car and it runs but the car does not move, chances are 1) the gears have slipped to the side and need to be moved on the axle, 2) the axle or motor has slipped out of its brackets and needs to be snapped back in, or 3) the gear teeth are broken.

Build Your Own Race Car

More than 90 percent of 1/32 scale model cars are sold ready to run. A few manufacturers do offer kits. You can also assemble your own collection of parts to create a kit to match a body. Usually,

if someone builds a car today rather than buying a ready-to-run, it is because the car he or she desires is not available. Even then, it is often possible to use the chassis from a ready-to-run car with a clear plastic body as shown in chapter 10.

MRRC, EJ's, Patto, Slot.it, Slot Classics, Maxi-Models, Electric Dreams, and others offer complete 1/32 scale race car kits. These kits can be assembled with just a screwdriver and pair of needle-nose pliers, but the bodies must be painted as described in chapter 10. There is also a wide choice of chassis from Slot.it, Pro-Track, MRRC, MJK, Plafit, Electric Dreams, and others. These same firms and others offer separate axles, gears, wheels, ties motors, and bodies so you can collect

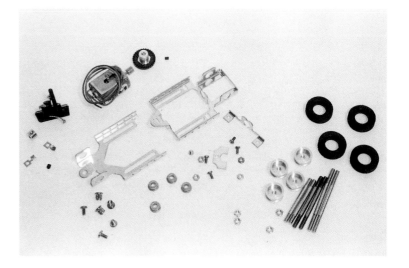

EJ's also offers their 2GC4 chassis as a complete kit that includes a VW Beetle body. EJ's usually offers a different body choice each year.

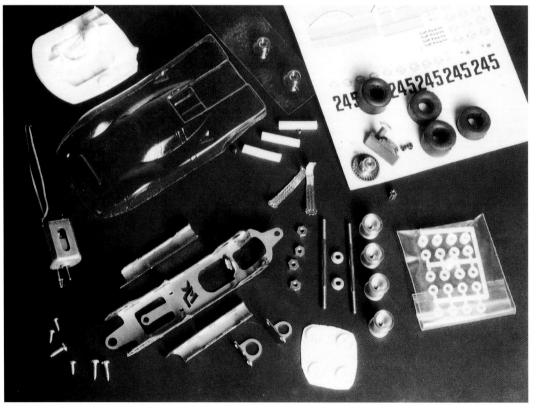

Patto offers a compete 1/32 scale kit with a wide choice of clear plastic bodies. This MJK chassis and other complete kits are also available from Slot Car World, Electric Dreams, and other dealers.

Slot.it offers chassis with either inline (shown) or sidewinder motor mounts, as well as an assortment of axles, gears, wheels, tires, motors, and magnets.

your own components for a "kit." The information on wheels, tires, gears, and motors in chapter 9 will help you make the best choices.

Ready-to-Run Chassis

The chassis used beneath Fly, MRRC, and Ninco ready-to-run cars are available as separate components, but you must also buy the pickup, front and rear axles, and motor to have a complete chassis. The Top Slot bodies are designed to fit specific Ninco and other ready-to-run chassis. I used a complete Fly car to build the Jaguar XJR9 in chapter 10. I also purchased a pair of Fly B74 rear view mirrors, Detail Master

MRRC offers a snap-in rear axle/motor mount and steering front wheels for the older Airfix bodies, and a brass inline chassis (center). The open-frame motor and chassis is EJ's number 2A inline-style.

2520 etched-metal windshield wipers and 2060 Quick-Turn fastener, Precision Scale 48102 pipe fittings (from a model railroad shop), and a Fantasy World body-mount kit. The 1988 Jaguar XJR9 body and decals are from Patto. The body fits the Fly chassis but the rear track is a bit too wide. To narrow the rear of the car, I used needle-nose pliers to hold the axle while I pulled off each wheel. I then shortened the ends of the axle 1/16 inch with a cut-off disc in a Dremel motor tool (wear eye protection). I used a razor saw to trim 1/16 inch from the back of each wheel and re-assembled the wheels. Chapter 10 describes how to mount, paint, decal, and detail the body.

The Jaguar body fits nicely over the Fly Joest chassis, but the rear track is about 1/8 inch too wide.

Above: Use a razor saw to trim 1/16 inch from the back of each wheel and push the wheels back onto the Fly axle.

Upper left: Use needle-nose pliers to grip the axle while you gently twist the wheels from the axle.

Left: Use a cut-off disc in a Dremel motor tool to trim 1/16 inch from each end of the axle, and gently grind all the corners you cut to remove any burrs. Wear eye protection.

Below: Chapter 10 explains how to mount, paint, decal, and detail a clear plastic or cast-resin body to look as realistic as this Jaguar XJR9.

Chapter Eight

RALLY CARS IN 1/32

Colin McRae's 2000 WRC Ford Focus was one of the two-wheel drive Rally cars from Scalextric. Like all Scalextric Rally cars, it has working lights.

Below: This single-lane, loop-to-loop Rally course includes a number of road hazard track sections for lots of Rally action in just 4x8 feet.

World Rally Cup could be the most exciting form of motorized racing on the planet. Yes, the cars compete against the clock one at a time, so the head-to-head element is missing, as is passing. But if you've seen it, either in person or on television, you know what I mean. This is legalized, out-and-out racing on public roads—public in the sense that they are the same roads on which you or I could drive. Some are paved, some are dirt, and some are covered with ice.

Rallies are divided into a series of several stages. The cars must reach each stage at a specified time, which limits the amount of time that can be spent on repairs. Your race track can obviously serve as one or even two of rally stages. Some model car racers assemble special tracks that are used specifically for rallying.

This Ninco Toyota Corolla is a replica of the one driven by Carlos Sainz in the late-1990s. Here, it slides under the arch bridges on the Monaco track from chapter 5.

Left: Classic Rally cars are also produced from time to time. This is Ninco's Jaguar XK120 with driver and co-driver (who is holding an actual 1/32 scale map) and the SCX Mini that won the 1967 Monte Rally.

Above: The Monaco Grand Prix course assembled from Carrera track as shown in chapter 5, but with the buildings removed and the trees relocated so the course replicates a special Rally stage through the woods. The cars are also running in the opposite direction with a crossover track so it takes two trips around the track to make a single lap.

Right: The Monaco Grand Prix course assembled from Scalextric and SCX track as shown in chapter 5. One straight has been replaced with a crossover track and the car is racing (against the clock on the timer/lap counter) over both lanes for an accumulated time from the readings from both lanes.

Road Hazards

Since rallies are run on public roads, and often minor roads at that, they encounter hazards that would be unthinkable on a road racing course. There are no safety fences or gravel traps—in fact, many of the special stages are lined with trees or fenced with sheer rock faces with cliffs rather than gravel traps at the edges of the road.

Scalextric has offered a C248 Hump Back Bridge for decades. It adds a nice touch of country-style realism and provides a place for the cars to fly (as the real Rally cars often do). SCX has a special number 88020 Adjustable Hump Bridge/Dip with a flexible straight track section that can be moved up or down to form a humpback bridge or a dip. You can use a string of 6 to 8 sections of 1/4-length track to make your own humpback bridge or dip, bending them up steep enough so a speeding car would fly off the edge. *Caution: you might ruin the sections for any other use.*

Scalextric also offers a C164 Rough Terrain Track with small rock-like bumps that can be rotated to just barely touch the car or to make a very good attempt to de-slot it. You can buy one of these sections and use the humps on any other brand of track by simply drilling the holes to accept the bumps in the new track.

The SCX 88020 Adjustable Hump Back Bridge/Dip can be set to provide either a hump back in the track or a dip. It's just right for the track to simulate the water-crossing fords that are part of some special test sections at real rallies.

Below: The Scalextric C248 Hump Back Bridge provides just the spot for Rally cars to do some "yumping" (as the Scandinavian Rally drivers say). This is the 4x8-foot Rally/hillclimb track shown later in this chapter.

You can rotate the bumps on the Scalextric Classic C164 Rough Terrain Track to produce more or less trouble for the cars. It's one more way to simulate the road hazards that face real World Rally Cup drivers.

Weather

One aspect of real-world rallying is that the cars run at night and in all kinds of weather. All the models of World Rally Cup cars include headlights and taillights. I do not recommend that you try to simulate real weather. Any kind of water will short out the motors and any type of powder will find its way inside the motors, gears, and bearings. SCX does offer a variety of Rally cars with snow and slush patterns painted on. You can add these touches yourself using acrylic paint. Put some white or dirt brown acrylic on a paintbrush and flick the brush at the model. Practice on a scrap of newspaper until you get it right.

SCX offers most of their Rally cars with the option of either simulated snow and slush–spattered or mud-spattered paint.

One-Lane Rally Tracks

While you can convert a two-lane track into a single-lane by simply installing a crossover track as described earlier, many modelers prefer to have a true single-lane track with a reverse loop at each end. Ninco offers a Rally set that includes two reverse loops and a single car. The reverse loops are also available separately as Kit 4, and you can adapt the Ninco track to Scalextric Classic or Scalextric Sport with the Ninco 10110 Adapter track. You will need two reverse loops, one for each end of the course.

Carrera track can be assembled with the joints offset half the width of the track so you can simply assemble a single-lane reverse loop for Carrera using four standard 20571 curves for the turn, two Number 20612 1/4-straights and two Number 20611 1/3-straights leading out of the curve, and two Number 29572 curves placed side by side to join to any Carrera track section as shown in the track plan later in this chapter. The advantage of this system is that the unused lane acts as a built-in border.

Lower left: You can assemble a reverse loop for a single-lane Carrera track using standard Carrera track sections.

Above: This Scalextric reverse loop can be assembled from standard Scalextric Classic or Scalextric Sport track sections, but the track joint at the connection to the loops must be permanently modified.

Left: When you try to join a Scalextric Classic or Scalextric Sport track to the reverse loop, you'll discover that the loop-to-loop and peg-to-peg connection will not work, so all three of these track sections must be modified.

Use heavy scissors to slice-off the loops from the end of the Scalextric 1/2-straight.

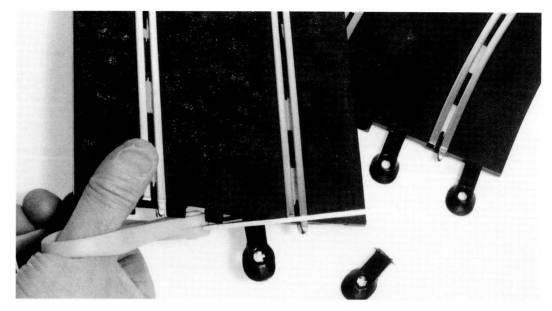

Use a pair of Testors Model Master sprue cutters to nibble notches and remove the excess tabs from the ends of the track.

Use stainless steel safety wire (from an auto parts store) to connect the two pegs that would normally have been joined by the Scalextric loops.

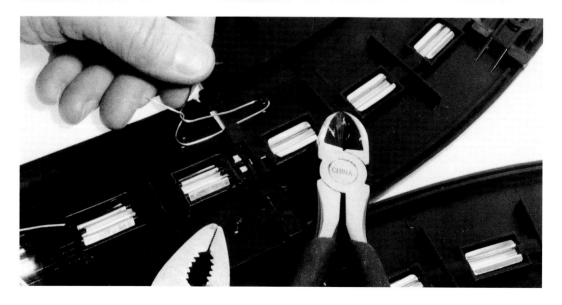

The Ninco Number 10213 track clips can be used to help hold the Scalextric track sections together. Note how the safety wire is twisted (top) to pull the track sections together.

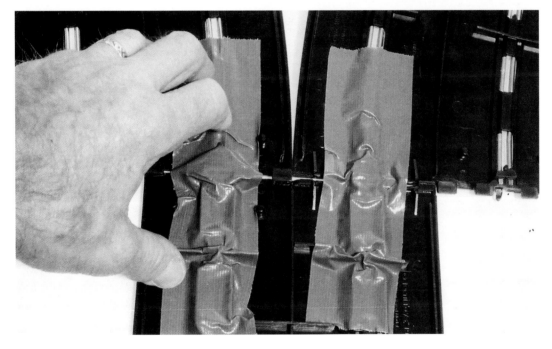

Finally, push duct tape tightly around the flanges and ribs on the bottom of the track to help hold it together. The flexible plastic used for Scalextric track resists epoxy and other cements, so these three mechanical means of holding the track together are used.

You can also assemble a reverse loop forScalextric Sport and Classic or SCX track. For Scalextric Classic (which can be joined to SCX) use two C156 45-degree inner curves and one C152 22-1/2-degree inner curve, plus two C158 1/4-length straights and two C154 22-1/2-degree standard curves and one 159 1/2-straight assembled to match the plan shown later in this chapter. For Scalextric Sport, use five C8202 inner curves, two C8234 curves, two C8200 1/4-length straights and one C8207 1/2-straights, assembled as shown in the plan later in this

chapter, except that it will take five of the 22-1/2-degree Scalextric Sport inner curves to make the end curves.

Scalextric and SCX use a track-joining system that is asymmetrical, so you cannot join the ends of the reverse loop without modifying the ends of the standard 1/2-length curves and the adjoining 1/2-track section. The joining faces of the 1/2-length straights and the facing curves in the reverse loop have to be permanently modified so they will work only with these reverse loops.

A COMPACT REVERSE LOOP WITH SCALEXTRIC CLASSIC OR SCALEXTRIC SPORT TRACK

Jeremy Dunning has a system that allows enthusiasts to assemble a very compact reverse loop. First, cut two 22-1/2–degree Scalextric Classic C152 or Sport C8202 R1 inner curves in half with scissors. The track is just soft enough so an adult can cut through it. Also cut two 1/4-straights in half to obtain four pieces of usable single-lane track. Next, join three pieces of 90-degree inner curves and assemble the two now–single-lane straight track sections and also the two now–single-lane 22-1/2–degree sections to make a reverse loop. It's very compact, but it forces the cars to use the tightest of Scalextric curves. The plans included here for a 4x8 Rally/hillclimb Scalextric Sport or Scalextric Classic illustrate the more complex reverse loop, but since it is larger than this one, either will fit in the space.

To make a more compact version of a reverse loop, cut the inner lane from two 22-1/2–degree pieces of Scalextric or Sport R1 inner curve.

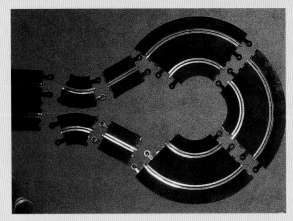

Arrange the now–single-lane pieces and three 90-degree R1 inner curves as shown to form the reverse loop.

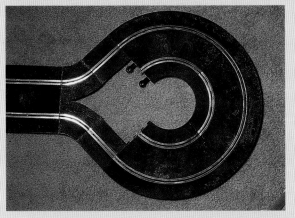

The more compact reverse loop forces the cars to use Scalextric Classic's or Scalextric Sport's tightest inner curve, but it's easy to make.

This single-lane track is assembled on a 4x8-foot tabletop. The tabletop is covered with green felt that has been touched up with spots of light brown applied with a roller to simulate grass and dirt. The trees are Life-Like. The tabletop is tilted to produce about a 4 percent grade.

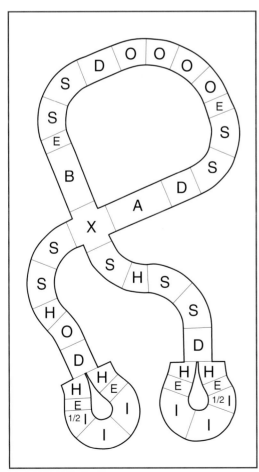

LIST OF SCALEXTRIC SPORT OR SCALEXTRIC CLASSIC TRACK REQUIRED FOR 4x8-FOOT RALLY/HILLCLIMB COURSE

Chapter 3 includes a list of part numbers for the track sections and borders identified by the key letters in this plan.

Key	Quantity	Description
H	6	1/2 Standard (R2) Curve
I	4	Inner-Inner (R1) Curve
I 1/2	2	Half-Inner-Inner (R1) Curve
S	9	Standard (R2) Curve
O	4	Outer (R3) Curve
OO	0	Outer-Outer (R4) Curve
E	6	1/4-Straight
D	2	1/2-Straight
B	1	Full-Straight
V	0	Crossover Track
A	1	Connector Track
C	0	Chicane
X	1	90° Crossover Track (see text)

You can also assemble this Rally/hillclimb circuit on a 4x8-foot tabletop using Scalextric Sport, Scalextric Classic, or SCX track sections. The two reverse loops have been replaced with three standard curves so you can run two cars at once or one lane at a time.

4x8 Rally/Hillclimb for Scalextric and SCX

These three tracks are about the smallest tracks you can assemble for 1/32 scale cars. Any of the three can become a hillclimb by merely tilting the entire 4x8-foot board so one end is 8 inches or so higher than the other end. If you elevate one end 8 inches, the average grade will be about 8 percent, although it will really only be 8 percent through the parts of the track that run straight up the slope. You can experiment to see how much farther you can tilt the board before the cars no longer climb the hill.

The track plan for Scalextric and SCX track can be assembled with two reverse loops, or the reverse loops can be replaced with a single standard turn. Since this is a one-lane course, there is a level 90-degree crossing at the "X" on the plan. The plan is drawn to accept the older half-length SCX crossover track, but SCX has replaced it with a number 84090 Crossover Track that is a full-length straight in both directions. If you use the 84090, you will need to substitute a 84040 1/4-straight and a 84050 1/2-straight for the full straights marked "B"

LIST OF SCALEXTRIC SPORT, SCALEXTRIC CLASSIC, OR SCX TRACK REQUIRED FOR 4x8-FOOT RALLY/HILLCLIMB COURSE

Chapter 3 includes a list of part numbers for the track sections and borders identified by the key letters in this plan.

Key	Quantity	Description
H	3	1/2 Standard (R2) Curve
I	0	Inner-Inner (R1) Curve
I 1/2	0	Half-Inner-Inner (R1) Curve
S	12	Standard (R2) Curve
O	4	Outer (R3) Curve
OO	0	Outer-Outer (R4) Curve
E	2	1/4-Straight
D	2	1/2-Straight
B	3	Full-Straight
V	0	Crossover Track
A	1	Connector Track
C	0	Chicane
X	1	90° Crossover Track (see text)

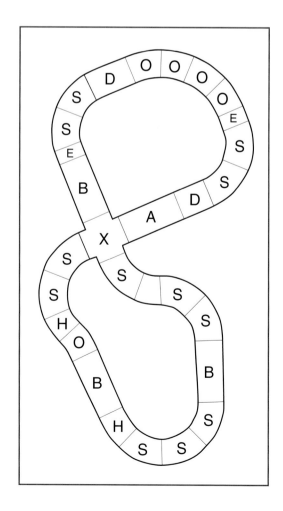

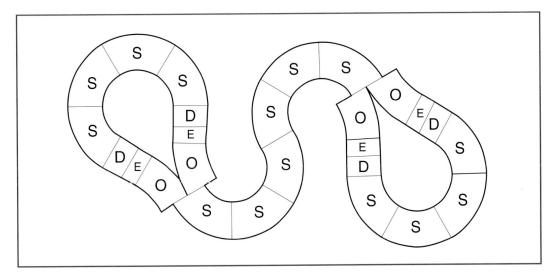

There is just enough room on a 4x8-foot board for a Carrera track if you assemble it with the reverse loops shown to produce a single-lane track. This one is more of a switchback hillclimb circuit than the other two 4x8 foot tracks in this chapter. Again, the 4x8-foot board is tilted so the track and cars really are climbing uphill.

on the plan, and replace the 1/2-straight marked "D" (the one next to the "A" straight) with a 84040 1/4-straight. If you assemble the circuit with Scalextric Sport track, use the C8210 Straight Crossover at "X" and replace the full straight at "B" with a C82057 1/2-straight and remove the 1/2-straight "D" next to the full straights at "A."

The two reverse loops can be replaced with standard curved track if you want the option of running two cars. You could, of course, replace any of the straight track sections marked "B" with a crossover track to make the figure-eight track a single lane, as shown for the Monaco track earlier in this chapter.

There is just enough room for a single-lane Carrera track in 4x8 feet. This circuit is really intended to be used as a hillclimb, with the 4x8-foot board elevated at least 8 inches on one end (and sometimes as much as three times that) to produce a truly challenging climb. The plan utilizes the reverse loops shown earlier in this chapter that can be assembled from standard Carrera track sections with no modifications. There is no room for a terminal track—in fact the only straight tracks on the entire circuit are the four short sections in each reverse loop. Chapter 14 explains how to assemble a 1/4-straight terminal track for Carrera. Except for a simple oval with, perhaps, a squiggle curve along one straight, this is about the only Carrera road course you will be able to squeeze onto a 4x8-foot board.

LIST OF CARRERA TRACK REQUIRED FOR 4x8-FOOT ONE-LANE RALLY/HILLCLIMB COURSE

Chapter 3 includes a list of part numbers for the track sections and borders identified by the key letters in this plan.

Key	Quantity	Description
S	14	Inner (1) Curve
O	4	Outer (2) Curve
E	4	1/4-Straight
D	4	1/3-Straight
A	0	Connector Track

Chapter Nine

RACE CAR SETUP

Three Scalextric Porsches and a Fly Viper hammer around the banked turns on the Daytona International Speedway from chapter 5.

A model racing car is very much like a real racing car in that the model responds to mechanical changes much like the real car. Changes in tires, weight distribution, motor power, play in the front and rear axles, and a host of other variables can make one model car considerably quicker going around any given track than another model car.

Tuned for Racing

The most important lesson you can learn from this chapter is to set up the car so it is balanced, so that when it is at the edge of its limit, its rear will leave the track just a millisecond before the front jerks the pickup out of the slot. I suggest that you tune the car by switching tires, trying different front wheel and tire setups, and adding or subtracting weight until you get the car to handle well without any magnets. That stable platform is a far better place to begin tuning a really fast car than by merely sticking on magnets so you need a more powerful motor, controller, and power pack.

Blueprinting Your Race Car

One real race car concept that is fundamental to maximum performance in a model race car is that of adjusting all the car's tolerances to perfection. Real race car tuners call this "blueprinting." Nearly every ready-to-run model race car has too much side-to-side axle play, out-of-round tires, poorly adjusted pickup brushes, and out-of-alignment chassis. There are several brands of aftermarket axles, wheels, gears, and tires that will help improve the performance of your car. The greatest gains that any of these components offer is that they are not as sloppy as the standard components they replace. So you have two choices: remove all the slop from the stock parts or buy new parts that don't have the slop in the first place. Crude, I know, but the concept is that simple: make your own precision or buy it.

Precision Tolerances

Precision means very little play or wobble. A piece of wrapping tissue is about .002-inch thick: try to envision how much that is and make it your goal to keep all the tolerances on your cars within that .002-inch range. There's no need to measure, only to get the feel for minimum wasted movement.

Every ready-to-run car I've seen needs at least some adjustment of its tolerances. First, be sure the pickup is free to swivel smoothly from side to side. If it rocks, replace it with a new Slot.it or similar pickup guide with a locking collar. Be sure the pickup does not hang up when it pivots to either side and if it does, move the wires inside the car to allow smoother movement.

Before you remove the body, check to see if there is any way the tires can rub against it. While you may need to shave a bit of plastic from the wheel wells, the rubbing can sometimes be eliminated by removing the side-to-side play in the front and rear axles.

If the rear axle moves more than .002 inches from side to side, remove one wheel so you can install a brass washer or two to eliminate the

Remove the body and push the axle from side to side to see how far it moves.

Grip both tires and twist and pull to remove the rear wheels. On this particular Fly Lola T70, two .010-inch-thick washers were needed to remove excessive side-to-side movement.

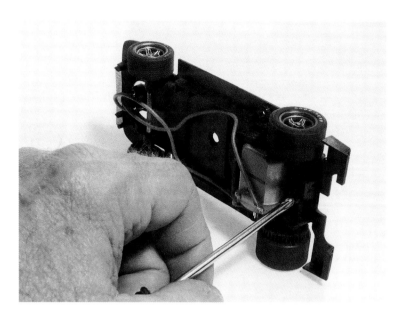

Remove the screw that holds the motor pod on most Fly sidewinders to reach the magnet.

have a flanged gear that controls its side-to-side play. Add one or more washers between the back side of each wheel and the outside of the bearing so the wheels, not the gear, keep the crow gear centered on the pinion gear.

Look at the magnet and decide if you want to lower it or leave it in the stock position. Some racing rules do not allow lowered magnets, so check the rules of the organizing group if you intend to compete. On most Fly cars you can lower the magnet .010 inch by installing a brass washer on top of the magnet to force it down into the cavity. If the rules allow it, cut out the bottom of the cavity and lower the magnet flush with the bottom of the chassis and hold the magnet in place with metal-filled epoxy.

Tuning the Front End

There is little agreement among model car racers about the best type of front axle. Some believe that all the weight of the car's front should rest on the pickup, with the wheels barely touching the track. Some Ninco and SCX cars usually have a spring-loaded pickup shoe that effectively transfers all the weight to the pickup. Others feel that independently rotating front wheels are essential. Still others prefer a solid front axle. Some SCX sports cars have nearly 1/8 inch of

play. Large hardware stores and some hobby shops sell number 3 washers for 3/32-inch shafts. You can also order them from some model car parts suppliers like NorthWest Short Line and EJ's.

If the car has spur gears, install the washers on the side of the axle that will force the crown gear on the axle to ride in the center of the pinion gear on the motor. Most cars with inline motors

Push the magnet out of its pocket.

Use one of the axle washers to force the magnet all the way down into the pocket. Place the washer on top of the magnet. If you want to decrease the magnetic downforce, place the washer in the bottom of the pocket so it is between the track and the magnet, in order to raise the magnet.

side-to-side play in the front axle. My opinion is that the front wheels should be as stable as possible. It may or may not make a difference if they are on a single axle or rotate independently, but the independently rotating wheels usually wobble so much that I replace them with a solid front axle when I can fit one. Decide if you want to retain independently rotating front wheels or side-to-side front axle movement. Personally, I prefer the way the cars handle with a solid front axle and less than that .002 inch of side-to-side play.

Balance and Vibration

Some modelers prefer to balance the front and rear weight of their cars with magnets or lead weights placed as close as possible to the pickup. You can use two food or postage scales to measure the front and rear weight of the car. The front/rear balance will obviously be affected by the amount of magnetic downforce you use and whether the magnets are just in the rear or also in the front. Generally, I find that 1/32 scale cars handle best with about 45 percent of their weight (and/or downforce) on the front tires.

When you replace the body, tighten the screws, then back them off about two turns so the body can rattle slightly. You may even want to grind some of the chassis' edges to allow the body to literally rattle. The car will handle much more smoothly because the rigid body amplifies any tire chatter. Again, some racing rules do not allow loose bodies, so check before you grind.

Top: I replaced the rather floppy front wheel/axle assembly on the Fly Lola T70 with a solid 3/32-inch (2.3-millimeter) steel front axle. Grip the pins that hold the front wheels with needle-nose pliers while you twist and pull the wheel to remove it.

Bottom: The replacement front axle should be about 1/16-inch shorter than the overall length of the original pins. The shorter axle will allow you to press the wheels a bit tighter to eliminate any excess side-to-side play.

Use two food scales or postage scales to weigh the front and rear of the car. The weight balance on this Scalextric Pontiac is about what most racers prefer. It's best to get the weight right, then add or move magnets.

If you replace the stock tires with silicone tires, be sure to lubricate the wheel with a single drop of dishwashing detergent so the silicone tire will not split as it stretches on the wheel.

Racing Tires

There are usually several choices of tires for 1/32 scale cars. Most often stock tires are about as good as you will get, particularly on plastic track with its relatively rough surface. Tires do age, however, so you may improve the performance of a car that is a couple of years old by buying new stock tires. Historic Scale Racing Replicas (HSRR) offers a line of replacement tires for modern sports and F1 cars. EJ's has tires for virtually all the classic metal wheels.

You can sand the rear tires to remove minor wobble. Put a piece of fine sandpaper on the track and lower the car onto the track with the throttle on about 3/4 speed. Gently lower the car so the spinning tires barely touch the sandpaper—you want to sand off just the high spots, not reduce the diameter of the tire. On some cars, you can temporarily mount the front tires on the rear wheels to sand the front tires round.

Some model car racers find better traction using silicone tires from Indy Grips, ScaleRacing, and others. When you mount silicone tires, use a small dab of dishwashing detergent as a lubricant so the tire will slip easily onto the wheel—if you use force the silicone tires will split.

Replacement tires nearly always allow the car to turn quicker lap times. But I am not completely convinced that replacement tires are why the car runs better. Most often, I believe it is a combination of fresh rubber and, often, a tire that is rounder than what was on the car.

Round Wheels

All plastic wheels wobble to some degree. I am usually willing to put up with it because they look so realistic. Spin the wheels and look for any wobble at the edges of the tire. Sometimes you can correct the wobble by using finger pressure to twist the wheel slightly; sometimes just rotating the tire 90 degrees on the rim will eliminate wobble. If you want performance, however, I suggest you replace the stock plastic wheels with metal wheels, which means replacing the axle and, perhaps, the gear as well. Slot.it and others offer replacement wheels, gears, and axles. HSRR, Pro-Track, BWA, MRRC, EJ's, Patto's, and others offer precision-machined aluminum wheels and true-running steel axles. Most also offer their own tire bearings to fit the more popular brands of cars. Indy Grips offers silicones for nearly all the aftermarket aluminum wheels.

The main reason to replace the axle is to obtain the closer-fitting bearings that go with it, although wobbly plastic wheels can be aggravating. Most ready-to-run cars have a 2.4-millimeter axle that is very close to 3/32 inch. NorthWest Short Line offers 2.4-millimeter ground-steel rod and bronze bearings to match. They also have 3/32 rod and bearings. Precision-machined aluminum wheels for 3/32 axles are available from Slot.it, BWA, Patto, Plafit, and others. The 2.4-millimeter axles also fit most press-on wheels. EJ's has a range of 1/8-inch axles, bearings, and wheels like those found on the classic 1/32 cars of the 1960s and 1970s.

The Magic of Downforce

On a real racing car, the body is shaped so the wind generated by the car moving along the track actually forces the car down onto the track. It's called "aerodynamic downforce," or just "downforce." Model cars do not travel fast enough for the wind to have that much effect. There is, however, a downforce adjustment that you can make on your model car that is even more effective than the downforce exerted on a real racing car. On a model car, it is magnetic downforce that so profoundly affects the handling and speed of the car. But as with a real car, the greater the downforce, the more power that is needed to achieve any given speed, so there is a limit.

The limit of magnetic downforce on a model racing car depends more on your concept of what a model racing car should look like in action than it does on any specific force. Most 1/32 and HO scale model racing cars are fitted with magnets. The exceptions are some of the Ninco 1/32 Classics and the Thunderjet HO cars. The more dedicated HO model car racers fit their cars with as much downforce as the most powerful motors will pull around the track. As a result, HO cars travel so quickly that you can barely move your eyes or head fast enough to focus on them. Most 1/32 scale cars are, proportionally, much, much slower, but the trade-off is that you can actually see the car start to slide, see when it begins to reach its limit, and have time to correct the throttle before you lose it.

Making the Most of Downforce

I have my own opinions about magnetic downforce. I like the concept of being able to make one car considerably quicker than another (with the help of magnets), because it allows me to improve the performance of my models just like mechanics and tuners tweak the real cars that model cars replicate. I removed the magnets for nearly all my pre-1969 era cars because these cars usually cornered in lurid power slides. I want my modern-era Formula 1 cars to be the fastest cars on the track so they have the strongest magnets, but I still want to be able to power slide them around some corners.

Usually I leave the magnets alone. Once in awhile, however, I find one brand of car that does

Carrera cars have this adjustable magnet that can be pushed forward (as shown) for virtually no magnetic downforce, or pushed all the way to the rear (which also moves the magnet closer to the track) for maximum downforce.

not perform quite as well as other models of the same class of car. There is, for example, much more downforce in an SCX Formula 1 car than in a Ninco Formula 1 car. In such cases, I use magnets to adjust the performance so they match, usually raising the magnet in the SCX car and lowering the magnet in the Ninco car (or replacing it with a stronger magnet). I also like the ability to make a smaller car match the performance of a larger car, especially when the two are equal in real life. The magnetic downforce scale

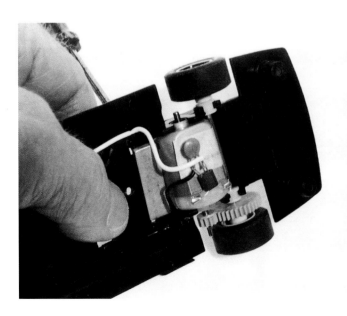

When you replace the body, tighten the screws then back off about two turns so the body can rattle a bit on the chassis.

The magnet in the Scalextric Ford Taurus NASCAR chassis is held in place with plastic tabs. Twist the chassis to pop the magnet out of its clips.

shown later in this chapter makes it easier to achieve equal downforce, regardless of whether you want to increase or decrease it.

Balancing the Magnets

Carrera cars feature adjustable magnets. If you slide the magnet all the way to the rear, it is also lowered closer to the track for maximum downforce. Slide the Carrera magnet forward and it is also raised to the point where it really only acts as a bit of extra weight on the pickup.

Scalextric Ford Taurus NASCAR cars and Mustang and Camaro Trans Am cars with sidewinder motors offer the choice of three magnet positions. For maximum downforce, the rear position works best because it transfers more of the downforce directly onto the rear tires. The Taurus NASCAR cars with sidewinder motors are also a bit quicker than the older Ford Tauruses and the Scalextric Pontiac. You can detune the sidewinders by merely moving the magnet to the middle position. If you want even more magnetic downforce, stick one of the Scalextric magnets right onto the bottom of the sidewinder car's motor (after cutting off the ribs on the plastic chassis) and move the stock magnet into the forward position.

Replacement and accessory magnets are available from Scalextric Classic, Scalextric Sport, ScaleRacing, SCX, Fly, Ninco, Slot.it, Tweaker, and others. Even Radio Shack sells suitable magnets. Most Slot.it magnets fit the pocket on Scalextric cars. In addition, most stock magnets are dull metal, while replacement magnets, including the ScaleRacing SM4039 and Slot.it SICNO2 notched magnets and the Ninco round 70179 magnets, are made from neodymium or "neo." Any of these are likely to be a bit more powerful than the stock magnets. You do not, however, need to replace the stock magnet—you can leave it in place and supplement it with additional magnets if you wish.

You can sometimes double the effective strength of stock magnets merely by moving them closer to the track. Cut a hole in the chassis the size of the magnet so the magnet can hang down to within about .020 inch of the track surface, and adhere the magnet in place with metal-filled epoxy.

The only limit to how much magnet you can add is the power of the motor. There are no rules or formulae here, but most model car motors are powerful enough to pull about twice the stock magnetic downforce without a noticeable loss in speed. The exception is usually SCX, whose cars

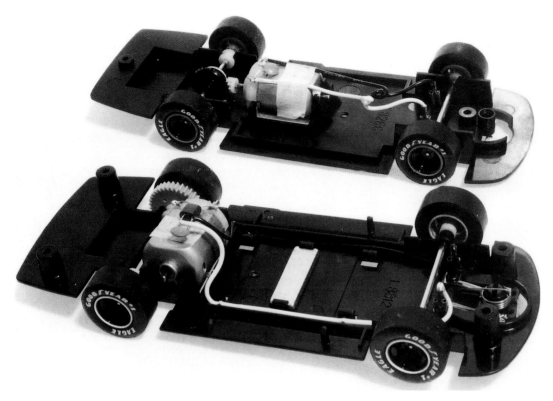

If you mount the magnet on the Scalextric sidewinder-style NASCAR chassis in the middle, the performance of the car will be diminished so it will be competitive with the older (top) inline-style NASCAR cars.

For maximum downforce on the sidewinder-style Scalextric NASCAR cars, put the stock magnet in the forward position to help hold down the pickup and install a Slot.it SICNO1 neodymium magnet on the bottom of the motor.

often have all the magnetic downforce the motor can handle. When you add so much magnetic downforce that the motor slows down, it's time to consider a more powerful motor. The more powerful motor will force you to use a controller with a lower ohm rating, and you may also need a larger power supply for the more powerful motor. You have exceeded the limit, in my opinion, with a 1/32 scale car that zips around the track as fast as an HO car—a car that sticks so well you need only lift the throttle for the ends of the longest straight and, perhaps, blip the throttle off for an instant in one or two corners.

You can use magnets to help force the rear of the car down onto the pickup strips and even at the front to help force the pickup into the slot. The magnets will work fairly well, but they can take the skill out of driving. With really strong

BUILDING A DOWNFORCE SCALE

The downforce scale track is supported on a pair of open CD jewel cases with a film canister to hold lead shot for precise measurement. The rectangular lumps are automobile balance weights in 1/4-ounce sizes. Use a terminal track so the scale can also be used to sand tires true. Pry off the Carrera bottom plate from its glued-on posts.

The large platform is 1-3/8x1-5/8 inches and is 1 inch from the end of the track. The smaller platform 1-3/8 x 5/8 inches and 4-1/2 inches from the end of the track. Mark the locations with masking tape and a ruler.

Use a Dremel motor tool with a cut-off disc to cut through the plastic track and the steel rails. Wear eye protection. Work quickly because the cut-off disc is actually melting the plastic. Cut about 1/4 inch beyond the ends of each corner to cut all the way through the plastic and the rails. Remove the two scale platforms. The shorter one will be useful if you decide to add a magnet to the front of the car as well as the rear (you can check the downforce at both ends at the same time). Use a hobby knife to scrape away the burrs left by the cut-off disc. The platforms must be about 1/16 inch smaller than the holes.

Open boxes support the shelves for the scale. Cut two pieces of the tube 1/2 inch longer than each platform and cement one to each of the extreme outer edges of each platform. Use Testors Model Master Cement for Plastics for all the glue joints on Carrera track. You will have to use 5-minute epoxy, Goodyear Pliobond, or Walthers Goo to cement the plastic tubes to the flexible plastic used for Scalextric, SCX, and Ninco track.

The vertical posts at each of the four corners of each platform are 1-1/2 inches long. Use a razor saw to cut the tube and to remove the end tabs from the track. Cut the shelves for each of the scale platforms from .010-inch-thick Plastruct or Evergreen Scale Models styrene sheet plastic and cement them, as shown, to the bottom of each of the scale platforms. Be sure to weigh each of the platforms and mark that number in a safe place because you will later use those weights to determine actual downforce.

The scale platform must be free to rattle loosely about 1/16 inch to either side or end, and free to move about 1/8-inch down—the white plastic tubes will prevent the platform from being pulled any higher than the level of the surrounding track. Hold the scale platforms to the track by merely inserting a piece of K&S 1/16-inch brass tube into the hollow of each pickup rail from the open end of the track. Pull the end of the tube up and bend it over 90 degrees with needle-nose pliers. Bend the opposite end of the tube over 90 degrees at the end of the track so the tube cannot fall out of the rail.

Position the car above the larger scale so the center of the scale is as close to the center of the magnet as possible. Test the scale by gently pulling down on the scale platform. You will hear a "click" as the magnet's force is overcome and the scale moves downward. With no weight, however, the scale will snap back up the instant you let go of the platform. Place two or three 1/4-ounce stick-on automobile wheel balance weights on the top of the .010-inch styrene shelf. Continue to add weight until the scale platform snaps free of the magnet. To get a more precise measurement, gently push the scale back up to see if you can coax the magnet to just barely grab hold—that's the most accurate reading for downforce. To be really accurate, use lead shot in a film canister for the final 1/4 ounce.

To obtain the actual downforce, add the weight of each scale to the weight of the balance weights and/or lead shot. My larger scale weighs .5 ounces and my smaller scale weighs .3 ounces, but yours may be much different. It takes about 50 pieces of the lead shot I use to equal 1/2 ounce, so effectively each lead shot weighs about .1 ounce. Actually, the scale and the shot are not that accurate, but it is accurate to about plus or minus .2 ounces. Remember that you are comparing one car to the next, and you are also using the same scale for each test. It is the comparison that will help you determine how to increase or decrease the magnetic downforce, not the precise measurement.

magnets, the only skill you need is determining—by practice—how much throttle to apply to any given corner. The whole concept of driving the car to maintain an endless flow of controlled power slides or brake slides gives way to steady throttle pressure to try to keep the magnets stuck.

Measuring and Race-Tuning Magnetic Downforce

You can build a scale to measure exactly how much magnetic downforce any car generates. Because it is made from a piece of track, the scale replicates the action of the car on the track. The principle is simple enough: the magnets are trying to pull the car down to the track, which is the same as trying to pull the track up to the car. The scale simply frees a couple of inches of the track so you can see how much force the car is exerting to try to pull up the track. Add lead weights to the small platform suspended beneath the scale until the scale pulls free from the car's magnetic attraction. The scale itself has a stop, so it cannot be raised any higher than the surface of the rest of the track.

You need to build a scale for each brand of track you use because each brand of track has different magnetic attraction. Scalextric Sport, Scalextric Classic, SCX, and Ninco track have plated steel rails to prevent rust, while Carrera and Artin track has rails made of a rust-free steel

alloy. As a result, the rails on the Scalextric Sport, Scalextric Classic, SCX, and Ninco track are nearly three times as powerful as the rails on the Carrera and Artin track. Scalextric Classic track provides measurably more downforce than its Sport counterpart because the pickup rails on the Classic track are about .005 inch above the track

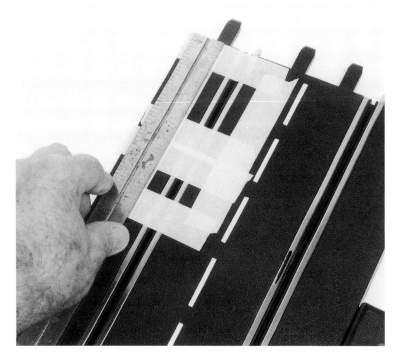

Mark the locations of the two scale platforms with masking tape.

Cut through the track, rails and all, with a cut-off disc in a motor tool.

Hold the motor tool as nearly parallel to the track as you can to minimize the bevel on the edges of each cut.

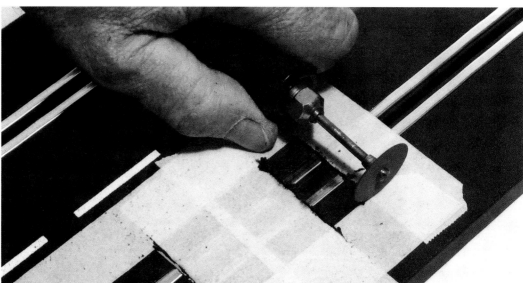

Shave the edges of the two scale platforms until there is 1/16 inch free side-to-side and end-to-end movement when they are placed back in their holes.

Cement a piece of .010-inch-thick plastic to each side of the slot boxes, then cement the rectangular tubes to the bottoms of the scale platforms as shown. These are the tubes that will stop the scale from moving upward any farther than the level of the rest of the track.

The open-crate boxes are as light as possible. Weigh each one before you install it.

surface, while the Sport rails are flush. A typical 1/32 car will have about 3 ounces of downforce on Scalextric Classic, SCX, and Ninco track, but only about 1 ounce on Carrera track. Since there are so many choices of magnets, it is easy enough to increase the car's magnetic downforce to be the same on Carrera or Scalextric Sport track as it is on others. It is equally possible to raise the magnets or fit weaker ones to reduce the magnetic downforce of the cars by up to one-third.

The scale can make it easier and quicker to determine just how much magnetic downforce you want for your particular track. Once you have a car or two with the handling you prefer, you can get very close to duplicating that by matching that car's package of front/rear weight balance and the magnetic downforce. The scale shows, for example, the true effect that raising or lowering a magnet just .010 inch can have on a car's downforce. If you are

Insert a piece of 1/16-inch aluminum tubing into each rail to retain the scale platforms.

The car's magnet will grab the scale platform and snap it up as far as it will go. Add weights to the platform until you can feel the platform break free from the magnetic attraction of the car's traction magnet.

experimenting with magnet position and type, leave other variables like tires, motors, and gearing alone so you can isolate the effect of just the magnets. If you find you want to change the gearing, motor, or tires, do so, but keep the same magnet setup until you find the effect of the gearing or motor change.

Racing Motors
By definition, the motor in your model racing car is a racing motor because it is, after all, a race car. Faster and more powerful motors are available. I question their value for home tracks, but the choice is yours. The Plafit Rabbit is about the same as most stock motors. SCX offers a 50120 "Pro Turbo" motor that snaps

into most of their cars. Ninco offers the NC-2 motor that is quicker than the NC-1 fitted to some of their cars. Patto's, Reprotec, and others have similar motors.

The Plafit Fox, Slot.it V12, and similar motors are probably the best choices for more powerful motors in cars that race on home tracks. Even with these, you will probably want to use a controller with a 30- or 45-ohm resistor (as described in chapter 13) because the controllers supplied with most race car sets won't provide the control needed with these more powerful motors. Motors like the Plafit Cheetah and those used for commercial raceways in 1/24 scale cars are far too powerful for cars raced on home tracks.

Pick a motor with care because they are not all interchangeable, some differ slightly in size and the motor shaft may protrude from the plastic end bell on some and from the metal case on others. Some motors have the shaft extending out both ends, like the Slot.it V-12 and the motors in the SCX four-wheel drive Rally cars. If the motor shaft interferes with the chassis or is so long it hits the boss on the crown gear, you can slice it off with a cut-off disc in a Dremel motor tool. The supply of motors changes constantly, so when you read this there will most certainly be motors available that are not shown here, and some shown here that are no longer available.

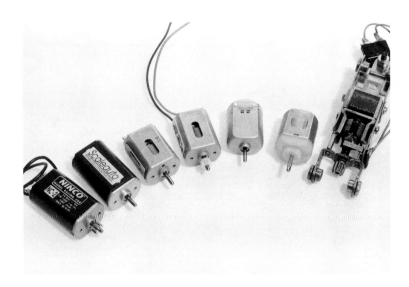

Racing Gears

The gear ratio in your car has been designed to obtain the optimum performance from the motor and magnetic downforce in the stock car on a typical home raceway. If your home raceway is not typical, or if you make any major adjustments to magnetic downforce or change the motor, you may find better performance if you change the gear ratio as well.

The gear ratio is the number you get when you divide the number of teeth on the larger gear by the number of teeth on the smaller gear. To find the gear ratio in your car count the teeth on the two gears and do the math or look at the chart provided here. If you want more acceleration (at the expense of absolute top speed), increase the gear ratio by fitting either a smaller pinion gear, or a crown gear (for inline cars) or spur gear (for sidewinder cars) with three more teeth. As a rough rule, one less tooth on the pinion gear produces the same result as three more teeth on the spur or crown gear. If you want more speed (at the expense of somewhat slower

There is a wide selection of motors available to replace your stock motor or to use in assembling your own car (left to right): Ninco NC-2, Scale Auto from Reprotec, Plafit Cheetah, Plafit Fox, MRRC, Slot.it V12, and EJ's open-frame motor.

Use a vise to press a pinion gear onto a motor. Insert a 1-inch-long piece of 1/8-inch brass tube between the gear and the vise jaw so the motor shaft can fit inside the tube for the final few fractions of an inch of the installation.

149

Gear Ratio Table

driven gear
──────── = gear ratio
driven gear

Number of teeth on driven gear (crown or spur gear)

Number of teeth on driven gear (crown or spur gear)

	28	30	32	34	35	36	38	39	40	42	44	45	46	48	50	60	80
6	4.67	5.00	5.33	5.67	6.83	6.00	6.33	6.50	6.67	7.00	7.33	7.50	7.67	8.00	8.33	10.0	13.0
8	3.50	3.75	4.00	4.25	4.38	4.50	4.75	4.88	5.00	5.25	5.50	5.63	5.75	6.00	6.25	7.50	10.0
9	3.12	3.33	3.55	3.78	3.89	4.00	4.22	4.33	4.45	4.68	4.89	5.00	5.12	5.34	5.56	6.67	8.89
10	2.80	3.00	3.20	3.40	3.50	3.60	3.80	3.90	4.00	4.20	4.40	4.50	4.60	4.80	5.00	6.00	8.00
11	2.54	2.73	2.92	3.09	3.18	3.27	3.45	3.54	3.64	3.82	4.00	4.09	4.18	4.27	4.54	5.45	7.27
12	2.34	2.50	2.67	2.83	2.92	3.00	3.17	3.24	3.33	3.50	3.67	3.75	3.83	4.00	4.16	5.00	6.67
13	2.15	2.31	2.46	2.62	2.69	2.77	2.92	3.00	3.07	3.23	3.38	3.45	3.54	3.69	3.84	4.61	6.15
14	2.00	2.14	2.28	2.43	2.50	2.57	2.72	2.78	2.85	3.00	3.14	3.21	3.28	3.42	3.57	4.27	5.72
15	1.82	2.00	2.13	2.27	2.33	2.40	2.53	2.60	2.67	2.80	2.93	3.00	3.07	3.20	3.33	4.00	5.33
16	1.75	1.88	2.00	2.12	2.18	2.25	2.37	2.44	2.50	2.62	2.75	2.82	2.87	3.00	3.12	3.75	5.00
18	1.55	1.67	1.78	1.89	1.94	2.00	2.11	2.16	2.22	2.33	2.44	2.50	2.56	2.67	2.78	3.33	4.44
19	1.48	1.58	1.64	1.74	1.84	1.90	2.00	2.05	2.10	2.21	2.32	2.37	2.43	2.52	2.66	3.15	4.21
20	1.40	1.50	1.60	1.70	1.75	1.80	1.90	1.95	2.00	2.10	2.20	2.25	2.30	2.40	2.50	3.00	4.00
22	1.27	1.37	1.45	1.52	1.59	1.64	1.73	1.77	1.82	1.91	2.00	2.04	2.09	2.18	2.27	2.75	3.63
24	1.17	1.25	1.33	1.42	1.46	1.50	1.58	1.62	1.67	1.75	1.83	1.87	1.92	2.00	2.08	2.50	3.36
26	1.04	1.15	1.21	1.31	1.35	1.38	1.46	1.50	1.54	1.61	1.69	1.73	1.76	1.84	1.92	2.30	3.15
27	1.02	1.11	1.18	1.26	1.30	1.33	1.41	1.44	1.48	1.56	1.63	1.66	1.70	1.78	1.85	2.22	2.96
28	1	1.07	1.14	1.21	1.25	1.29	1.36	1.39	1.43	1.50	1.57	1.61	1.64	1.72	1.78	2.19	2.86
30	0.93	1	1.07	1.13	1.17	1.20	1.27	1.30	1.33	1.40	1.47	1.50	1.53	1.60	1.67	2.00	2.67
32	0.88	0.94	1	1.02	1.09	1.12	1.19	1.22	1.25	1.31	1.38	1.41	1.44	1.50	1.56	1.87	2.50
34	0.84	0.88	0.94	1	1.03	1.06	1.12	1.15	1.18	1.23	1.29	1.32	1.35	1.41	1.47	1.76	2.35
35	0.81	0.86	0.91	0.97	1	1.03	1.08	1.11	1.14	1.20	1.26	1.28	1.31	1.34	1.43	1.71	2.28
36	0.79	0.83	0.89	0.94	0.97	1	1.05	1.08	1.11	1.17	1.22	1.25	1.28	1.33	1.39	1.67	2.22
38	0.75	0.79	0.84	0.89	0.92	0.95	1	1.03	1.05	1.11	1.16	1.18	1.21	1.25	1.31	1.58	2.11
39	0.72	0.77	0.82	0.87	0.90	0.92	0.97	1	1.02	1.08	1.13	1.15	1.18	1.23	1.28	1.54	2.05
40	0.70	0.75	0.80	0.85	0.88	0.90	0.95	0.98	1	1.05	1.10	1.13	1.15	1.20	1.25	1.50	2.00
42	0.67	0.71	0.76	0.81	0.83	0.86	0.91	0.93	0.96	1	1.05	1.07	1.09	1.14	1.19	1.43	1.90
44	0.64	0.68	0.73	0.77	0.80	0.82	0.86	0.89	0.91	0.96	1	1.02	1.05	0.09	1.14	1.36	1.82
45	0.63	0.67	0.71	0.75	0.78	0.80	0.84	0.87	0.89	0.94	0.98	1	1.02	1.07	1.11	1.33	1.78
46	0.62	0.65	0.69	0.74	0.76	0.78	0.83	0.85	0.87	0.91	0.96	0.98	1	1.04	1.09	1.30	1.74
48	0.58	0.63	0.67	0.71	0.73	0.75	0.79	0.81	0.83	0.88	0.92	0.94	0.96	1	1.04	1.25	1.67
50	0.56	0.60	0.64	0.68	0.70	0.72	0.76	0.78	0.80	0.84	0.88	0.90	0.92	0.96	1	1.20	1.60
60	0.47	0.50	0.53	0.57	0.58	0.60	0.63	0.65	0.67	0.70	0.73	0.75	0.77	0.80	0.86	1	1.33
80	0.35	0.38	0.40	0.43	0.44	0.45	0.47	0.49	0.50	0.53	0.55	0.57	0.58	0.60	0.65	0.75	1
	28	30	32	34	35	36	38	39	40	42	44	45	46	48	50	60	80

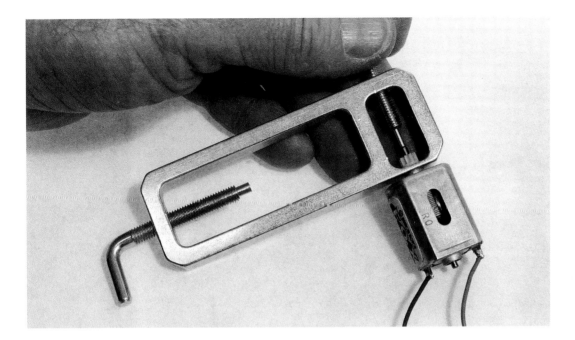

The Ninco 70201 gear puller makes it much easier to remove and install gears and wheels on axles and to install and remove (as shown) gears from motors.

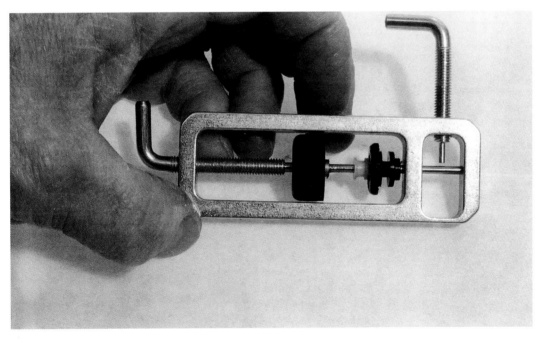

Here, the Ninco 70201 tool is used to press a crown gear onto an axle.

acceleration), fit either a pinion gear with one more tooth or a crown or spur gear with three fewer teeth than stock.

Always buy gears in sets of matched pinion and crown or spur gears from the same maker. If you mix brands, there is a very good chance the teeth will not mesh properly. If the car has spur gears, you will also have to buy matched sets of gears that have precisely the same shaft-to-shaft spacing for the gears to mesh properly. Slot.it, EJ's, Scale Racing, Parma, REH, NorthWest Short Line, and other manufacturers offer gears.

Also, if you change the motor, you may need to change the pinion gear on the new motor. Slot.it, Parma, EJ's, MRRC, Patto, REH, North-West Short Line, and others offer new pinion gears if one is not fitted to the new motor.

Finally, the Ninco 70201 gear puller tool makes it much easier to remove and replace the wheels and gears on axles and gears on motor shafts. You can use a small vise and a piece of 1/8-inch tube and a 1/16-inch drill bit, but it's often difficult to get everything lined up properly.

Chapter Ten

THE BODY SHOP

The winners of the 1985 and 1988 Le Mans endurance races re-created in 1/32 scale.

You can race model cars without ever building or painting a thing. For some of us, though, part of the enjoyment of the hobby comes from building or, at least, from painting. Somehow, the model manufacturers never seem to make exactly the car I want. If they re-create the car that won Le Mans, I want the same car that ran at Daytona. The good news is that I can have an accurate replica of just about any car I want if I am willing to at least paint it, if not build it from the track up.

Real Racing Cars in Miniature

I enjoy watching real-life racing about as much as I do driving the model. But I know that I enjoy building the model much more if I truly understand the real car. I strongly suggest that you buy whatever book or magazine you can to provide photos of the car you are modeling. For example, I wanted to have an accurate model of the McLaren F1 that won Le Mans in 1995. The book, *Driving Ambition,* by Doug Nye (ISBN 1-85227-841-2) has the complete story of the

McLaren F1, with plans and color photos of the Le Mans–winner as well as dozens of other racing McLaren F1s.

Custom Paint

You do not need to build a complete car. You may not even need to build a car at all. When you find a car you want but cannot buy it in the color scheme you desire, find out what the alternative may be. For example, I wanted a model of that McLaren F1 that won Le Mans in 1995. Ninco made the car around 1999, but they are all collectors' items now. Ninco continues to offer McLaren F1s with different paint schemes, but they will never offer the Le Mans winner again.

The answer is simple enough: buy any Ninco McLaren and paint it. Patto offers the correct decals. This one is relatively simple because the body is black except for some dark silver panels on the sills and the tail. Any black will do, and these lower panels are very close to gunmetal, which is available from Testors Model Master as a non-buffing metallic, as well as from other brands. After looking at the photos, I decided that Ninco had selected a metallic color that was much too light a shade of silver. In fact, I mixed in about one part black to three parts gunmetal before I sprayed the model.

Before painting, disassemble the model and remove the windows, headlight, and taillight lenses. Paint the black, then mask off the lower panels and tail and spray on the gunmetal. Apply decals and a clear coat as shown later in this chapter.

Body Builders

The primary sources of 1/32 scale bodies include firms that supply complete model car kits with chassis and body, like MRRC, Maxi-Models, Slot.it, Slot Classics, Patto, and EJ's. In addition, Top Slot provides bodies to fit existing plastic

Any Ninco McLaren F1 body (right) can be painted black and lettered with Patto decals to re-create the car that won Le Mans in 1985 (left).

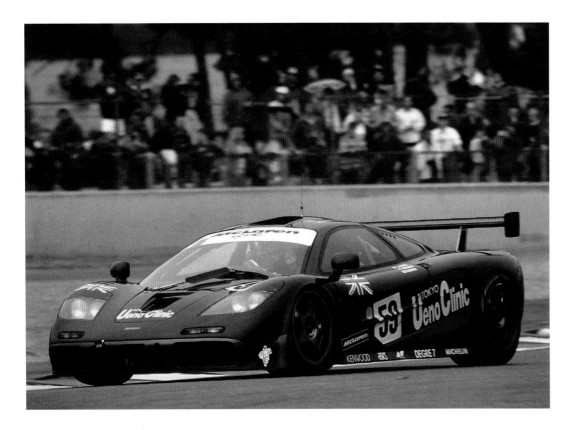

The McLaren F1 on its way to victory at Le Mans in 1985. *LAT photo*

153

The Jaguar XJR9 on its way to winning Le Mans in 1988. *LAT photo*

chassis. These products are all relatively easy to assemble, but you will need to know how to paint and apply decals.

Clear plastic bodies like the one on the XJR-9 Le Mans–winning Jaguar in this chapter are available from True Scale, EJ's, Patto, Betta, and others. Resin bodies similar to the Top Slot but with no provision for mounting and far less detail are available from A2M, Betta and Mundaring. When you order a clear plastic or cast-resin body, be prepared for a wide range of quality. Some barely resemble the real car while others are very close to the correct shape except in one or two areas. The quality control is about the same for all; if one Corvette Grand Sport is bad, all the firm's Corvette Grand Sports will be bad. However, the same firm might have a superb Chaparral 2C, for instance. Be prepared to be both thrilled and disappointed. Bodies are relatively inexpensive, so I order assortments of a half-dozen or more different bodies and when I get them, about one of six, on average, is worthy of being built into a car.

Cast-Resin Bodies

The cast-resin bodies in the Top Slot, Slot Classics, and Maxi-Models kits are virtually ready to paint right out of the box. Wash them in detergent and follow the steps shown later in this chapter.

The cast-resin bodies from A2M, Beta, Pre-Ad, and Mundaring, however, must be trimmed, the

windows opened or cockpit removed, and the body fitted to your choice of chassis. It's all work that can be done with small grinding wheels on a Dremel motor tool. Wear eye protection and respirator so you do not inhale the resin dust. Once the body is fitted, follow the painting and decaling steps in this chapter.

Clear Plastic Bodies

The clear plastic body is a relic of the 1960s when someone (probably Ron Klein of Knight Bodies and, later, Shark, Russkit, and Aurora) discovered that clear plastic could be vacuum-formed over a pattern of the model. The clear body was designed to be painted on the inside so the tough plastic would protect the paint. The clear plastic is, however, far too thick and it detracts from the realism of the car. The standard set by the Fly cars in the mid-1990s have been met and exceeded by both Fly and their competitors. If you want your custom-made model to look as good as your other out-of-the-box racing cars, you have to paint the clear body on the outside. The techniques for painting clear bodies are the same as for painting injection-molded plastic or cast-resin bodies; the major difference is that you must mask off the windows on a clear body, while you usually have to remove them from a cast-resin or injection-molded body.

You will also need a chassis like those described in chapter 7. My research indicated that

the Joests that won Le Mans in 1996 and 1997 had very similar chassis and wheels to the Jaguar XJR9 I wanted to model. Fly makes a fine 1/32 scale model of the Joest. I had to narrow the rear track width 1/8 inch, lower the rear wing, re-shape the ends, lower the driver, and modify the headlights to make the chassis fit.

Modeling the 1988 Le Mans–Winning Jaguar XJR9

My choice for a model was the Jaguar XJR9 that won Le Mans in 1988. Scalextric made an injection-molded model of the car in the early-1990s, but they are difficult to locate today and lack the skirts and some details of the real car. You have your own choice of a favorite car to re-create, so just substitute the body, chassis, and other components of your choice. After much shopping, I discovered a clear plastic body from Patto that was very close to the shape of the real XJR9. I used the book *Le Mans 1975–1999* (ISBN 1-855-2507) as my primary reference. It was not enough, as it turned out. After I completed my model, the book *Jaguar at Le Mans* (ISBN 1-85960-632-6) by Paul Parker was published, and I discovered that I had not extended the purple on the nose back far enough and that the bot-

tom of the windshield should have been painted about 1/8 inch higher. If you are going to try to duplicate my efforts, try not to duplicate my mistake—buy the book first.

Clear plastic bodies are trimmed from their molding sheet, but the final fitting is left to the modeler. The bottom edges of the real Jaguar XJR9 are perfectly straight. I used a combination of tools to trim the lower edges, including a Dremel motor tool with a 1/8-inch milling

This 1/32 scale replica of the Le Mans–wining XJR9 Jaguar has a Fly chassis with a Patto clear plastic body.

Below: Use a paper cutter to perfectly cut a straight edge along the bottom of the clear body.

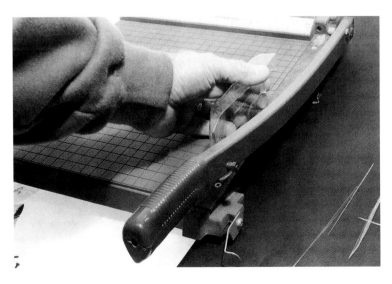

155

Use a cabinetmaker's or a machinist's file to file the bottom edge of the body flat and smooth.

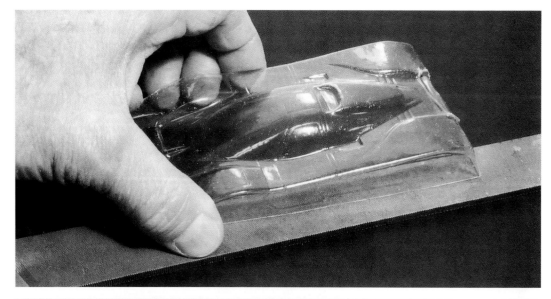

Use scissors to trim the body so it will clear the wing supports.

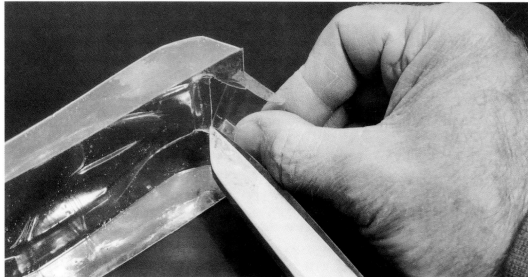

File the sharp edges of the cuts near the rear-wing cutouts.

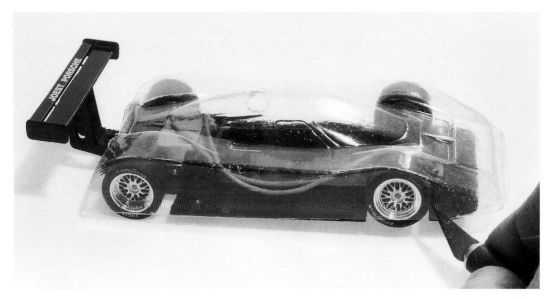

Mark the exact locations of the wheel cutouts with a hobby knife.

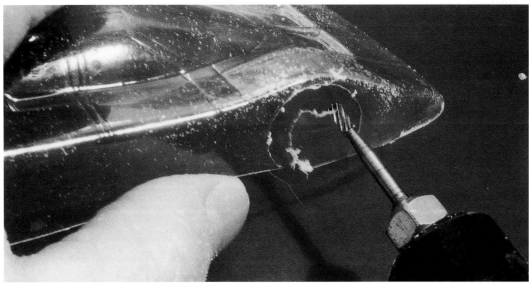

Use a 1/8-inch milling bit in a Dremel motor tool to trim the body, including the wheel wells.

Wrap 400-grit emery paper around a hobby knife to smooth wheel cutouts.

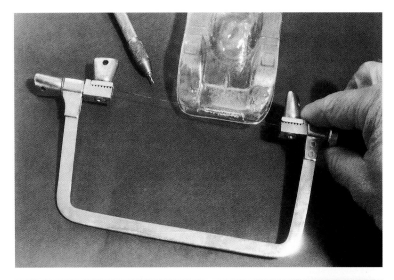

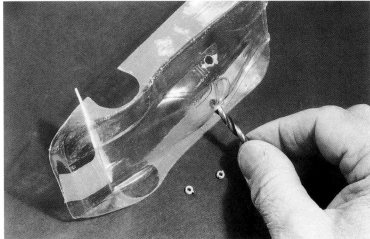

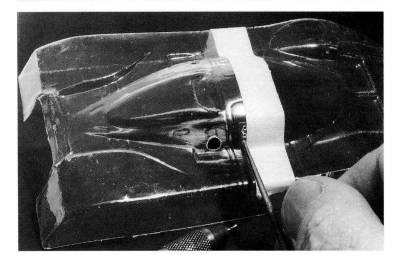

Top: Use a jeweler's saw to cut across the top of the front grill opening.

Center: Use a pin vise with a 1/4-inch bit to drill the holes for the fuel fillers.

Bottom: Mark the edges of the side windows' vent holes with tape, drill them with a 1/16-inch bit in a pin vise, then enlarge them with a jeweler's file.

bit, a paper cutter, and a flat file. I cut the rear spoiler area to clear the support for the rear wing on the chassis, bent the clear plastic over, and filed the outside corners smooth. Position the body over the chassis and, using photos of the real car as reference, mark precisely where the front and rear wheel cutouts should be located on the sides of the body. Trace the area with a hobby knife. Use a 1/8-inch milling bit in a Dremel motor tool to grind out the material from the wheel cutouts. You can also use the tool to trim the bottom of most bodies. Wrap some 400-grit emery paper around a hobby knife handle and sand the wheel cutouts so they are perfectly round.

I wanted the grill in the nose to be open, so I drilled 1/16-inch holes in each corner, holding the drill bit in a pin vise. I then used a jeweler's saw to cut across the top edge of the opening. I folded the remaining flap down and in and filed the edges of the opening smooth with flat and round jeweler's files.

Precision Scale makes a Number 48102 pipe fitting for model railroads that is very much like the fuel fillers on modern racing cars. You can order the part through your local hobby dealer. I drilled a 1/4-inch hole in each side of the cockpit to locate the fuel fillers. The XJR9 has a series of vent holes in the side windows. I drilled them with a 1/32-inch drill and filed them to size with a round jeweler's file. When you are satisfied with the way the body fits and all the detail holes are drilled, mask off the windows with tape and sand the body with 400-grit emery paper.

Mounting a Clear Plastic Body

I elected to use the complete interior from the Fly Joest. Trim off the tabs that retain the interior and remove it. The driver sits about 1/8 inch too high, so I used a razor saw to remove about 1/8 inch from the bottom of the interior and the bottom of the driver. You can cut the body-mounting posts from the Fly Joest with the Dremel and the milling bit. If you do, leave about a 3/4-inch round portion of the body still attached to each of the posts. I used the body-mounting kit offered by Fantasy World to make mounts similar to those I would have cut from the Joest body. This body-mounting kit is simply three pieces of telescoping Evergreen or Plastruct styrene tubing with a wood screw and a .020-inch thick square with a hole punched in it. You can make your own. The tubes telescope to build

Left: Sand the body with 400-grit emery paper, but do not touch the paper to the clear windows.

Below: Slice off the tips of the pegs that hold the interior into the body.

Bottom: Use a razor saw to cut off the bottom of the interior and the driver so the interior piece sits low enough to clear the inside of the Jaguar body.

a thick mounting post, and the plastic flange gives it a bit better support inside the body.

Attach the three posts to the chassis and lower the body in place. Note how much material needs to be removed from each post to lower the body to the correct height. Use a razor saw to cut the posts, but make at least two tries. Remove about 1/8 inch *less* than you think you should and test fit the body. Then remove the necessary amount to get the body down to the precise height. For the final body height adjustments, file the tops of the mounting posts as shown. The front mounting post actually sticks up in the windshield, so it needs a mounting surface. I cut a 1-1/2x1-inch piece of .020-inch-thick Evergreen styrene for the top of the dashboard and used that as the support for the front mounting post. When the body is resting on the posts at the correct height, cement the squares and the dashboard to the tops of the posts with Testors Model Master Liquid Cement for Plastic. Remove the screws and cement the tubes inside one another. Let the supports dry for a week.

The rear wing on the Joest is bout 3/8 inch higher than the wing on the Jaguar. Use a razor saw to cut the wing from the Joest chassis and to remove the necessary amount for the support posts. Refer again and again to the photos of the real car to get the height right. File the ends of the wing to match the shape of those on the Jaguar XJR9. Reattach the wing to the chassis with metal-filled epoxy.

Remove the two inner headlights from the headlight brackets and position them in the forward corners of each bracket. Cut two small

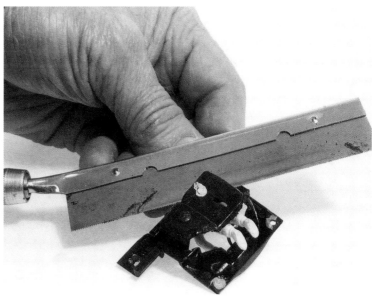

159

Fantasy World body mounts are three telescoping sizes of plastic tube held to the chassis with a wood screw.

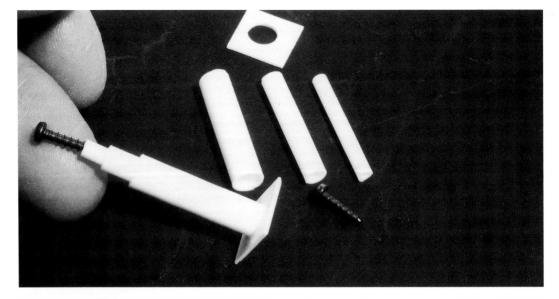

Attach the body-mounting posts and test the fit of the body.

Use a razor saw to shorten the body-mounting posts, then file them to the correct height.

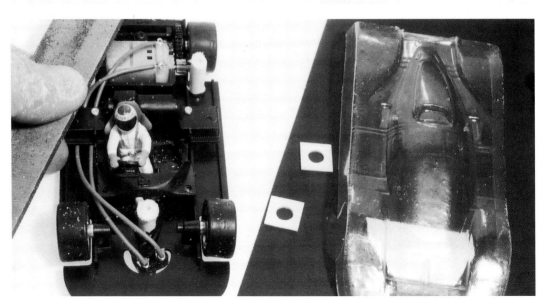

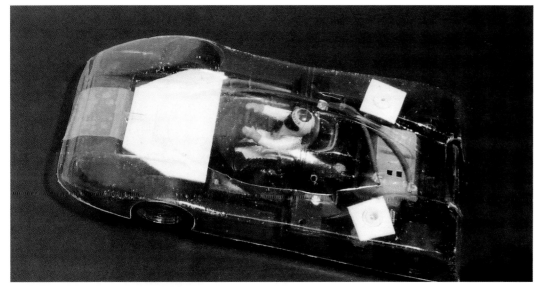

A piece of 020-inch styrene sheet is used for the dashboard that also supports the front body-mounting post.

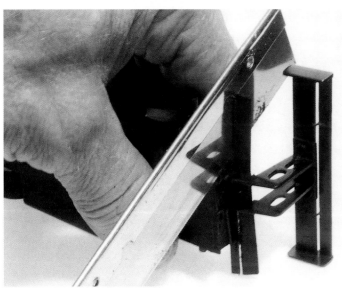

Use a razor saw to cut the rear wing off at the base.

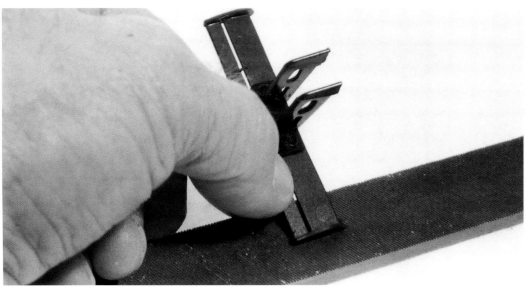

File the ends of the wing to match the shape of the ends of the wing on the Jaguar.

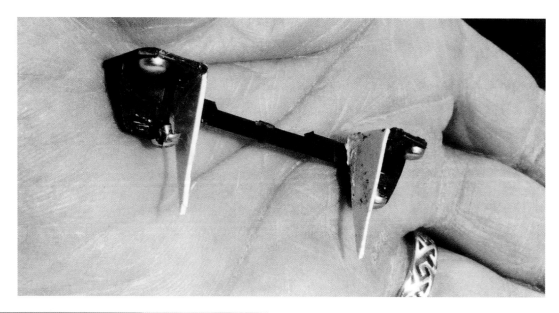

Move the inner headlights on the Joest headlight bracket farther forward and add two small triangles cut from .020-inch styrene.

Above: Cover the clear windows and headlights with Microscale Magic Mask fluid and let it dry.

Slice around the edges of the dried Magic Mask fluid and peel off any excess from outside the window frames.

triangles of .020-inch plastic to serve as side panels for these headlight boxes. Cement the parts together with 5-minute epoxy.

Masking Clear Windows

I use Microscale's Micro Mask to mask off windows and headlights. Brush the fluid over the areas you want to remain clear. While you should try to get the fluid right on the edges of the window frames, it's okay if you slop over a bit. When the Micro Mask dries, trace around the window frames with a hobby knife and peel off any dried masking fluid that was outside the frames. Be sure to mask the inside of the body, too, so paint cannot reach the clear windows or headlights while you are painting the outside of the body.

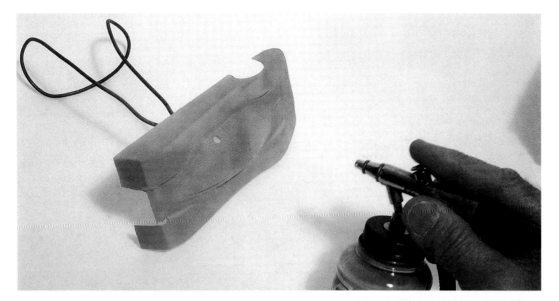

Tape the body to a handle fashioned from a coat hanger while you spray the primer coat.

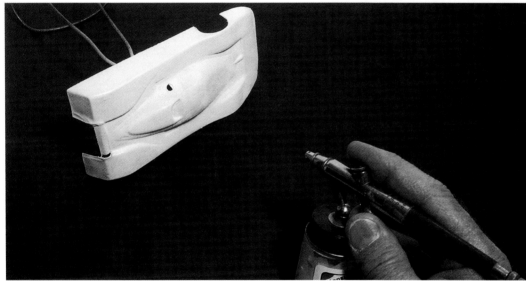

When the primer dries, spray the entire body.

Use 600-grit sandpaper to sand any imperfections from the paint, then apply another coat of white.

163

Mask over the white
to leave the areas
to be painted
purple exposed.

Painting with an Airbrush

It is possible to achieve a reasonable paint surface with aerosol cans. There is not, however, the choice of colors you will need. I used MCW lacquer paints and primers on this Jaguar: Number 1004 Light Gray Primer and Number 2068 Silk Cut Dark Purple. I elected to use an off-white, but I would select a lighter shade, like MCW 2501 White, if I were doing it again. Bend a coat hanger to use as a handle and tape the body to the wire. If you are going to use lacquer, I recommend a cheap external-mix airbrush. Thin the paint with one part lacquer thinner to four parts paint. If you want to use an internal-mix airbrush,

buy a special slow-drying thinner like Sherwin Williams Sher-Lac R7K 200 Slow Thinner so the paint will flow properly. Hold the airbrush about 6 inches from the model and use about 15 pounds per square inch of pressure. Apply the primer first and let it dry overnight, then apply the white and let it dry overnight.

Use the green Scotch brand automotive masking tape in a 1/8-inch width for the edges of the purple, and cover the remainder with drafting tape (it's less sticky than regular masking tape). Spray the Silk Cut Purple on the body and on the rear wing.

When the paint dries,
slide along the edge of
the masking tape with
a hobby knife, then
peel back the tape.

Left: Slice around the edges of the window frames and headlights, then gently peel back the dried masking fluid.

Below: I found it easiest to scrape the dried masking fluid from the centers of the headlights with my fingernail.

Bottom: Cut the decals as close to the color as you dare.

Removing the Masks

Slice along the edges of the color separation lines with a hobby knife before you peel back the masking. Peel the tape back over itself to minimize the chance of lifting the paint beneath the tape. Use a hobby knife to slice all round the edges of the windows and lights (again), then pick at the edges of the dried masking fluid until you can lift a corner with tweezers. I found that it was easiest to just use my fingernail to scratch the paint off the centers of the headlights.

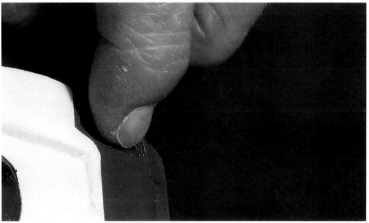

Lettering and Striping with Decals

Decals for 1/32 scale cars are available from Patto, MRE, Monarch, Slixx, Electric Dreams, Top Slot, Pro Slot, and others. There is also a variety of 1/24 scale decals (including those from display model kits) that you can reduce to 1/32 scale in an ink jet color copier onto special sheets of decal paper from Microscale and other brands.

I needed two sets of Patto decals to have enough stripes for this model. Practice these techniques on an older model with some scrap decals before you start on the final project. Cut the decals as close to the color as you dare with scissors. Place one decal into a cup of warm water for about a count of three, then lift it out and rest the decal on a paper towel for a few minutes while the water soaks through the paper backing to reach the glue beneath the decal. Coat the area that will be covered by the decal with decal-softening fluid like Micro Scale's Microsol or Testors Model Master Decal

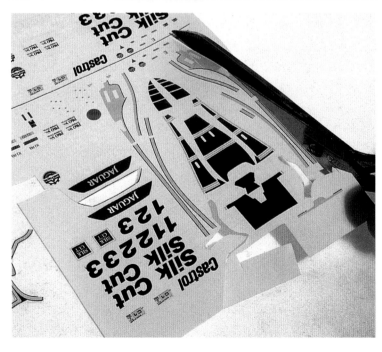

Dip the decal in warm water, then rest it on a paper towel while the water soaks through decal backing.

Apply decal-softening fluid to the area you will cover with the decal.

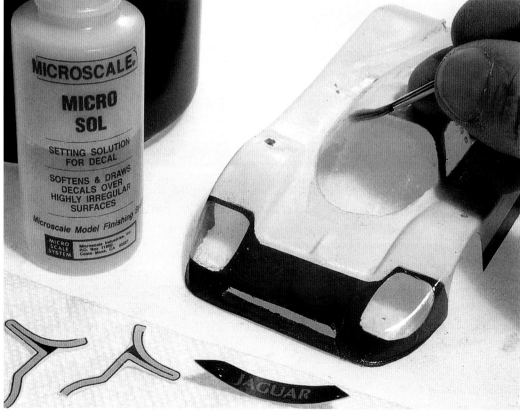

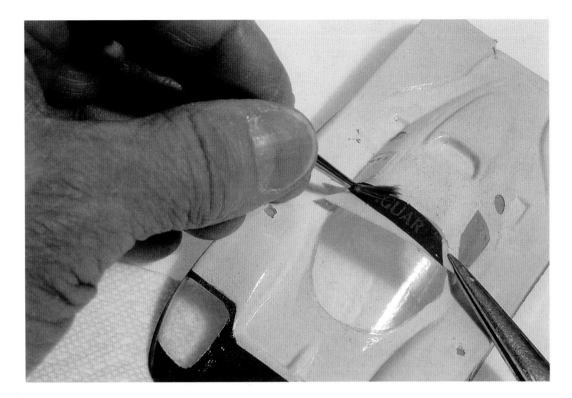

Hold both decal and paper in place, then pull the paper from beneath the decal.

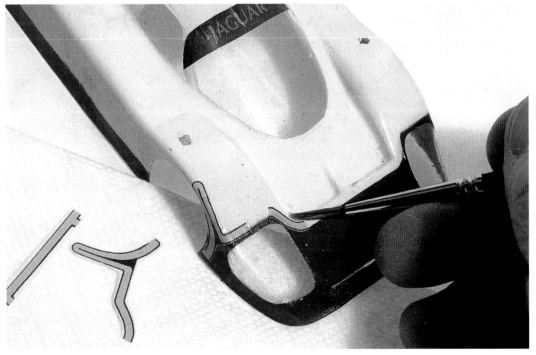

Add an extra length of stripe material to allow the stripe to run all the way across the car.

Softening Fluid. When the decal can be moved, position both the decal and the paper exactly where you want the decal. Hold the edge of the paper with tweezers and pull the paper backing from beneath the decal while you hold the decal itself in place with the tip of a hobby knife. Use gentle pressure so you do not tear the decal.

Press gently on the decal with a wet paintbrush to position it perfectly. I cut two of the stripe decals to flow the yellow lines down into the grill but I was wrong—the yellow stripe should go straight across the top of the car so there is purple paint down inside the vent on the top of the nose of the car. When the decals are all in

167

Spray the finished
model with a single
coat of Testors
Glosscote clear paint.

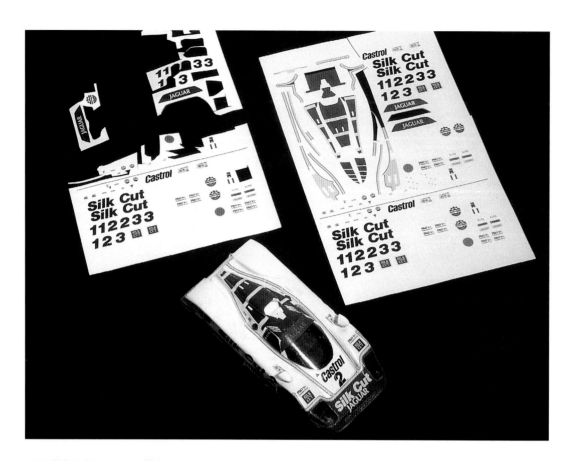

Use a round key as a
template to trace the
lines for the rear
wheel covers.

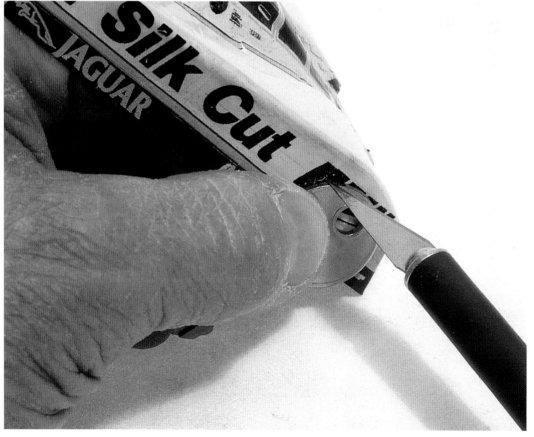

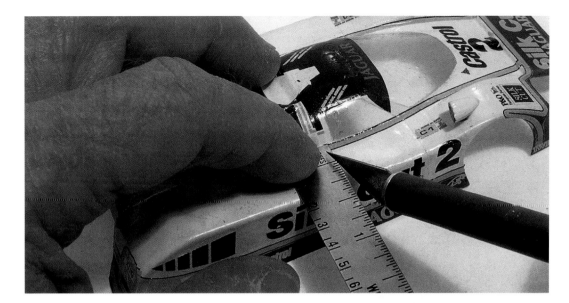

Use a ruler to guide your knife when making slices along the straight panel lines.

Use a number 0 paintbrush to flow black India ink into the panel lines you just sliced with the hobby knife.

Below: Use a damp tissue to wipe away the ink for the body—it will remain in the sliced panel lines to simulate a realistic shadow line.

place, let them dry overnight, then gently wash the surface to remove any decal glue and let the model dry. Finally, spray the car with a thin coat of Testors GlossCote.

Superdetailing Tips

You can make any model racing car more realistic by accenting its panel lines. Slice along the panel lines with the tip of a hobby knife. On the XJR9, the wheel covers over the rear wheels are round, so I used a key to guide the hobby knife when slicing those lines. Use a small ruler to guide the knife when slicing straight lines. Use a number 0 brush to flow black India ink into the lines you just cut. Use a damp cloth to wipe the surface of the model so the ink remains only in the sliced lines. Work with only a

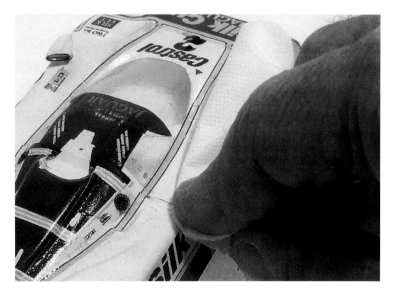

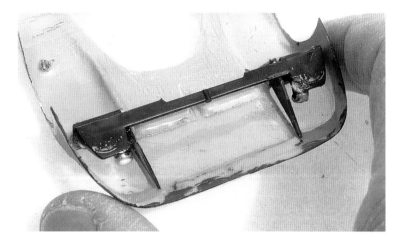

few inches of lines at a time so the ink does not dry completely.

The headlight bracket can be installed in the body and held in place with 5-minute epoxy. Paint the dashboard flat black. I used a Detail Masters 2520 etched-metal windshield wiper on the windshield (although it should be parked off the windshield) and 2060 Quick-Turn fasteners near each wheel well. The fuel fillers are Precision Scale 48102 pipe fittings (from a model railroad shop, as detailed earlier), and the mirrors are Fly B74. Detail Master has a few other etched parts, as well as turned-metal carburetor intakes and 1/24 scale wire wheel inserts.

When the body is complete, it can be mounted permanently to the three body mounting posts with metal-filled epoxy.

Bullet-Proof Clear Finish
Most clear paints will yellow. Some acrylic floor coverings, however, seem to remain clear for years. Protect the finish on your model racing car by brushing on a coat of clear acrylic floor covering like Future brand.

Top: Use 5-minute epoxy to hold the headlight bracket inside the body.

Above: Paint and decal the wing and paint the dashboard flat black.

Right: Protect the finish of any model racing car with a brush-on coat of Future clear floor covering.

Chapter Eleven

HO RACE TRACKS

This was one of the tracks that Aurora used in the 1960s for organized championship races. You can build grandstands like these. Model railroad shops can order the seated figures and sheet and strip styrene plastic to build the grandstand structures.

I t's the race track, even more than the cars, that makes HO scale the choice for many model car racers. You can get a lot more HO track in any given space. And, ounce for ounce, gram for gram, the HO cars are much faster than the 1/32 scale cars. Somehow, for many fans, that makes HO scale racing more realistic than 1/32 scale racing.

Realistic Racing in HO Scale

I have to provide a personal observation here: I've seen race tracks by the hundreds during my half a lifetime in model car racing. Beyond any doubt, the most realistic track I have seen so far is the Katz-spa-ring. The track itself is a very nice design and it has scenery that is as realistic as any model railroad, and far beyond the scenery of most model car racing tracks. What makes this track so incredibly realistic, however, is the speed of the cars relative to the size of the track. It really and truly does look like a real race track as seen from, perhaps, a helicopter. But unlike a spectator's view from a helicopter, you are actually in full control of your car down there on the track. The HO scale G-Plus cars feel about like you'd expect a real Formula 1 car to perform, while the HO scale Thunderjet cars run about like real production C5R Corvettes. (And the super-power Super G-Plus and Patriot cars look like toys.) And, yes, you can almost feel the cars' acceleration and cornering g-force because the whole movement

Brad Bowman, from Brad's Tracks, is custom-building the Katz-spa-ring 8x26-foot track for Greg Katz. The track is routed from sheets of expanded PVC plastic. The scenery is still under construction, but the track has hosted dozens of races.

matches what you'd expect if you were driving the real car. Incredible!

Few HO scale racers have enough space for a track that's as large as the 10x31-foot Katz-spa-ring, but you can build an HO track that performs at least as well as a 1/32 scale track in half the space of a 1/32 scale track. Put another way, the Katz-spa-ring would require a whopping 20x60-feet if built with 1/32 scale sectional track. So, a relatively small 4x8-foot HO scale track can have all the realistic action of an 8x16-foot track in 1/32 scale—and the largest 1/32 scale track in chapter 5 is the 9x16-foot Daytona International road course for Carrera track.

Selecting Sectional Track

Tomy A/FX, Life-Like, Mattel, and Model Motoring are the four most common brands of HO sectional track. All use the same geometry and

Max Trax produces large plastic track sections that are combined to create custom-designed tracks like "Slugger" Canady's. The lap counters/timers are from Trix Trax.

footprint, so you can use any of them with any track plan, assuming that the brand you choose makes all the sections shown on the plan. The geometry is clever, with the track being 3 inches wide and curves with 6-, 9-, 12-, and 15-inch outside radii. None of the brands are interchangeable, although Life-Like does offer a set of adapter sections for Tomy A/FX, Mattel (ex-Tyco), and older snap-lock Aurora track. The simple geometry means that you can substitute a 12-inch, 90-degree curve for a 15-inch, 90-degree curve by simply adding a 3-inch piece of straight track on each end of the 12-inch curve to make up the difference. Since the track only curves in 45-degree (or with some double-length curves, 90-degree) segments, the track never moves so far out of alignment that you cannot connect the final two pieces, even if you have to go back and replace one or two 9-inch straight track sections with a 3- or 6-inch piece.

TRACK SECTION KEY TO HO TRACK PLANS

Each plan in this book has letters on every track section to help you identify the track sections that are required. This chart will show you which pieces are used. Remember that you can mix HO brands as long as you buy an adapter track that joins the two brands you are using, but that you must also then include that 3-inch adapter track in your plan.

Key	Description	Tomy (A/FX) Part No.	Life-Like Part No.	Mattel (Tyco) Part No.	Model Motoring Part No.
E	3-inch Straight	8632	none	K	none
D	6-inch Straight	8641	none	5830	none
C	9-inch Straight	8622	9930	5829	9452
B	15-inch Straight	8621	9934	5836	9405
A	15-inch Terminal	8627	in set*	5832*	9453*
J	6-inch Curve	8656	none	none	9451
H	9-inch 90° Curve**	8623	9927	5831	none
I	1/2 9-inch Curve**	8624	none	5846	9408
K	9-inch Bank Curve	8628	9929	5852	none
G	12-inch Curve	8642	none	5844	9407
M	12-inch Bank Curve	8991	9928	none	none
F	15-inch Curve	8663	none	none	9406
ADAPTERS (all are 3-inch straights)					
	Tomy (A/FX) to Life-Like	none	9931	none	none
	Mattel (Tyco) to Life-Like	none	9932	none	none
	Tomy (A/FX) to older Aurora Snap-Lock Track	8626	none	none	none

The letters L, W, and Y on track plans indicate places where matched pairs of straight track can be inserted to expand the size of the track for a larger space.

* Tomy A/FX terminal track is 15 inches long, but Life-Like, Mattel (Tyco), and Model Motoring terminal tracks are 9 inches long, so an additional 6-inch straight track must be joined with the 9-inch terminal track to make a 15-inch pair of track sections, counting the 15-inch terminal. Also, the 6-inch straight will have to be added to the quantity of track needed for those three brands.

**NOTE: You can substitute full 90-degree 9-inch curves for most pairs of these 45-degree curves.

You can certainly race on a two- or four-lane track on the floor. It's a whole lot easier to see the fine details on the cars, however, if you can find even a temporary space for a portable door-size track. Rick and Sandy Schleicher are competing on the Suzuka track from this chapter.

Track Plans for Larger Spaces

You can add length or width to nearly any sectional track plan by simply inserting equal-length pieces of straight track on opposite sides of the track. Thus, any of these 4x8-foot plans could be lengthened to 4x12 feet or more by inserting additional pieces of 9- or 15-inch straight track along the two long sides of the track. You might want to add some extra straight pieces to some of the inner tracks that parallel the long sides.

You Create the Action

Please do not consider any of the track plans in this book, or anywhere else for that matter, to be the only way to assemble a track. Experiment on your own. Every HO racer has his or her own idea of what is the best track configuration. Some racers prefer a dozen or more tight 6-inch curves twisting around the infield with just one or two broader curves. Others prefer banked turns wherever possible, and some folks like to use as many 12- or 15-inch radius turns as possible to get as much "drifting" action as they can in any given space. The plans for HO scale versions of the flat (not banked) Daytona Road Course, for Suzuka, and for Monaco are a combination of tight and broad curves. The plans for the banked Daytona track include banked turns on the appropriate corners with as many 12- and 15-inch flat turns as would fit.

Try all the plans in this book. I have designed them so they represent the feel of the tracks as much as the appearance. If you want to match the appearance of real race tracks, particularly the Formula 1 tracks, use the plans furnished with the Tomy A/FX International Super Challenge four-lane set. There are different versions of Suzuka (Tomy calls it "Japan") and Monaco in the manufacturer's A/FX series of plans. These plans focus on the shapes of the tracks and use a large number of the tight 6-inch radius curves to get the shape of the track as accurate as possible.

Permanent Tabletop Race Tracks

If you can find the space, install your track on a permanent tabletop so you can race whenever you wish. A 2-1/2x6-1/2-foot door is large enough for a variety of HO scale layouts, including all those in *Racing and Collecting Slot Cars*, and most of the 18 tracks in the Tomy A/FX International Super Challenge set. If you are really cramped for space, you can fit an HO layout on a 15x48-inch coffee table—there's always enough room somewhere for HO race track. Remember that you can store a door or the 4x8 piece of plywood on its edge with the track attached, or you can remove the track and reassemble it in less than half an hour. Once you understand how the track plans work, it takes very little time to assemble the track, with its snap-together track sections. It takes me longer to add the guardrails, in fact, than it does to assemble the track.

There are a variety of 4x8-foot panels available, including 1/2-inch plywood and MDF, as well as the lightweight but expensive foam-filled Gatorfoam panels sold by firms specializing in trade show displays. Gatorfoam must be edged with plastic as shown in chapter 3. There is also, of course, the ultimate permanent HO track: one custom-made from PVC sheet like the Katz-sparing or Shaun Lee's Shaunadega tri-oval. I do not recommend particleboard unless you support it with a framework of 1x2 boards as shown in chapter 3. You can use this framework to support plywood, MDF, or Gatorfoam but these boards are also strong enough to be self-supporting with just a pair of sawhorses or card tables to serve as legs. For a really large layout, you can use a Ping-Pong table as shown in chapter 3. If the track must be portable, you can attach it to the tabletop with wood screws (you can remove them more easily than with nails) for those times when you want to change the track.

If the track constantly slides around, you can install a half-dozen flathead wood screws around the extreme edges. If you simply drape the tabletop with felt to provide a somewhat more finished track as shown in this chapter, you may not even need to bother with the screws because the felt will keep the track from sliding. Or you can cement the felt to the tabletop with odorless contact cement. Coat the tabletop with the cement and press the felt in place while the contact cement is still wet. It's best to work with about 2 square feet at a time so the cement does not dry before you can press the felt in place.

Borders, Skid Aprons, and Shoulders for HO Track

No HO scale track maker offers extensions for the curves so the cars will not slide off the edge on the outer lanes. Boye's Models offers cast-resin borders for most HO curves and some straight sections. Sliding off is not really a problem with cars that have magnets for downforce because they only slide about as far as the pickup rails before flipping. More and more HO racers are finding that cars without magnets are at least as much fun to race as those with magnets. The original Aurora Thunderjets are still available to dealers through REH and BSRT, while Model Motoring and Playing Mantis produce similar chassis without magnets. You can always

pull the magnets from the cars that have separate traction magnets. If you race cars without magnets, you will find that the cars will fall right off the outer edges of the curves unless you add an extension to the width of the track.

All the 1/32 scale track makers offer extensions for the outside of curved track sections called "aprons", "shoulders", or "side curves." I will refer to them as "borders." You can add borders to HO scale track by cutting the next-larger radius turn in half lengthwise. You can then cement the cut outer half to the edge of the track. I suggest using metal-filled epoxy for the strongest joint, although black automotive trim cement should work about as well. You may want to paint the borders grass green or sand beige like the custom-painted borders on the Carrera 1/32 scale tracks in this book. Microsport decals (available from BSRT) even offer red and white rumble strip vinyl stick-on

You can squeeze an interesting and exciting HO track in a space as small as 15x48 inches. This is A/FX track painted concrete gray.

Use spare track sections as borders for straight or curved track. Mark the cut line with masking tape. Hold the track in a vise and mount the saw blade at 90 degrees to the saw so you can cut the full length of the track.

borders for HO track sections. If you do paint them, it is easier to apply the paint before you glue the border to the edge of the track. You should also make borders for the straight sections leading out of curves to give the fishtailing cars space to straighten out without falling off the edge of the track.

There is no HO curve larger than a 15-inch radius, so you have to fabricate borders for these largest of curves. You also have to fabricate borders for the banked turns, although you may not need them. You can use HO scale model railroad cork roadbed for the borders. The roadbed comes in two halves, and you only need to use one of the 7/8-inch-wide halves. You will likely need two layers, however, to match the thickness of the track. The cork roadbed is flexible enough to conform to the outside of the curve but it must be cemented in place. If you have mounted the track permanently onto a tabletop (in spite of my suggestion not to), you can simply cement the cork to the tabletop with odorless contact cement. If you want to attach the borders to the track sections themselves, cut a piece of .020-inch-thick Evergreen or Plastruct sheet styrene, or even a cheap plastic "For Sale" sign, to the size of the track section plus the extra 7/8-inch width on the outside for the border. Cement the

.020-inch-thick plastic sheet to the bottom of the track with metal-filled epoxy. When that dries, cement the cork roadbed to the 7/8-inch-wide protruding lip of .020-inch plastic. You can, of course, also use this method for adding borders to any curved or straight HO track section.

There is no built-in provision for guardrails on these borders around the curves. You can simply ignore the borders and surround the entire track with a 2-inch-tall fence made from a 3-inch-wide piece of wood or plastic baseboard nailed to each of the four sides of the tabletop. If you want guardrails on each corner, use the standard Tomy A/FX, Mattel, or Life-Like guardrails and cut off the clip-on base of each vertical post. Drill 5/32-inch holes in the borders to match the spacing of the guardrail posts and push the posts into the holes. You can leave the guardrails loose or cement them in place with metal-filled epoxy or black automotive trim cement.

Tuning the Track

Chapter 12 explains why a car with magnets for traction has more magnetic downforce and, therefore, corners faster if the magnets are closer to the rails. The plastic sectional track is all mass-produced by machines. The mass production techniques allow the edges of the two steel

The borders on these HO curves are model railroad cork roadbed cemented to the tabletop with contact cement.

pickup rails to protrude between approximately .007 and .027 inch above the track surface. With this kind of manufacturing tolerance, however, the magnets are sometimes a full .020 inch farther from the rails at some parts of the track than at others. The custom-made tracks have much closer tolerances; Brad Bowman's custom hand-routed tracks maintain a pickup rail height between .009 and .013 inch. The section on "How Low Can You Go" in chapter 12 explains how to test the track with a car using layers of Scotch Magic tape on the bottom of car to find the places where the rails are too high. You can replace the offending track sections to reduce the range of high and low rails consider-

ably. Or you can merely accept the higher rails as places where the tires get extra traction like rougher pavement on real track, and the lower rails as places that simulate slippery spots like spilled oil. You are the only one who needs to decide just how perfect you want the track to be.

Custom-Made Plastic Track Sections
The curved track sections for HO scale cars have relatively small radii, but most of the cars have such strong magnetic downforce that larger curves are really not necessary. It is fascinating to watch a car power slide through a really broad curve, however. You can make a curve of any radius you desire by using a hacksaw to cut up a

To make flexible track sections for large-radius curves, first cut straight track into individual lanes. Then make cuts into both sides of the track at every inch, cutting to within 1/16 inch of the metal rails.

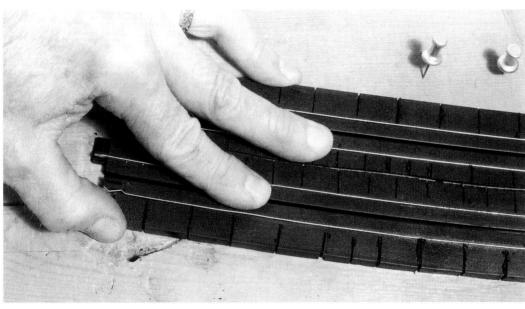

There's no prize for neatness with the flex track. Bend the track to the curve you desire and cement it to the tabletop. Fill in the gaps with automobile body putty.

For reliable joints between the track sections on a permanent track, solder each joint. Use acid flux and 50/50 tin/lead solder. Heat the two rails where they touch while you push solder at the joint. Let the metal melt the solder, not the soldering iron itself. Rinse the track thoroughly with clean water.

Wizzard and others make 20-foot lengths of replacement rail for permanent tracks. If you want to use continuous rail, clamp each track section in a vise and use pliers to pull the rails from the track.

12- or 15-inch HO scale straight track section. First, cut the track in half lengthwise with a hacksaw to produce two single-lane sections. If you use the finest-tooth blade you can buy, a minimum sanding or filing will be needed to make the cut edges smooth. Use a medium-cut flat machinist's file or a cabinetmaker's file to smooth the cuts. Next, make a series of cuts inward from both edges of the track to within 1/16 inch of the outer edges of the metal pickup rails. Cut from both sides of the track and make the cuts about 1 inch apart. You will find that you can force the cut track into a large-radius curve.

The track will not hold the curve, however, unless it is cemented to a tabletop, so the method is not really practical for portable track sections. You could cement the custom-bent track to a piece of thicker .040-inch sheet styrene as described earlier for making track sections with borders. You will find that the custom-made curves do not match the geometry of the standard track so you will have to custom-make additional curves and straights to connect the large-diameter curves into the track. This is the method Jason Boye used to build his 12x16-foot Le Monzaco track—all the track is made from either standard or custom-cut and curved pieces of Tomy A/FX track. Each joint between track sections and beside adjacent track sections was filled with styrene and body putty so the track surface is smooth all the way across, including the 1-1/2-inch-wide borders around the outside of all the curves.

Some serious racers go a step further and pull all the rails from the slots. Each of the four steel pickup rails is then replaced with a continuous 20-foot-long piece of rail sold by Wizzard expressly for this purpose. The continuous rail makes it possible for you to have better control over the distance the edges of the steel pickup rails protrude above the surface of the track than with hundreds of separate pieces of rail. Obviously, you cannot use continuous rail with portable track; the track must be mounted permanently to a plywood or MDF tabletop. It is a lot of work, but some people find it a better choice than trying to route their own tracks as shown in chapter 6.

Custom-Made Race Tracks
Custom-made HO race tracks are available by Brad Bowman's Custom Tracks, Max Trax, and others. It takes extreme skill to make an HO scale track—much more than a 1/32 scale track. I strongly suggest you buy a track rather than cut your own. Brad Bowman's Custom Tracks offers complete, individually designed racing circuits. Max Trax offers prefabricated CNC-machined track sections that can be linked together like standard track sections. Either can

be assembled on your own tabletop. The custom-made track offers two primary advantages: the curves can be much larger than the 15-inch maximum possible with sectional track and, for serious racers, the height of the pickup rails can be better controlled.

The techniques for routing 1/32 scale tracks shown in chapter 6 can be used to route a track for HO scale cars. The narrower slots for HO scale, however, are easiest to cut if you use 7/32-inch-thick expanded PVC sheet from the track surface. This material is about as light as cardboard and

Above: You can have a track custom made or buy a custom-made track in sections. Most custom tracks are routed from 7/32-inch thick PVC sheet like this sample from Brad's Tracks. The slot is 3/32 inch wide and 1/8 inch deep. The two steel pickup rails are held in their slots with colored insulated wire and Loctite.

Left: Shaun Lee's Shaunadega is a six-lane, 10x16-foot tri-oval custom-routed from PVC plastic sheet by Brad's Tracks.

is usually available from industrial plastics suppliers. If you do route an HO track, the slot should be 1/16-inch wide and 5/32-inch deep, with the two parallel slots for the steel pickup rails also 1/16-inch wide and deep enough so the top edges of the steel pickup rails protrude between .007 and .027 inch above the surface of the track. Match the dimensions of Tomy A/FX slot, slot spacing, rail positions, and rail heights as closely as you can. The rails themselves can be purchased from Wizzard and held into the too-wide slots with 22-gauge insulated wire. The wire serves as both a wedge and a color code for each lane. The wire and rails can be cemented in place with Loctite.

Daytona in HO

There are three choices of tracks for an HO scale version of the Daytona International Speedway. The first plan is a traditional flat layout that bears only a passing resemblance to the real Daytona road course. This is one of the plans that was featured in the long out-of-print issues of *Model Car & Track* magazine in the mid-1960s.

The track section sizes are marked on the plan for the curves. The straight sections are all 9 inches unless marked otherwise.

The real Daytona International Speedway offers the option of the banked tri-oval that is used by NASCAR sedans or the road course that is used by sports cars for the Rolex 24-hour race, as well as other road racing events for both automobiles and motorcycles. Tomy A/FX offers banked-turn curves with 9- and 12-inch radii, as well as a broad 15-inch radius flat curve section. Those are the components for the two banked versions of the Daytona track. If you need to assemble the track from other brands, you will have to settle for a smaller radius for most of the turns. The banked tri-oval nicely fills a 4x8-foot plywood tabletop.

The Daytona International Speedway is designed so you can quickly remove portions of the track to change it from the tri-oval to the road course and back again. In the photographs, the unused portion of the road course has been left in the infield, looking very much like the infield at the real Daytona.

The Daytona International Speedway road course to fit a 4x8-foot area. This plan originally appeared in *Model Car & Track* magazine in the 1960s. The curved-track sizes are marked on the plan and all unmarked straight sections are 9 inches.

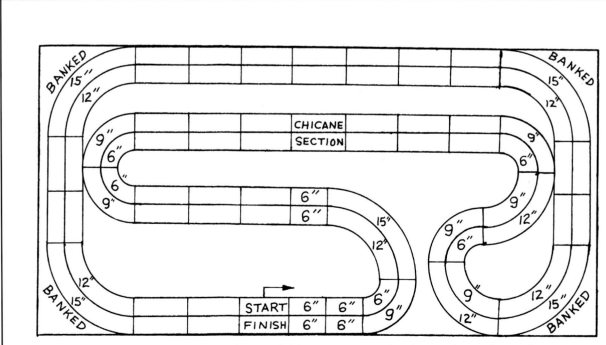

FIG. 203 This Daytona Raceway plan is scaled for HO construction but the same layout idea can be used with any set track using 45-degree or 90-degree segments of a circle.

The track sections that make up the road portion of the Daytona International Speedway are resting in the infield, looking very much like the used portions of real track during the NASCAR Daytona 500.

LIST OF HO TRACK REQUIRED FOR 4x8-FOOT DAYTONA 500 TRI-OVAL

Key	Quantity	Description
E	0	3-inch Straight
D	4	6-inch Straight
C	0	9-inch Straight
B	16	15-inch Straight
A	2	15-inch Terminal
J	0	6-inch Curve
H	0**	9-inch Curve 90°
I	0	1/2 9-inch Curve
K	6	9-inch Bank Curve
G	2	12-inch Curve
M	6	12-inch Bank Curve
F	2	15-inch Curve

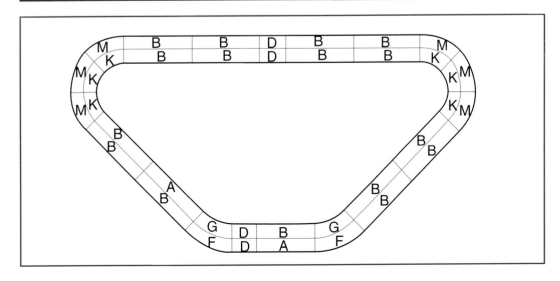

The road portion of the Daytona International Speedway is installed as it would be used for the Rolex 24 Hour road race. The unused portion of the oval is resting on the table in the upper right.

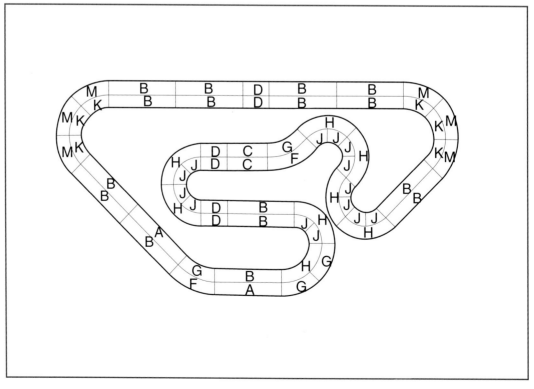

LIST OF HO TRACK REQUIRED FOR 4x8-FOOT DAYTONA INTERNATIONAL RACEWAY ROAD COURSE
(PAGE 182)

Key	Quantity	Description
E	0	3-inch Straight
D	6	6-inch Straight
C	2	9-inch Straight
B	16	15-inch Straight
A	2	15-inch Terminal
J	14	6-inch Curve
H	8	9-inch Curve 90°
I	0	1/2 9-inch Curve
K	6	9-inch Bank Curve
G	4	12-inch Curve
M	6	12-inch Bank Curve
F	2	15-inch Curve

The 9- and 12-inch radius "high banks" on the Daytona International Speedway are assembled from snap-together Tomy A/FX track components.

Monaco in HO

This plan is also available in the Tomy A/FX International Super Challenge four-lane set's plan sheet with even tighter curves, but is a much closer match for the shape of the real Monaco track. This plan is also from the original *Model* *Car & Track* series. If you want a truly realistic Monaco, I suggest using the Tomy A/FX plan but replace all the 9- and 12-inch curves with 12- and 15-inch curves and add as much straight as you can. It would fit very nicely on two door-size

Above: The Monaco Formula 1 Grand Prix track fills nearly every square inch of the 4x8-foot tabletop. The 1/2-inch sheet of plywood is draped with a 6x10-foot piece of green felt. The brown is latex wall paint rolled on at random to simulate bare earth.

Right: The center portion of the Monaco Formula 1 track (marked "Chicane Section" on the plan) looks like a 12-lane track but it's really just three segments of the four-lane track that are side by side.

panels arranged in an "L" shape. You could then install photo mural profiles like those on the 1/32 scale track in chapter 4 to create a true replica of Monaco.

Suzuka in HO

The Suzuka plan is the third one from the original *Model Car & Track* series of plans for 4x8-foot areas. The shape of the real track is reasonably close on this HO scale version. The plan in the Tomy A/FX International Super Challenge is a bit more like the real track but requires more than 4x8-feet. You could also use the Woodland Scenics Risers to make up-hill and downhill grades like those shown in chapter 4.

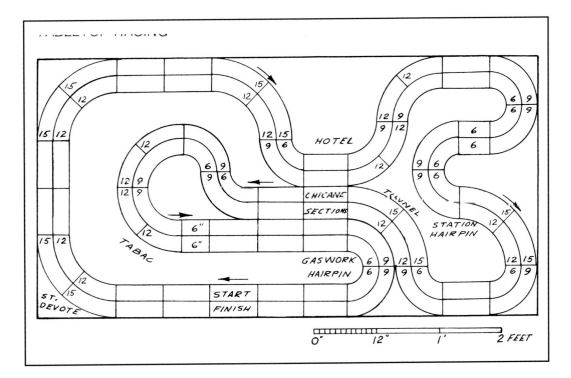

TABLE OF RACING

ST. DEVOTE

TABAC

6"
6"

CHICANE

SECTIONS

HOTEL

TUNNEL

STATION HAIRPIN

GASWORK HAIRPIN

START

FINISH

0"   12"   1'   2 FEET

The plan for the HO Monaco Formula 1 Track for a 4x8-foot area, originally published in *Model Car & Track* magazine in the mid-1960s. The area in the Chicane Section is actually six pieces of 9-inch straight track laid edge to edge. The use of two chicane tracks as marked on the plan is optional. This is the kind of tight and twisty course that many HO scale racers find most exciting.

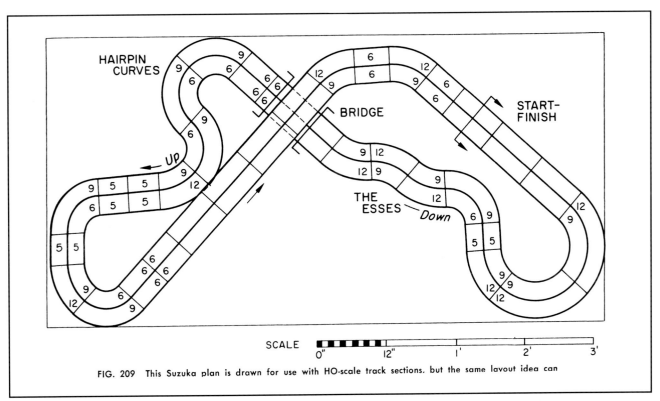

HAIRPIN CURVES

UP

BRIDGE

START-FINISH

THE ESSES — Down

SCALE   0"   12"   1'   2'   3'

FIG. 209 This Suzuka plan is drawn for use with HO-scale track sections, but the same layout idea can

The HO Suzuka Formula 1 course for a 4x8-foot area. This plan, from *Model Car & Track* magazine in the mid-1960s, captures the general shape of the real track but wastes a lot of table area. This would be an interesting track to treat with scenery and up and down grades using the Woodland Scenics Risers as shown in chapter 4.

Chapter Twelve

RACE CARS IN HO

Custom-made Daytona Charger, Tyco Plymouth Superbird, and 429 Fairlane NASCAR racers compete on Carl Schorle's Aurora track. Playing Mantis' Johnny Lightning series of friction cars includes a Daytona Charger that can be mounted on a Thunderjet or Playing Mantis HO racing chassis. Life-Like also has a Plymouth Superbird.

For many model car racers, HO is the perfect size. You are aware that you are driving a miniature replica of a specific real car, but it is just large enough that you can easily see the details and the shapes of the cars. These HO cars are the smallest practical size for tabletop racing. There's just enough room inside the body for a motor and gears that can be mass-produced at a reasonable cost.

HO Racing Car
As tiny as they are, the HO cars offer a full range of performance, from exact reproductions of 1960s-era Model Motoring cars to commercial race cars that zip around plastic track curves at more than 10 real miles per hour. The use of magnets to provide downforce and, hence, more

traction for the tires which in turn means more cornering speed, originated with HO cars. You can expect the HO racers have perfected the tuning art of magnetic downforce, and indeed they have, as you will read later in this chapter.

There is an ever-growing number of HO racing cars, but most of the newer releases are new paint schemes on existing plastic bodies. There are far too many to catalog here. NASCAR sedans are available from Mattel and Life-Like, and the Tomy A/FX series includes some older model NASCAR cars. Mattel has a generic Formula 1 body that they decorate to match a half-dozen real F1 cars. Tomy A/FX, Life-Like, and Mattel all offer a variety of sports cars and sedans. Model Motoring, Playing Mantis, and Mini-Models have series of

186

1960s sedans and hot rods. Some of the Johnny Lightning friction-drive cars from Playing Mantis have plastic bodies and fit on a Thunderjet or Playing Mantis chassis.

If you are willing to paint your own bodies, there are replicas of most of the Aurora T-Jet cars as well as modified sedans and hot rods from Furuli Models and others. Boye Racing Models and others offer a series of cast-resin sports and GT cars.

What Is HO Scale?

There is essentially only one size chassis for all HO cars, regardless of who makes the model. The pancake-style motors of the original Aurora Model Motoring cars are still available as Thunderjet chassis through REH and Playing Mantis, and all the other cars from Tomy A/FX, Mattel (ex-Tyco), Life-Like, and Wizzard have inline motors with the motor axis running the length of the car. The Thunderjet and Playing Mantis chassis are a bit narrower than the others and the chassis that Mattel fits under their Formula 1 cars has a bit shorter wheelbase. The body dimensions for the model are adjusted to suit the chassis. In real life Formula 1 cars are huge, as are modern sports racers, both about the size of a Camaro, Firebird, or NASCAR sedan. The HO versions of these two cars are approximately

1/72 scale. An HO model of a full-size sedan like Ford Fairlane, however, is about 1/87 scale. Since most HO cars are replicas of F1 cars, NASCAR cars, or pony cars and all three real cars are similar in size, the HO versions are all very much in proportion to one another, at about 1/72 the size of the real cars. It's only the HO models of the larger cars like the Fairlane, Dodge Intrepid, and Daytona that look somewhat out of place, but even these are proportional to one another at close to 1/87 the size of the real cars.

Model Motoring offers a series of musclecars. This is their 1987 Buick Grand National in unpainted form.

BSRT has a series of non-magnetic cars with inline chassis. The cars include this Camaro and a Mustang Trans Am, as well as a series of sports and GT cars, each with a clear plastic body painted and decorated by BSRT.

Six of the most common HO scale chassis, five with inline motors and the sixth with a pancake-style motor (left to right): Wizzard's Patriot, Tomy's G-Plus and SRT, Mattel's 440-X2, Life-Like, and Thunderjet.

The Johnny Lightning Corvette Grand Sport body will screw onto the Thunderjet chassis, but it sits too high because the clear windshield interferes with the chassis.

Thunderjet Chassis for Playing Mantis Bodies

Playing Mantis offers in their Johnny Lightning series a variety of musclecars that have metal friction-drive chassis but plastic bodies. The bodies are designed to mount on the original Aurora Thunderjet chassis (which are still available to hobby dealers through REH) or on the new Playing Mantis or Model Motoring chassis. You simply remove the two screws from the Johnny Lightning body and install the body on a Thunderjet chassis. Some of the bodies, however, have windshields that interfere with the chassis, like that on the Grand Sport Corvette shown here. Use flush-cut diagonal cutters, like Testors Sprue Cutters, to trim away the portions of the chassis that interfere with the windows. With a bit of trimming, the Grand Sport will sit at a more realistic height on the Thunderjet chassis. You may need to perform similar modifications on the other Johnny Lightning bodies to adapt them to the Thunderjet chassis.

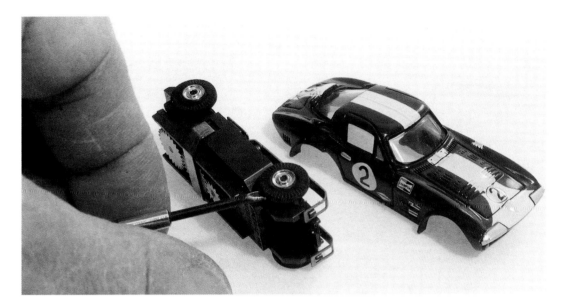

Remove the body. Pry the front wheels a bit farther apart so they fill the wheel wells.

Use Testors Model Master Sprue Cutters to trim off the flanges on the tops of the chassis where they interfere with the clear windshield inside the body.

With the chassis trimmed, the body sits almost 1/8 inch lower on the chassis. To correct the rear-offset chassis, file small notches in the mounting posts to move the body forward about 1/16 inch.

To adapt the Life-Like NASCAR body to a Mattel chassis, apply a drop of Testors Model Master Liquid Cement for Plastics to each of the body-mounting posts inside the Life-Like NASCAR body. Then cement two 7/8-inch-long pieces of 1/16x1/8-inch adapter strips of styrene to the mounts.

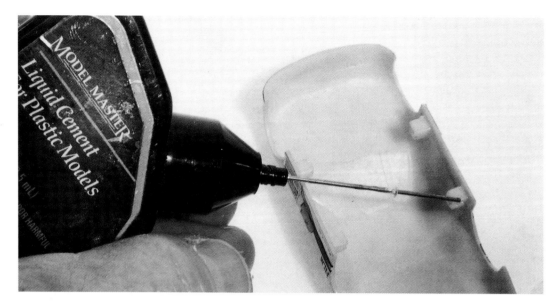

The two 7/8-inch pieces of 1/16x1/8-inch Evergreen or Plastruct styrene strip inside the Life-Like body will fit the notches on the Mattel chassis. Use a hobby knife to trim the rear edges of the wheel cutouts to clear the Mattel tires.

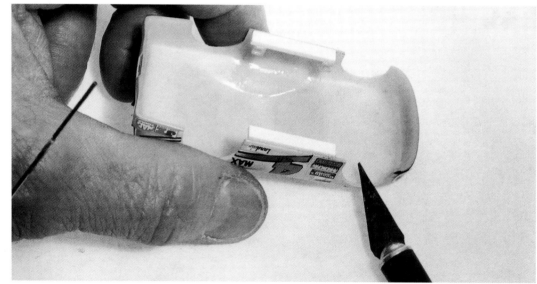

The Mattel chassis should snap into the modified Life-Like body, with the two pieces of 1/16x1/8-inch plastic fitting into the body-mounting slots on the Mattel chassis.

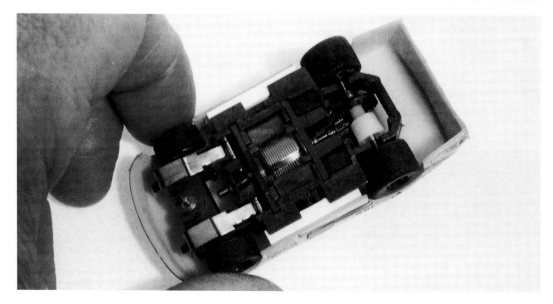

Life-Like NASCAR Bodies on Mattel Chassis

Both Mattel and Life-Like offer a range of NASCAR sedans. There are certain paint schemes available on one brand that are not available on the other. It is possible to fit the Life-Like chassis into the Mattel bodies and hold it there with a couple of small dabs of rubber cement. The rubber cement is flexible enough so the body can be removed for maintenance.

It is a bit more difficult to install a Mattel chassis beneath a Life-Like body, but it can be done. You need some 1/16x1/8-inch strips of Evergreen or Plastruct styrene plastic. Cut two 7/8-inch-long pieces and cement the 1/8-inch-wide edges to the bottoms of the Life-Like body-mounting posts with Testors Model Master Cement for Plastics and let the cement dry for about a week (yes, a week). The body should snap into the Mattel chassis, but you may need to trim the edges of the rear of the front wheel wells a bit so the tires spin freely,

Scale Chassis for Mattel F1 Racers

Mattel has a special short-wheelbase chassis that they fit to their Formula 1 cars. Unfortunately, the chassis wheelbase is about a scale foot short, so the noses of the cars hang out in a most unrealistic pose. The pan chassis used beneath the Mattel NASCAR cars can be installed beneath

Mattel Formula 1 cars are all fitted with chassis that have wheelbases too short for their bodies (top). Modify the body and the Mattel NASCAR pan chassis to provide a more realistic longer wheelbase (bottom).

The Mattel Formula 1 chassis (left) is lower in the front and shorter than the Mattel NASCAR "pan" chassis (right).

Left: Use a razor saw to remove the angled reinforcing flange from the corners of the Mattel NASCAR chassis so it will fit below the nose area of the Formula 1 body.

the Mattel F1 bodies if you are willing to do a bit of carving. The resulting model is within about 5 percent of being an exact 1/72 scale replica of a typical modern Formula 1 car and the change in appearance is well worth the effort.

Hold the Formula 1 body over the NASCAR chassis and note where the tapered body is likely to interfere with the square edges of the front of the chassis. Use a razor saw to trim off the top flanges on the chassis between the motor and the front axle. Also mark the lower edges of the body where they still interfere with the cut-down front of the chassis and gently whittle slivers of plastic from the bottom of the body with a hobby knife until the body will snap over the chassis. Use the same technique to open up the notch in the body for the front axle so the body clears the new chassis' front axle. If you slice the simulated front suspension carefully, you can reinstall it above the relocated front axle. The back edges of the front wing will have to be trimmed a bit to clear the front tires. Finally, you may need to trim down the body-mounting flanges a bit so the body will snap over the new chassis.

The notch for the front axle in the Formula 1 body will have to be relocated to match the new longer chassis. The bottom edge of the body will also have to be trimmed and about 1/32 inch removed from the rear of the front wing.

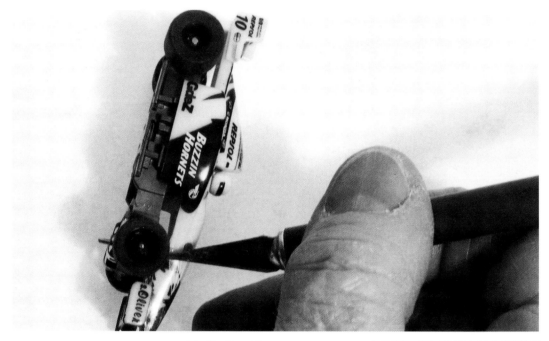

Carefully slice off the simulated front suspension so you can reinstall it over the new forward axle location.

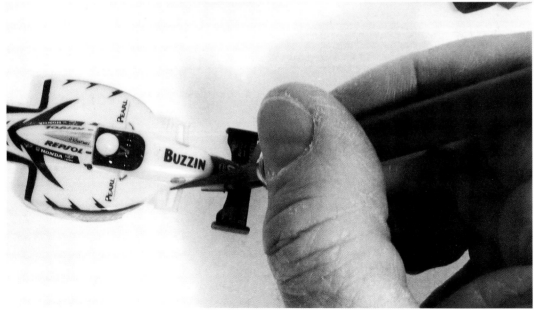

New Bodies for HO Cars

BSRT, Wizzard, and others offer a wide choice of clear plastic bodies for HO model racers. Most of the bodies are extensively modified for all-out commercial or "neo" racing and they barely resemble the real cars. There are, however, a few bodies that are nicely proportioned replicas. BSRT offers a new range of prepainted bodies, including a replica of the Porsche 917K in the paint schemes of the car that won Le Mans in 1970, as well as the Gulf-sponsored cars. The bodies are painted on the outside so the thickness of the clear plastic does not distort the paint. Racers who are more interested in speed paint clear bodies on the inside so the clear protects the paint in the high-speed crashes, but the effect is much less realistic.

BSRT also offers a new series of ready-to-run cars with clear plastic bodies painted and decorated on the outside. These cars have a BSRT chassis with an inline motor but no traction magnets, so they handle like the Thunderjets, but with more speed and better control. The series of ready-to-run models includes Camaro, Mustang, and a series of sports and GT cars.

Painting HO Bodies

The painting techniques in chapter 10 can be used to paint any HO car. The HO cars are small enough that you can mask the windows with Testors Model Master Parafilm M rather than masking fluid. This is the technique that Jason Boye uses to paint his magnificent HO sports and GT cars. The Boye's Racing Models' bodies are cast resin to fit Mattel 440-X2 chassis. To paint these cast-resin bodies, first spray the entire car with a thin coat of primer. Let that dry overnight, then apply Floquil Grimy Black to the window areas and let it dry for a day. Mask off the windows by covering the entire window area with Parafilm M. Stretch the material to pull it snugly over the window frames and push it down firmly with your fingers. When it is perfectly tight, use a hobby knife to trim along the visible edges of the window frames and remove the excess Parafilm. Paint the body your color of choice. When the paint has dried for an hour, trace around the edges of the window frame with a hobby knife to slice between the paint and the masking. Peel the Parafilm from the windows. Apply decals and protect the model with a coat of Testors GlossCote. When that dries, brush on a thin coat of Future vinyl floor covering fluid sold in grocery stores.

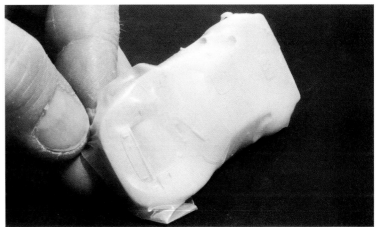

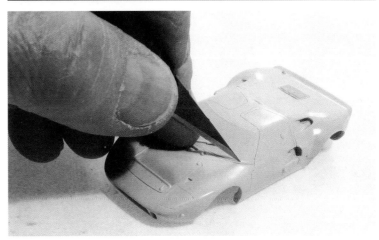

Top: BSRT offers a wide range of painted and decorated clear plastic bodies that must be trimmed with fingernail scissors to match the chassis and tire locations. BSRT also offers special mounting-post kits to mount these bodies on Tomy A/FX or Mattel chassis.

Middle: Use Testors Model Master Parafilm M to mask the entire window area of a cast-resin body. This is Boye's Models Ford GT40 body to fit the Mattel 440-X3 chassis.

Bottom: Carefully slice through the Parafilm around the edges of the window frames with the tip of a hobby knife and remove all the Parafilm but that covering the windows. Paint the body, then slice through the paint around the window frames again. Peel off the Parafilm from the window areas and apply decals as shown in chapter 10 to finish the body.

Tuning and Maintenance

HO cars usually require very little maintenance to keep them in action. Clean the track with a damp rag—never use solvent because it can attack the plastic. The guide pins are replaceable but it takes hundreds of hours of racing to make a noticeable mark on the sides of the pin. Lint can accumulate around the pickup shoes, their pivot points, and around the guide pin. Clean these areas thoroughly with a toothpick to remove any loose hairs or lint. The track can work loose at the joints to cause erratic running, so it's also a good idea to examine every joint before a race.

Troubleshooting HO Cars and Track

Troubleshooting begins with isolating the problem: is the track itself at fault or just one car? If you have problems with a car, try another. If that still does not help, try another controller. If the problems persist with just a single car, then there is likely to be a problem with just that car. Conversely, you can isolate problems with the track using this system. If there is a problem with the track, it can usually be traced to a loose joint or a bent pickup strip that is not making contact across the track joint.

If a car fails to run, it is nearly always because one of the pickup shoes has lost its contact spring or the shoe itself has slipped from the chassis. Erratic performance is often caused by the same pickup shoes becoming dirty. Use a hard rubber eraser to clean the working faces of the pickup shoes and rub over the track pickup rails with a hard rubber eraser or even a coin to remove oxidation. Sometimes the wheels will be accidentally moved in close enough to rub on the chassis or far enough out to touch the body. You can pry the wheels back into place with a screwdriver.

Race-Tuning HO Cars

Brad Bowman conducts the performance track tests on HO cars for *Model Car Racing* magazine. He tests the cars on the 50-foot per lap Shaunadega tri-oval as well as on the 171-foot-per-lap 8x26 Katz-spa-ring (there's a photo of that track in chapter 11) and the much tighter 32-foot-per-lap 4x8 HO DL Challenge Track. He also tests the cars on a circle of 12-inch Tomy A/FX track using the inner lane. The lap times around the Katz-spa-ring range from 29.22 seconds for a Thunderjet car (no magnets) to 11.50 for a Tomy Super G Plus F1 car. The BSRT G2 is an example of the supertuned high-performance HO cars: its lap time is 8.15 seconds—a third of the Thunderjet. The Patriot by Wizzard and the G3 from BSRT are even quicker. The newer Life-Like cars and the Tomy A/FX SRT cars are within a few

The BSRT G2 car (left) has a longer chassis for more realism, but also has the toy-like O-ring front tires that some commercial racers prefer. The BSRT G2 car also has stronger magnets, a quicker motor, and gold-plated pickup shoes for improved speed and handling. The Mattel Formula 1 car with the longer NASCAR chassis is in the center and the stock Mattel car is on the right.

tenths of a second of the Super G-Plus cars. Around the skid pad, the Thunderjet runs about 2.12 miles per hour (that's real miles per hour, not HO scale—these cars are quick) to 7.01 miles per hour for the Tomy A/FX car, while the Mattel, Life-Like, and Tomy A/FX cars run in the 5.39 to 7.15 miles per hour range. The Patriot almost flies around at 10.01 miles per hour and BSRT G2 cars zing to an incredible 11.68 miles per hour—that's far too quick for many model car racers. Still, it's incredible to think that matchbox-size cars can run faster than you can!

Downforce for Model Racing Cars

Aurora engineers John Wessels and Bob Bernard were working with Jim Russell in 1972 to develop new products when they discovered that it was possible to use motor magnets strong enough that they served to pull both the rotating armature at higher speeds and the car downward onto the steel pickup strips. Aurora introduced Thunderjet-style chassis with taller magnets to reach down closer to the track as the Magna-Traction car in 1974. In 1975, Jim Russell got his way and the G-Plus car with the inline motor appeared to establish the standard of HO scale slot car design that has been improved only in detail in the intervening quarter century. In 1975, engineer Pat Dennis at Tyco (later sold to

Mattel), introduced separate traction magnets with the Curve Hugger HP-2 chassis.

The Aurora engineers knew that the magnetic attraction of the car to the rails was stronger the closer the magnets were to the rails. The designs were limited, however, by the strength of the motor—it takes more and more power to drag the car along when what it really wants to do is stay stuck. In effect, the magnets increase the weight of the car by a factor of as much as 100. Back in 1972, they were pleased just to double the effective weight of the car—the early Magna-Traction cars barely equaled the effective weight of the model, enough so you could turn the track upside down and the car would hang on. That was plenty for a race car that would be sold in the mass market. Any more power would require a more powerful motor and that, in turn, would require a more powerful transformer that would mean larger hand controllers—a cost-increasing spiral that was just not practical.

Model car racing enthusiasts, however, are not quite as concerned about cost, so they soon discovered stronger magnets. The racers perfected the art of rewinding the motor's armature (the rotating portion of the motor with all those bundles of little copper wires) with larger wire for more power to match the stronger magnets.

You can use layers of paper to determine the clearance between the bottom of the car (the traction magnets) and the tops of the steel pickup rails. The closer the magnets are to the steel pickup rails, the greater the magnetic downforce and the better the tire grip for faster cornering.

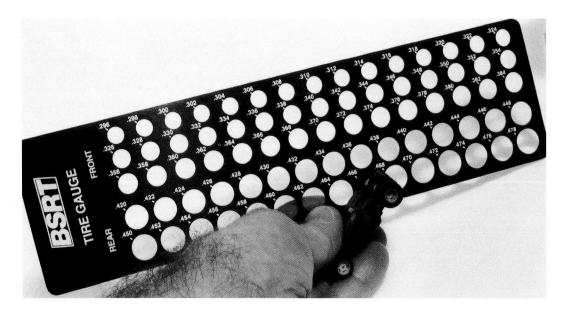

To some extent, the major manufacturers followed this same path, with Super G-Plus cars replacing the G-Plus cars at A/FX in 1990, 440-X2 cars replacing the 440 at Mattel (formerly Tyco) and, in 2001, Life-Like's new Pro Tracker-SS (called the "T" chassis) replacing the original Life-Like car. Today, all three of these cars are very similar performers, although if you really want to beat a G-Plus car you need to slightly modify the Mattel or Life-Like cars by replacing the stock tires with silicones or by allowing them to run slightly smaller-diameter tires.

How Low Can You Go?

The simplest way to lower the magnets in a HO car is to lower the entire car. And the simplest way to do that is to use smaller diameter tires. BSRT, Wizzard, and Slottech offer a range of hop parts that include replacement tires molded from either foam or silicone (or in some cases, foam tires coated with a silicone tread). Each track, even the custom-made tracks, have slightly different rail heights at various parts of the track. There's no easier way to find out how close your car is to the track than to lower it a few thousands of an inch at a time and test it to see if it is so low it actually rubs the rails. That's precisely what the serious HO race car builders do.

For a home racer, I suggest an alternative: place five layers of Scotch Magic tape over the bottom of the car. Press each layer firmly onto the car. The tape is about .002 inch thick, so the five layers will decrease the ground clearance (the distance between the bottom of the car and the top edges of the rails or strips) by about .010 inch. Use a black felt-tip pen to color the bottom of the tape. Run the car around and see if the ink is scraped off the tape. If it is, remove a layer of tape and apply more ink, then retest. If the ink was not rubbed off the bottom of the fifth layer of tape, try adding another layer of tape and color it, then retest the car to see if the color rubs off. Repeat the process of adding or removing tape and marking it with the pen until the car makes a complete circuit of the track with only a trace of ink having rubbed off on the pickup strips.

You can skip the tape method if you are willing to buy a set of five or six wheel-and-tire combinations so you can try ever-smaller tires until the bottom of the car actually rubs (you will have to use this trial-and-error system on any new track).

Be sure to run in both lanes and if you are racing in both directions, run in both directions. If you notice that the car is so low it gets hung up on one particular piece of track, take a close look at that piece to see if the rail is somehow dislodged. If you can, replace that track section and test again. You can use this test method to minimize the variation in rail height by replacing what are usually only a few offending pieces of track. Once you have determined the highest rail position on a particular track, you can decide how much (if any) lower you are willing to modify the cars.

Downforce Test Track

There's a downforce scale test track for 1/32 scale cars in chapter 9. It is possible to build a similar test rig for HO cars, but the try-it-on-the-track method I just described works well. You can, however, have a section of HO test track to save testing every car. When you have finished testing that first car with tape on the bottom, set it on a piece of 6-inch straight track. Measure the clearance between the tape and the rails on the test track. Pick a particular spot on the track and mark the position on track where you will measure the clearance so it is always measured at the same spot.

You can measure the clearance between the bottom of the car and the tops of the pickup rails with metal automotive feeler gauges, but they tend to get stuck on the magnets and give a false reading. It is easier to use paper as a feeler or clearance gauge. Tissue paper is usually about .001 inch thick and the pages of *Racing and Collecting Slot Cars* and this book are .004 inch thick and their covers are about .014 inch thick. You can have a machine shop use a micrometer to check the samples of paper and card you want to use as feeler (clearance) gauges. Many layers of paper are needed to fill the gap between the bottom of the car and the section of test track. You will likely find that the rails on the test track are at least .005 inch lower than the highest rails on the actual track, but the test track's rails could be higher or lower. Once you know the minimum clearance, you can then set up every car with that same clearance by simply measuring the clearance on the test track, then fitting tires that are two times the distance smaller than stock.

As an example, you may measure that low-as-you-can-go car and determine that it has .006 inch of clearance on the test track. The next car you check has that .006-inch clearance *plus* another .020 inch of clearance. The rear tires on that second car are .470 inch in diameter. You can measure the tires with a micrometer but it's tricky. You want to lower that car .020 inch, so you need tires that are 2x.020 inch or .040 inch smaller. Subtract .040 inch from .470 inch, and you'll see the tires you want to lower that car are .430 inch in diameter. Replace the stock tires (and perhaps the wheels) with .430-inch diameter tires and that second car should just clear the highest rails on the track described earlier. None of these numbers is likely to apply to your specific cars or test track, but they should be reasonably close.

BSRT and Wizzard make tire gauges for tires all the way from .296- to .450-inch diameter. To use the gauge, simply push each hole over the tire until you find the one that just fits without binding or rattling.

Racing Tires and Wheels

Replacement silicone tires in the stock diameter are available for A/FX, Mattel, and Life-Like wheels. The A/FX wheels have a depression at the center, however, that makes it difficult to mount a tire squarely, so most racers replace these wheels with aluminum wheels. The aluminum wheels are always more true-running than the stock plastic wheels anyhow, so serious racers also replace at least the rear wheels on their Mattel or Life-Like cars. Also, the aluminum wheels have a flange on both sides while the Mattel and Life-Like wheels have a flange only on the inside of the wheel rim.

There is often a choice of wheel diameters for the rear wheels. Stock Mattel wheels are about .255 inch in diameter and the stock Life-Like wheels are about .285 inch in diameter. The replacement silicone rear tires from BSRT, Wizzard, and others are flexible enough to fit either stock rim (but not the A/FX rim) or a range of sizes of replacement aluminum wheels. Replacement wheels are available in .250-, .275-, and .300-inch diameters. The tires are available in minimum .420-, .424-, .428-, .432-, and .436-inch diameters when mounted on the .250-inch-diameter wheels, but they will stretch to fit the larger wheels. The tire makers provide a chart that illustrates the size of each of the five tire sizes on the three common wheel sizes. If you want a .430-inch-diameter tire to lower the car described earlier in this chapter, you can use a .250-inch rim with a BSRT 383 or 393 tire and get a diameter of .428 inch, or use a 384 or 394 tire and .250 wheel to get a .436 diameter. A .380 tire, when mounted on a .250-inch-diameter rim, will also provide a .436-inch-diameter tire.

Beware, however, that there is definite limit as to how low you can make an HO car and still have enough motor to pull the downforce. You may need to use a faster armature or stronger motor magnets if you lower the car too close to the pickup rails. You will most certainly have to use a stronger motor if you fit stronger traction magnets. The stronger motor will require a controller with a lower ohm rating. You will most likely have to have a separate power pack for each lane (always a good idea), but each pack may need to have as much as 5 amps.

The tires are usually color-coded so you know at a glance which size you are using. The color coding doesn't do much for realism, but it makes it a lot easier and quicker to tune a car for an unfamiliar track. Serious racers have rear axles prepared with all three wheel diameters and an assortment of all five tire sizes. If you are concerned about color, the BSRT 391 tires are black, and when mounted on one of the three different choices of wheels, allow a .424-, .440-, or .458-inch diameter tire choice. The tires are also available, from most makers, in a soft compound for plastic track and a harder compound for continuous rail track. There are more choices of silicone tire compounds and even fine-pore foam tires. I strongly recommend that you purchase a BSRT and a Wizzard catalog so you can see the choices of tires and wheels, as well as gears, motor and chassis parts, and bodies if you consider modifying your HO cars for racing.

Performance Parity for HO Racers

"Performance parity" is my term for making two or more very different cars perform nearly the same so the two can race against each other competitively. It's the same general idea that is used by NASCAR and all other full-size car racing organizations. Generally, Tomy A/FX G-Plus cars are faster than Life-Like cars, which are, in turn, faster than Mattel cars. You can decrease the performance of any G-Plus car by fitting larger tires so there is less magnetic downforce. Conversely, you can increase the performance of any Mattel or Life-Like car (or for that matter any HO car) by lowering the car for more downforce. Often there is a noticeable and measurable difference in performance when you fit a different body to the same car. You can even achieve performance parity by stipulating that the better body has slightly less clearance between the track and the traction magnets.

Commercial Racing in HO

Really serious racers remove the injection-molded plastic body from their cars and fit a clear body. The front tires and wheels are replaced with new wheels with O-ring tires and, often, the rear tires are colored foam or silicone. The super-quick machines like the BSRT G2 and Patriot cars that are effectively twice as fast as out-of-the-box Tomy A/FX, Life-Like, or Mattel cars with magnets are just the beginning of the upper limits of HO performance. Stronger magnets, hotter motors, and special tires are available to make even the BSRT G2 and Patriot cars seem slow by comparison. There's no question these cars are quick, and you can find a wealth of information on them and on places to race them on the Web. This book, however, is designed to provide information for folks who are interested in racing replicas of real racing cars—replicas that are as accurate (if not as fast) as possible. Yes, it is possible to install a realistic body, wheels, and tires on a "hot" chassis like a BSRT G2 or Patriot if you want both speed and appearance, but the injection-molded body will add about 10 percent to your lap times.

Racing Classes for HO Cars

Serious HO racers divide the cars into classes. Each club has its own specific rules, so don't tell club members you read it here or that they are wrong. Generally, the classes are divided into these general categories:

• **T-Jet**—Based on the Aurora Thunderjet cars with pancake-style motors and no traction magnets. The Playing Mantis chassis may fit into this class as well. Generally, these are the cars that have the most realistic bodies, wheels, and tires because O-ring front tires and silicone or foam rear tires are usually not allowed.

• **Stock Class**—Includes the out-of-the-box Tomy A/FX Super G-Plus and SRT, Mattel/Tyco 440-X2, and Life-Like cars, all with their original injection-molded plastic bodies. The traction magnets must be stock (those that came with the car). Some clubs allow replacement of the front axle and wheels with O-ring tires and metal wheels and the use of new armatures and new rear wheels with silicone tires. For some clubs, this is a subgroup of stock.

• **Super Stock Class**—Cars are generally the same as the stock class cars except that a clear plastic body is allowed. Again, some groups allow replacement of the front and rear wheels and tires.

• **Modified Class**—Can include a variety of subclasses, depending on the club's rules. Most clubs have a list of approved motors, armatures, and traction magnets for each subclass of modified car. Motor and traction magnets are sometimes limited to the polymer material magnets that are usually much stronger than stock magnets. Often, modified cars in this class are called polymer class cars. The ultimate modified cars are allowed to use the fastest armatures and strongest motor magnets and traction magnets that are made from the incredibly powerful neodymium alloy and, thus, this is usually called the "neo class." These cars often have motors with adjustable motor brush timing, and ball bearings on both the motor and axle shafts.

Chapter Thirteen

DRIVING A RACE CAR

A Scalextric NASCAR Ford Taurus and Pontiac Grand Prix trade paint on a road course. If the driver of the Taurus punches the throttle, the rear of his car will swing out to hit the Pontiac's front fender and probably knock the Pontiac out of the slot—model car racers call it "nerfing."

There's more to driving a model racing car than just pulling the trigger on the hand controller. There are, as you would expect, driving techniques that can induce one of two equal cars to be faster around the track. The techniques in chapter 9 will allow you to be sure the car is performing at its best. Now it's up to you to get the best out of that car. There are also better, well-designed controllers that can give you more precise control and better feel for how your car is cornering. And if you want somebody to race with when there's no one around—choose the Pacer, Scalextric's system that allows you to race against yourself.

The Art of Driving
It would seem that you can learn to drive one of these cars by merely practicing enough to know

how much throttle the car needs for any given corner. You can apply increasing throttle to force the car to accelerate just short of breaking traction and fishtailing from side to side. At best, you can only maintain that speed with a learned amount of practical throttle. While that's one way to drive reasonably fast, you can learn more advanced techniques.

Lose It and Gas It
If your track and controllers do not have a brake circuit, buy a terminal track and controllers that do have brakes as described later in this chapter. Without brakes, the cars coast into the corners with very little response to the hand controller. When the car nears the next corner, you merely wait until the car coasts down to a speed low enough to negotiate the corner.

SCX offers cordless hand throttles that utilize an infrared signal from the controller to the control tower. The controller must be pointed at the tower to produce a clear signal.

When you have brakes, the car can be driven at full or nearly full throttle to within a few inches of the corner, then you can snap off the throttle trigger to apply the brakes. The brakes will slow the car down and unsettle it slightly, if not actually starting a slide. When that slide begins, you apply as much throttle as possible and the car will usually catch traction and rocket around the corner. You are, in effect, bouncing-off the braking point on the track. I call the technique "lose it and gas it." In reality, you do not really lose control of the car as it slides into the corner: it just looks like you've lost it.

To turn really fast laps you need to keep the car on the absolute limit of its available cornering, braking, and accelerating performance just short of spinning out. There are several factors at play: the traction or grip of the rear tires is important but it is only one element. You are also pushing the limit of how much force the guide or pickup shoe will take before it snaps out of the slot. (There is some debate among model car racers about whether the front tires actually help hold the car or if they are merely along for the ride, and that it's the pickup that makes all the difference.) And you are balancing centrifugal force, trying to move the car out of the corner with the momentum and acceleration force of the tires trying to drive it forward.

You can carry this lose it and gas it power sliding stuff to an extreme. If you constantly lean on the pickup through every corner, you will not turn as quick of lap times as you would if you control the car, so a bit more of its energy is used to propel it forward than is used to pry the pickup around the slot. On a Ninco track with lots of traction, using soft tires with maximum magnetic downforce, you probably won't slide the rear end of the car out anywhere except on the exit of corners and even that should be well-controlled. Run a Ninco Classic Jaguar or Austin-Healey with no magnets on a Carrera track with low friction and you'll likely be power sliding around every corner, as well as three feet down the straight.

Nerfing and Leaning

Sometimes, you can use the car in the adjacent lane as a leaning post to boost your own cornering speed. It takes a considerable amount of skill, but you can, if you time it just right, tap the front fender of the adjacent car (assuming the two cars are not open-wheeled cars) with your rear fender. Get it right and the ricochet effect can help launch your car down the next straight. Frankly, it's better as an idea than as a reality because you will usually knock the other car out of the slot and you may even de-slot your own car. If you do use your car to knock another car out of the slot, model car racers call it "nerfing," and it is not nice. Some race rules provide a one-lap penalty for anyone caught nerfing another car. Even if you do not get caught, your racing partner is not going to be pleased. But, hey, NASCAR drivers revel in the concept of trading paint, so why not try it?

Race against Yourself

Scalextric's Classic and Sport systems both offer a special terminal or connector track section called a Pacer. The Pacer is really a small computer. To operate it, you drive a car around Lane 2 as quickly as you can and the Pacer repeats your best lap for 99 more without you ever touching the car again. The Pacer even has a speed-adjustment knob in case you discover that your qualifying lap was just a bit too fast or too slow. Set a car running in Lane 2 and use Lane 1 for the car you are driving as you try to keep up with the programmed car. You will be amazed at how difficult it is to keep up with the car you just programmed because it never makes a mistake.

The Scalextric Sport lap counter/timer and the Sport terminal or connector tracks are 1/2-straights, but one end of each has the same loop-and-peg joining system as Scalextric Classic track. Effectively, that means that the Sport Pacer and lap counter/timer must only be used on a full-length straight, which can make it difficult to insert into a cramped track circuit.

The Pacer will work with just about any car. If you want a Pacer for Carrera, Ninco, or Artin track, however, you have to adapt the Scalextric Classic or Sport Pacer as shown in the photos. You can use the Pacer with Ninco track by using the Ninco 10110 adapter track.

continued on page 206

Top: This may be the most important accessory for anyone racing at home. Scalextric Sport and Classic offer this Pacer track section that allows you to program a car on one lane so you can literally race against yourself.

Middle: Since only Scalextric Sport and Classic offer the Pacer, you will have to adapt it to other brands. To fit a Pacer to Carrera track, first remove the plastic panel from the bottom of the Scalextric Classic or Scalextric Sport Pacer track section.

Bottom: The Pacer is a conventional terminal track with two wires to each lane plus a third wire to lane 2 (bottom) to receive the electronic signals for the computer chip.

Heat the connection for that third (usually yellow) wire and remove it from the tab. Use needle-nose pliers to straighten the tab as shown, then push the tab out through the top of the track.

Use a cut-off disc in a Dremel motor tool to cut a notch in the Carrera rail to match the size of the notch in the Scalextric Sport or Scalextric Classic rail. Always wear eye protection when working with a motor tool.

Use the cut-off disc to cut up through the bottom of the track so the notch is the same size through the metal and the plastic.

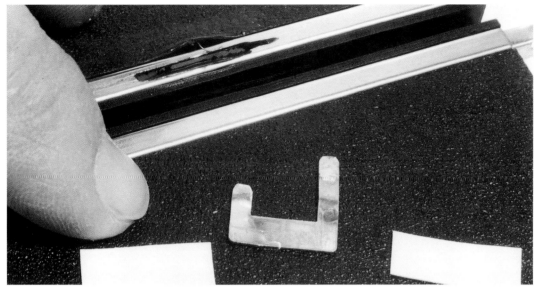

This U-shaped tab is the contact for the Pacer. Cut two pieces of .010-inch-thick Evergreen or Plastruct styrene about 1/8 inch longer than the tab to act as insulators on either side of the tab when it is installed in the notch in the rail.

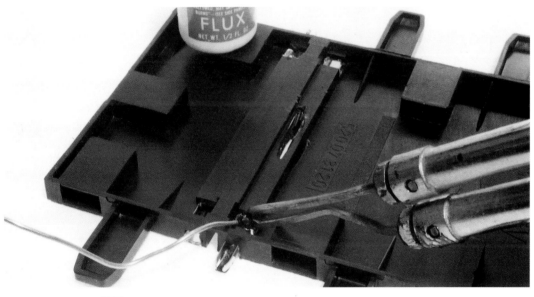

I used a 1/4-length Carrera track section so it could be inserted almost anywhere in the track. Carrera rails are a steel alloy that is very difficult to solder. Use acid flux and 50/50 solder. I found that it was easiest to solder near the contact tabs. Heat the rail, not the solder, and push the solder against the heated rail until it melts, then remove the soldering gun immediately.

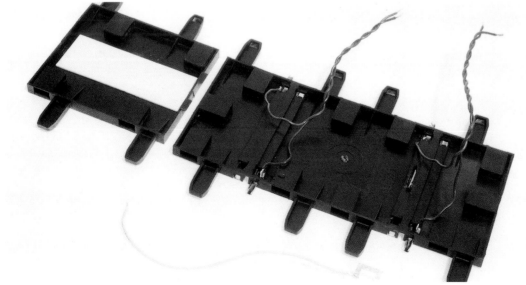

Make the two sets of two-wire connections to the pickup rails. I wanted the option of locating the Pacer near a curve so I cut and fitted a 1/4-length border as shown in chapter 2. All the wires must be long enough to reach across the border.

Upper left: Heat the Scalextric Sport or Scalextric Classic wire connections and join them with the two wires to each rail that was soldered to the Carrera track.

Above: Solder the Scalextric Sport or Scalextric Classic Pacer contact to the yellow wire.

Lower left: Place the two pieces of .010-inch styrene insulation on each side of the Scalextric Sport or Scalextric Classic contact piece and insert the sandwich through the slot you cut in the rail so the top of the contact is just .005 inch or less above the top of the Carrera rail. Hold it in place with thickened Super Glue.

Below: The contact must be at the same level as the pickup strip so the brushes on the car can touch both the rail and the contact simultaneously. Gently file the contact strip until it is at the exact height of the pickup rail.

The finished Pacer contact tab inserted in a Carrera track section.

The Scalextric Classic or Sport Pacer control box can be mounted to the Carrera track, but a half-dozen plastic tabs must be cut away from the underside of the Carrera border for the two brands to fit. Use Testors Model Master Sprue Cutters to cut off the tabs.

There are no assembly tabs or clips. You could attach the Scalextric Pacer control box to the track with 5-minute epoxy, but that would make it almost impossible to correct any loose wires that might occur later. I used automotive safety wire, twisted into pigtails with pliers, to hold the assembly together.

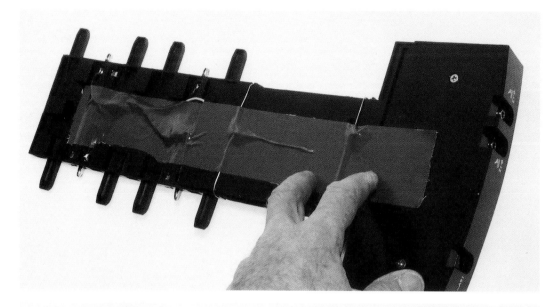

Protect the loose wires on the bottom of the Pacer/Carrera unit with duct tape.

The completed Pacer/Carrera track section can be inserted almost anywhere in a Carrera track if a second 1/4-straight is inserted on the opposite side of the track to match it and maintain the track alignment.

Continued from page 201

The Best Hand Controllers

Every race car set includes a hand controller for each lane. Carrera and MRRC offer plunger-style controllers that you hold like a ski pole and depress the throttle button with your thumb. Scalextric Sport, Scalextric Classic, SCX, Ninco, Artin, Tomy A/FX, Life-Like, and Mattel all provide pistol-style controllers with a trigger you operate with your forefinger. The Scalextric Classic and Sport controllers are designed so you can hold them upside down for comfortable operation by pushing the trigger with your thumb. Back in the dawn of slot car racing, all the manufacturers offered push-button controllers. In the mid-1960s, the Russkit pistol-style controller appeared and most drivers discovered they had more control with their forefinger than with their thumb. You might prefer a thumb-operated controller, so try both styles before you decide. Most hand controllers operate by moving a contact strip across a wire-wound ceramic resistor like the Ninco controller in the photographs.

Match the Controller to the Car

The perfect controller is one that allows you to actually control the car through the entire movement of the trigger. If you must depress the trigger three-fourths of the way before the car responds, the controller likely has too much resistance and you need a resistor or completely new controller with a lower ohm rating. Parma offers a wide range of replacements for their controllers. Scalextric offers a C800 30-ohm controller. SCX offers the Pro hand controller with replaceable 20- and 45-ohm resistors. If the car hits almost full speed with only a light touch on the trigger, you need a controller with more ohms. Most of the controllers furnished with home racing sets have about 60 ohms of resistance. This is probably perfect for cars with no magnets or relatively weak magnets. If the car has a stronger magnet, like the Fly, SCX, and Scalextric Sport cars, you may want a resistor with slightly fewer ohms.

Ninco, Professor Motor, Pro Slot, Parma, BSRT, Wizzard, and others offer special versions of the trigger-style hand controller. Some, like the Ninco Vario and the Professor Motor controller, have adjustable ohm settings. Ninco has the Vario 16 Dual hand controller with a choice of 16 ohm settings. Carrera offers a thumb-operated

Above: Ninco, Scalextric Sport, Scalextric Classic, and SCX controllers have a simple copper strip that rubs across the individual wires on the rheostat coil. Remove the three screws that hold the two halves of the Ninco controller together.

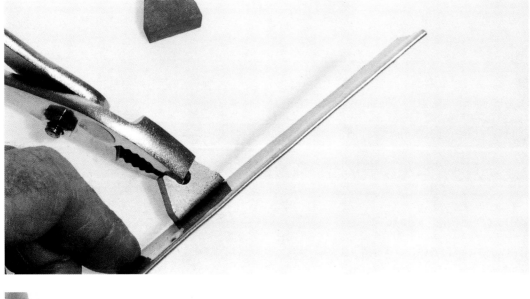

Upper left: The sintered copper material used for automotive starter brushes is perfect for the rubbing face of the contact strip in a model car controller. Use a razor saw or hacksaw to cut 1/4-inch-long, 1/8-inch squares for each controller.

Left: The sintered copper brushes are a bit difficult to solder. Tin one of the 1/8-inch sides of the brush by heating it with a soldering gun and flowing a coat of solder over just that one side of the brush.

Rub the contact faces of the copper wiper with emery cloth to polish it. Hold the sintered cooper square in place over the brush and heat the side of the square until the solder flows.

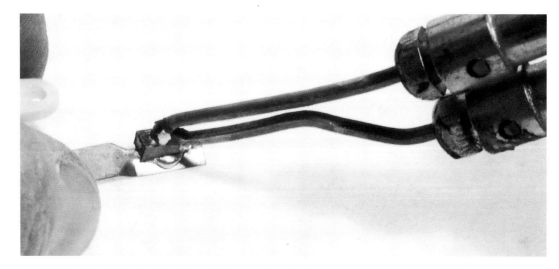

Inspect the solder joints and the wires that lead to the wiper on the controller trigger. If the wire is frayed or loose, cut it off and remove about 1/8 inch of the insulation, then resolder the fresh wire end to the copper contact strip.

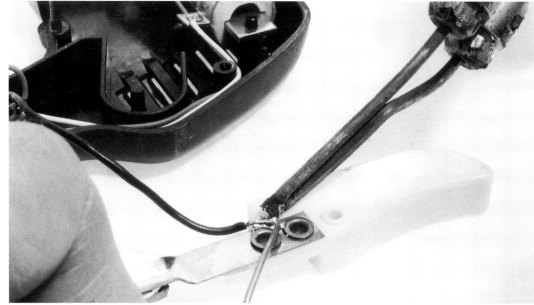

Reassemble the controller trigger and copper wiper and inspect the new sintered copper brush to be sure it is making full contact with the rheostat coil (far right).

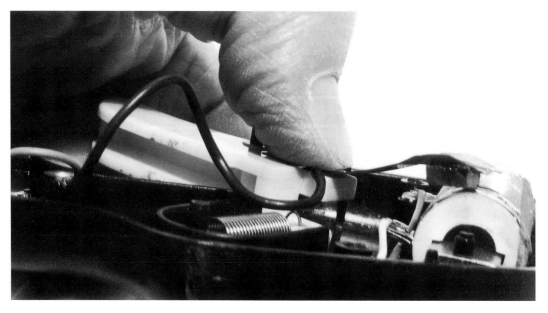

Bend the copper brush up or down until the sintered copper makes smooth and even contact.

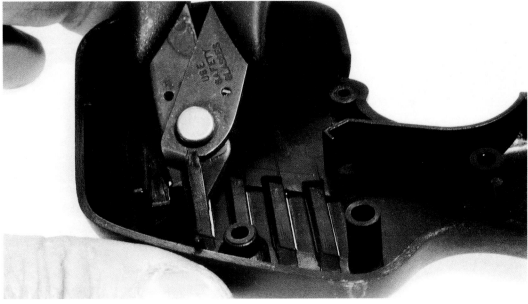

The thicker sintered brush pushed the copper strip out far enough to foul the inside of the controller. Use diagonal cutters to remove two of the ventilation ribs so the wiper arm cannot catch on them.

Xtreme-Control controller with adjustable settings. The majority of these controllers also have special heat-dissipating devices that are necessary for racing on commercial tracks but are not really needed for most home racers. If you have decided to add stronger magnets for more downforce in your cars, they will likely need more powerful motors to pull the magnets around the track. And you will likely need one of these special controllers. You can upgrade the less-expensive controllers by installing a sintered copper contact as shown in the photographs.

Apply the Brakes

Brakes are standard with Carrera, Ninco, Tomy/S/FX, Life-Like, and Mattel tracks and controllers. The Scalextric Classic, SCX, and Artin sets usually do not have brakes. You can check for brakes by looking at the number of wires from the control to the track: if there are three wires, the controller probably has brakes. The brake wire is connected to the off end of the resistor inside the controller so the motor acts like a generator when the controller is in the off position. There's a wiring diagram in chapter 6 to install both brakes and a lane-reversing switch. There's a diagram for the brake circuit in *Racing and Collecting Slot Cars.* Sport and Scalextric offer an accessory terminal track called Advanced Track System that includes both the brake circuit and reversing switches for each lane. The reversing switches can be added to standard Scalextric Sport, Scalextric Classic, Carrera, or Artin track as described in chapter 14.

Chapter Fourteen

LET'S RACE!

It all starts at the start. You can re-create any real car race or rally, including both the cars and the driving challenge.

There's really no other form of motorized competition that can fulfill that wish to race easier than tabletop model car racing—what we used to call slot racing. It's nice to have a garage-size track, but you can have truly exciting races on a 4x8-foot oval or Rally track. The cost to life and limb is minimal, the risk to ego as great as with any kind of racing. To state the obvious, it is fun!

Start Here

You can race all by yourself using the Scalextric Sport and Scalextric Classic Pacer in chapter 13. Model car racing is a bit more fun, however, if you can get four or more people together so at least two can race while the other two act as corner marshals and replace de-slotted cars. Actually, with the crash-and-burn system, two is enough for a race.

Who Won?

Racing implies that there is a winner, and usually the winner is the car that completed the most laps. It is possible to have someone count your laps (the real race car teams do it), but there's usually nobody to spare for that task. All the track makers offer lap counters. The least-expensive usually have a lever inside the slot that triggers either a ratchet mechanical counter or sends a signal to a small computer chip like the Scalextric Sport and Scalextric Classic counters. Carrera and SCX offer inexpensive photocell lap counters on bridges that hang over the track.

The lap counter can also be triggered by the cars passing over a dead spot in the track. The dead spot is a 4-inch-long area where the pickup rails receive no power. The pickup rails in the dead spot are connected to the lap counter so the dead spot serves as the sensor. When the car passes over the dead spot it completes an electrical circuit to trigger the lap counter. Dead spots are very reliable sensors, but they only function with the cars traveling in one direction—when you decide to run the opposite way, the lap counter track must be removed and rotated 180 degrees and replaced.

You can make your own dead-spot lap counter for Carrera or any brand of track as shown in the photos. DS offers ready-made, full-length sections of track with built-in dead spots for Scalextric Sport, Scalextric Classic, Carrera, Ninco, Tomy A/FX, and Mattel (Tyco). DS also offers just the wiring for a dead spot, so you can use their lap counters with hand-routed track. The DS infrared bridges and dead-spot lap counters are wired to fit the DS electronic lap counters/timers, but you can buy plugs to connect them to other lap counters.

The most reliable lap counter sensors are infrared with a bulb below and above each slot. DS makes a bridge with the bulbs spaced to match the slots in Scalextric Sport, Scalextric Classic, Carrera, and Ninco track in a choice of 2, 4, 6, or 8 lanes. You will need to drill 1/8-inch holes through the bottom of the slots in Carrera track to match the locations of the below-track lights.

The electronic lap counters usually include a lap time option, even on the inexpensive Scalextric, SCX, Ninco, and Carrera lap counters. The more expensive lap counters, like the DS model 300 and the Ninco 10402 Pole Position, provide more accurate lap timing to within 1/1000 of a second. Trix Trax also offers an electronic lap counter/timer.

DS offers a modular system of lap counters/timers that can be expanded for up to eight lanes.

The SCX 88090 Digital Speedometer provides a miles per hour average per lap, time-per-lap, or cumulative race time per lap for two lanes.

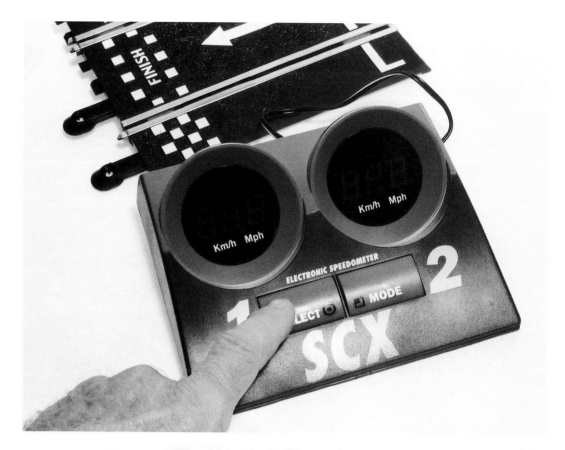

The dead spot lap counter sensor can be made by cutting two gaps, about 4 inches apart, through the pickup rails. Use a motor tool with a cut-off disc and wear eye protection.

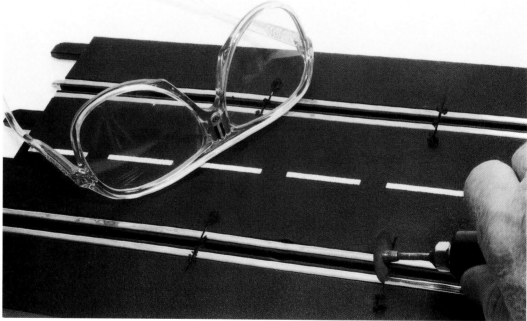

Computer-Controlled Racing

Scalextric has a Race Management System (RMS) lap counter system with a CD and a special connector track. The CD is inserted into your computer so the screen displays the laps as well as a half-dozen other displays. The RMS sys-tem is much more than a lap counter because it also has programs to provide mandatory pit stops, with fuel consumption variables, and it records practice, qualifying, and race times. You can use RMS to duplicate the fuel load and pit

Use a hobby knife to scrape any oxidation from the last 1/16-inch of the Carrera track-mounting tabs to prepare them for solder.

Apply a drop of acid flux to the rail and heat the rail with a soldering gun while you press 50/50 tin/lead solder against the hot rail. Remove the soldering gun the instant the solder flows. This will tin the rails and make it easier to solder the wire connections.

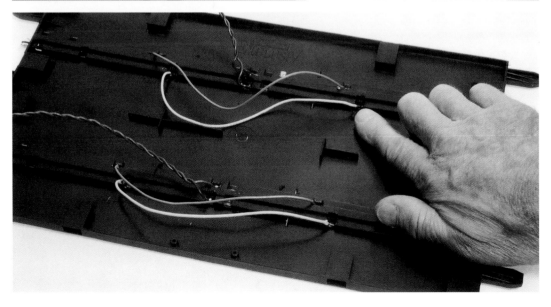

Eight wires must be soldered to the rails, two each to the dead-spot rails in the center and two more jumper wires to carry the electrical current around the dead spots in the middle of the track.

Check the slots carefully and use the cut-off disc in the motor tool to remove any excess melted plastic that may have bulged into the slot.

Fill the gaps in the track and rails with 5-minute epoxy.

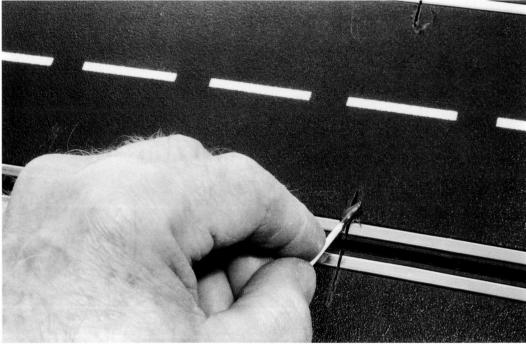

stop strategies that are so important in modern Formula 1 racing. It also has a race track design program for Scalextric Sport or Scalextric Classic track.

Trakmate offers a CD and a power cable to plug into your computer so the computer program (for the CD) does the lap counting and timing. The Trakmate power cord must be connected to your choice of sensors. It works best with an infrared like the DS Bridge Sensor but it can also be used with a dead spot sensor.

Running the Wrong Way

You can double the life of any race course by running both directions. The track is completely different when run in the opposite direction (unless, of course, it's a simple oval). Carrera has reversing switches on the bottom of each of

You can buy small DPDT reversing slide-style reversing switches from Radio Shack, or the Atlas Twin from model railroad shops.

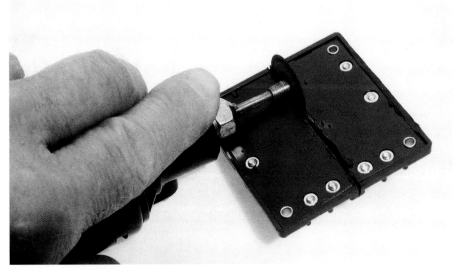

Atlas "Twin" switches are wired together internally; use a cut-off disc in a motor tool (or a razor saw) to cut right through the box to break the connection.

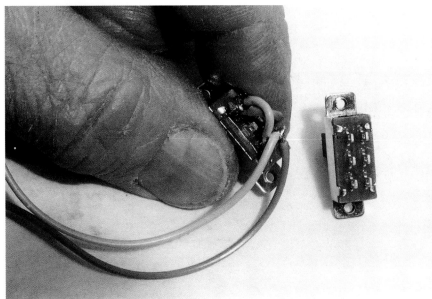

Solder short pieces of wire to diagonally connect the four outermost terminals on the Radio Shack DPDT switch. The two longer wires to the track are soldered to the two end tabs. The Atlas Twin is already connected internally.

Use a milling bit in a Dremel motor tool to cut two rectangular boxes in the Carrera connector track to fit the slide-style Radio Shack DPDT switches. Shave the edges of the holes to make them a precise fit around the DPDT switches.

Two Carrera control boxes. The one on the left has one of the two DPDT reversing switches soldered to the proper terminals. The box on the right has sockets to fit Ninco or Parma controllers wired to the Carrera terminals. I managed to squeeze both into a single connector box, but I'd advise adding a separate box.

their cars, but no reversing switches for the track itself. Only SCX sets have reversing switches, but optional connector tracks with reversing switches are available for Scalextric Sport, Scalextric Classic, and Ninco. If you want reversing switches for Carrera track, you will have to make your own.

Radio Shack and similar electronics hobby stores sell small DPDT slide switches, or you can buy Atlas Twin slide switches from a hobby

George Szmuda purchased a small black plastic box from Radio Shack and fitted three posts for controllers with alligator clips and DPDT reversing switches for Fed Martin's Carrera track from chapter 3. He installed sockets for Parma or Ninco plugs in the Carrera control box.

You can install the sockets to accept the Ninco or Parma plug on a Carrera controller cord. Cut off the controller and solder the wires to the Radio Shack socket to make an adapter cord to plug Ninco or Parma controllers into a standard Carrera connector track.

dealer. The Atlas switches can be mounted on the edge of the table with screws. I handmade special connector track sections for Carrera track that squeeze a socket for Scalextric Sport, Ninco, or Parma controllers, and DPDT reversing switch for each of the two lanes into the Carrera connector track's control box. George Szmuda bought separate boxes to house the reversing switches, as well as external screws for drivers with controllers that use alligator clips to connect to the track. The third (and easiest) option is to use the Atlas switches and make a socket adapter cord to plug into the Carrera-controlled sockets as shown.

Power Packs

I recommend that you have a separate transformer for each lane, regardless of the size of the track. If you try to run two cars from one transformer, one of cars can be affected by full-power application from the other car, which violates my rule that the track should never be the cause of a wreck. You can have separate power supplies by simply buying a second connector track and plug-in power supply. Artin and the standard Carrera power supplies are divided internally to produce separate power for each lane, but there is barely enough. Carrera offers a more powerful 20734 Exlusiv power supply that is also divided internally to provide separate power for two lanes.

Most model racing car motors only need 1 amp per lane. If you fit very strong magnets with a faster motor like a Slot.it V12 or Plafit Cheetah, the motor may draw closer to 2 amps. The older Mabuchi and similar slot car motors from the 1960s also need 2 amps. Some of the really fast motors used on commercial tracks need even more. The Artin pack delivers about .15 amp per lane, Scalextric about 1 amp (which is okay if you use one per lane), the standard Carrera about .24 amp, and the Exlusiv about .6 amp.

Super Power Packs

If you push the motors to the limit with magnetic downforce and lots of use, any of these power packs can cause the motor to overheat, because all allow at least a bit of alternating current to flow through the circuit. Voltage is not a particular problem—Artin has 12 volts, Carrera's standard pack has 14, the Carrera Exlusiv 18, and Scalextric 16. The more expensive power packs filter out the AC current to deliver pure DC current like an automobile storage battery, but I do not recommend storage batteries because the recharging cycle can create explosive gases and the total energy can create fire-starting sparks.

Radio Shack offers a Regulated Power Supply transformer that delivers 3 amps of well-filtered DC current. There's enough power for two lanes,

The Radio Shack Regulated Power Supply has 3.0 amps. The bare wires can be folded over and twisted to plug into the Carrera connector sockets with two short jumper wires to connect the power to both lanes.

This Crest Switching Power Supply by Aristo-Craft has a full 20 amps of pure DC current—as much as some automobile batteries.

When the cars slide out of turns, they can smack the control box. I assembled a special Carrera connector track with a built-in border to avoid this problem.

but I recommend one for each lane so the power surges from one car won't effect the other car. Crest, by Aristo-Craft, has the CRE-55465 Switching Power Supply that delivers a full 20 amps and 13.8 volts. The circuits inside the pack automatically provide for surges up to about 22 volts. This pack is plenty for any four-lane home-racing track.

Connector Tracks with Borders

My personal philosophy of model car race track design includes a fundamental precept: the track should never be the cause of a wreck or de-slotted car. Usually, that means keeping the slot clean and open and avoiding bridges or fences too close to the track. I am a confirmed "border man" in that I believe there should be no place on the track where a sliding car can fall off because there is no border. Take a look at any of the tracks in chapter 5 and you'll see very few places where there are no borders. I do not use them just for appearance: the borders are there because cars have fallen off the edge of the track, even on the inside of some curves.

This severely limits where you can put a conventional terminal or connector track because the control boxes are always right up against the edge of the track. The tower-type lap counters or sensors can also have support legs too close to the track. I use a four-lane lap counter bridge on a two-lane track just to keep the side of the bridge away from the track. You can move the control box away from the edge of Scalextric Sport or Scalextric Classic using their multi-lane connector tracks designed so the connector has wires that are to be plugged into the rails of the third and forth lanes from below the track. You can use these multi-lane terminals with two-lane tracks to move the control box away from the edge of the track.

I made a special terminal or connector track for Carrera using just the control box from a Carrera connector track and a 1/4-length straight track with a border cut to fit as shown in chapter 2. I epoxied the control box, the border, and 1/4-straight into a single track section. The 1/4-straight can be inserted into the track just about anywhere. I made two for my two-lane track so that two driver positions could be used. I made a third for a four-lane track. The same system could be used to make a custom connector track for Ninco, but I would start with their 10401 Double Power connector track that has

Use a screwdriver to pry the cover from the bottom of the Carrera connector track. The cover is glued to the posts, so you will break it.

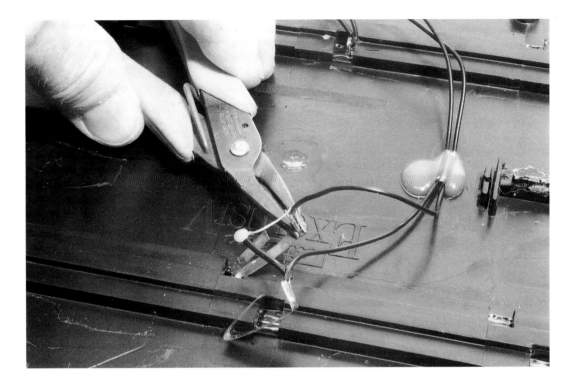

Use needle-nose pliers to pull the bent copper strips from inside the rails.

The Carrera control box can be removed from the track. Cut a 1/4-length track border as shown in chapter 2 and use diagonal cutters or sprue cutters to cut notches so the border will fit beside the Carrera control box.

built-in sockets for the controllers, brakes, and reversing switches. I installed sockets and reversing switches in the Carrera control boxes as shown in this chapter.

Running a Race Program

Okay, you and two or three friends are ready to race. Now what? First, you will want the cars to be more or less equal. The information in chapters 9 and 12 will help you select or modify cars so they are all similar performers. If you are a fan of real racing cars, you may want to divide the cars into classes based on both their performance as models and their prototypes. The obvious classes would include NASCAR, Formula 1, Rally, sports, touring, and vintage. *Racing and*

The wires can simply be plugged back into the Carrera rails with the clip from Carrera's connector track, or if you want a more secure connection, solder them to the rails as shown earlier in this chapter. Attach the control box and border with metal-filled epoxy.

Collecting Slot Cars has a dozen different classes you might want to consider. Generally, if there is a class for real cars, you can either buy or build replicas of most of the cars in that class. Specify equal-performance chassis and you can re-create just about any race in history, from an SCCA National to the 1954 Le Mans to the 2001 Daytona 500...the races go on and on.

Crash-and-Burn Racing

You already have a lap counter (or someone volunteered to count laps) and two of you are ready to race on a two-lane track. What if one of your cars comes out of the slot? There are several options: the simplest is called "crash-and-burn" and it means that if your car comes out of the slot you are out of the race.

Run a few dozen crash-and-burn events and you'll improve your driving skill considerably. The other alternative is to have at least four people available for a two-lane track: two to race and two to serve as corner marshals who put the cars back on the track. You can color code the track with stick-on dots and affix a similar dot to the

bottom of the car—or you can just yell which car and which lane and hope the marshal understands—you'll soon see why the dot system is essential if you are running four lanes.

The Driver's Championship

If there are four of you, how do you determine the champion? Again, choices: have a race-off so drivers A and B compete, then drivers C and D. The winner of the first race competes with the winner of the second for the championship.

You will, however, discover that one lane is always faster than the other. To make it truly fair, each driver should drive half the race on one and half the race on the other. So now you have six races, Driver A on Lane 1 and Driver B on Lane 2, then Driver A on Lane 2 and Driver B on Lane 1, and so on. Running half the race in each lane negates the need for a lane-equaling, figure eight-style track design. In fact, this simple six-race event allows truly equal competition, especially if the cars have similar performance.

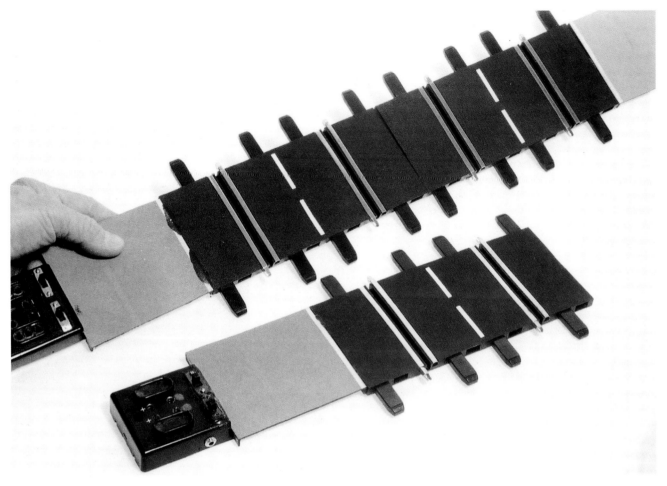

If you really want to see who is the best driver, repeat the whole process but mandate that the two losing drivers get the two winning drivers' cars and repeat the six-race series. Carry it to the extreme and each driver can drive each of the four cars. Or, do a model car version of IROC (the International Race of Champions): leave the cars in the lane and mandate that each driver completes an equal number of laps in each car, that way, as in IROC, the fastest *driver*, not the fastest *car*, wins.

The Racing Program

There is another slightly more complex system for an organized race meet: first, the distance around the track is divided into tenths of one lap. The races are run for a specified time, say 5 minutes. Use an outlet timer that shuts off the whole track (some electronic lap counter systems will also turn off track power). At the end of the 5 minutes, the laps on the lap counter are recorded *plus* any additional tenths of a laps each driver completes. The cars and drivers then change to the next lane to their right. Each driver gets to drive 5 minutes in each lane. The total numbers of

laps and tenths of laps for each driver are then added and the driver with the most laps wins. If there are more drivers than lanes, run heat races: the top two drivers (if it's a two-lane track) or the top four (if it's a four-lane track) qualify for the main event. The main event is also run in four sections, but usually 10 minutes each so every driver gets 10 minutes in each lane. Again, the total number of laps for each driver are recorded *plus* the tenths of lap and the total for all four lanes to determine the winner. We do inform the drivers of their totals so they know as the race progresses how they are doing in their quest for a win. There's a chart in *Racing and Collecting Slot Cars* that illustrates the system for eight drivers on a four-lane track. The same system can be used for any number of drivers on 2-, 3-, 4-, 6-, or 8-lane tracks.

These cars are not just models, nor are they just models of racing cars: these are true miniature racing cars that you control. The cars are precise replicas and their performance a close match to the real thing. The challenge is for you to drive them as well as the champions that drove the real racers.

Super Carrera connector tracks must be custom made. Each has sockets for Scalextric Sport, Scalextric Classic, Ninco, or Parma controllers (with brakes) and reversing switches. I made one for four-lane and two more for two-lane tracks.

Resources

These manufacturers supply everything you need to pursue the hobby of racing replicas of real cars on home slot car tracks.

Where to Buy Model Racing Cars

Most of the firms listed below sell through hobby dealers. I have even listed some of the major distributors that sell only to dealers in the United States, including Scalextric-USA, REH, LGB America, Imex, and Stevens: you can offer this contact information to your dealer as sources. If you are searching for a specific brand, contact the manufacturer and they may be able to provide a list of dealers. Or you can search the Web. The *Model Car Racing* magazine Website lists all the dealers that carry the magazine, with addresses, phone numbers, and links to their Websites.

Below are the addresses that each firm provides, including the mailing address, phone, and the Website, if available. If you contact these firms by mail, include a stamped, self-addressed envelope if you expect a reply. Many of them charge for their catalogs. You have our permission to scan this page and download it into your computer to make it easier to search and contact Website addresses.

• • • • • • • • • • • • • • • • • •

A2M (see Sports Car World or Rad Trax for U.S. orders) - 1/32 scale resin bodies
Productos para Modelismo S.L.
Uruguay, 32
08320 El Masnou
Barcelona, SPAIN
(34) 93 540 11 11
www.a2mweb.com

Airfix (see MRRC)
www.airfix.com

Any Slot (see Electric Dreams and other dealers) - 1/32 scale cars and bodies

Annie Minnie (see Electric Dreams and other dealers)

Aristo-Craft
698 S. 21st St.
Irvington, NJ 07111
973-351-9800
www.aristocraft.com/catalog/crest/power

Artin - 1/32 scale sets
200 Fifth Avenue, Rm. 200
New York, NY 10010
www.artin.com.hk

Aurora (see Racemasters)

Auto Art - 1/32 scale ready-to-run cars
www.autoartmodels.com

Bauer - HO scale cars (see New Jersey Nostalgia for U.S. and German dealers; also see Umpfi's Slotbox for dealers)

Betta & Classic - Cast-resin and clear plastic bodies
61 Larkfield Lanes
Southport
Merseyside PR9 8NN
UK

Booth (see EJ's, Parma, and other dealers) - Clear plastic bodies

Boye Racing Models - HO scale bodies and decals
www.lemonzaco@aol.com

Brad Bowman's Custom Tracks - Custom-routed HO and 1/32 scale tracks
www.origin8.com/bradstrack

BSRT - HO scale cars, bodies, hop-up parts
20807 NE 8th St.
Redmond, WA 98053
www.scaleauto.com

Bumslot - 1/32 scale cars
www.bumslot.com

BWA Wheels - 1/32 scale aluminum wheels and inserts
www.trak.to/bwaslotcars

Carrera (see LGB America for U.S. dealers) -
1/32 and 1/24 scale cars, track, and sets
STS Racing GmbH Carrera
Postfach 1652, 90005
Nürnberg
GERMANY
www.carrera-toys.de

Classic (see Betta)

Cox (out of production; see EJ's and Electric Dreams)

Detail Master - Etched-metal and cast-metal parts, 1/24 scale adaptable to 1/32
Modeltyme Designs
146 Halstead St., #117
Rochester, NY 14610
716-482-0970
www.detailmaster.com

DS Electronic Racing Products (see MRRC or Scalextric-USA) - lap counters and timers

Eagle Distributing - Pro Slot, 1/32, and 1/24 scale commercial cars and parts
www.eagledist.com
Design manual for home-built routed tracks
www.oldnslo.com/track

EJ's Hobbies - 1/32 scale cars, parts, bodies, and decals
7017 Cascade Rd. SE
Grand Rapids, MI 49546-7304

Electric Dreams
3190-H Airport Loop Rd.
Costa Mesa, CA 92680
www.electric-dreams.com/elecdrms.htm

E-R Model Importers - Preiser wholesaler
100 South Main St.
Newark, NJ 14513

Etzel Speed Classics - 1/32 scale cast-resin CART and IRL bodies and 1/24 scale cast-resin static model kits
P.O. Box 5195
Lafayette, IN 47903-5195

Fantasy World Hobbies - 1/32 scale body-mounts and components
7901 South Hosmer, Ste. A-6
Tacoma, WA 98408
877-318-7144
www.fantasyworldhobbies.com

Fisher Model and Pattern - 1/24 scale cast-resin static model kits
5290 Buckboard Ln.
Paradise, CA 95969

Fitzpatrick (see Betta)

Fly Car Model (see Scalextric-USA, REH, and Stevens for North America)
S.L., Ronda de la Bugavilla del Rey, No. 31
Madrid 28023
SPAIN
www.flycarmodel.com

Furuli Models - HO scale cast-resin bodies
4432 W. Hayward Pl.
Denver, CO 80212

Highway Pioneers - 1/32 scale plastic display kits
Dapol Limited
Lower Dee Exhibition Center
Llangollen
Derbyshire LL20 8RX
UK
www.dapol.co.uk/cgid
apol/store/commerce.cgi?page=highway
pioneers.html

Historic Scale Racing Replicas - 1/32 scale Can Am cars, wheels and tires
P.O. Box 769
Ukiah, CA 95482
www.p-b-l.com/can-am/canamhistorics.html

Hot Wheels Racing (see Mattel) - Diecast HO scale cars

Imex Model Company - Ninco wholesalers
15391 Flightpath Dr.
Brooksville, FL 34609

Indy Grips - Silicone tires
2034 Woodcrest Rd.
Indianapolis, IN 46227

LGB America - Carrera in North America
6444 Nancy Ridge Dr.
San Diego, CA 92121-2296
800-669-0607
www.62.128.3.117/frames/store_top.html

Life-Like - HO scale cars and track
1600 Union Ave.
Baltimore, MD 21211

Johnny Lightning (see Playing Mantis)

Magnatech SRP - Magnetic track braid material for custom-routed tracks
7702 Briaridge
San Antonio, TX 78230
210-308-6909

Mattel - HO scale cars and track
333 Continental Blvd.
El Segundo, CA 90245
www.mattel.com/our_toys/ot_hotw.asp

Maxi-Models - 1/32 scale kits, handbuilt ready-to-run cars, and detailing parts
The Antiques Shop
Main Street, Tingewick
Buckinghamshire MK18 4NL
UK

Max Trax - Custom-built HO tracks
831 Trommer Rd.
Spencerport, NY 14559

MCW Automotive Finishes - Lacquer paint
P.O. Box 518
Burlington, NC 27216-0518

Mini-Models - HO scale cars
7326 Jetty Ln.
Houston, TX 77072
www.nu-rora.com

Model Car Masterpieces - 1/24 scale cast-resin static model kits
1525 W. MacArthur Blvd., #20
Costa Mesa, CA 92626

Model Car Racing Publications, Inc. - Bimonthly magazine devoted to 1/32, HO, and 1/24 home racing
6525 Gunpark Dr., Ste. 370-142
Boulder, CO 80301
www.modelcarracingmag.com

Model Motoring - HO scale cars and track
P.O. Box 10725
Newport Beach, CA 92658
www.modelmho.com

Monarch Lines - 1/32 cars and parts
www.monarchlines.co.uk

Monogram Models (no longer makes 1/32 scale; see MRRC)
www.revell-monogram.com

MRE - 1/32 scale cars, books, and decals
www.mre.co.uk

MRRC International Hobbies Ltd. (see Scalextric-USA for North America) - Cars, hop-up parts, and decals
P.O. Box 790
St. Heiler
Jersey JE4 0SW
UK
www.mrrc.com

Mundaring Hobby Center - 1/32 scale cast-resin bodies, chassis, and parts
Shop 3, Mundaring Mall
7025 Great Eastern Highway
Western Australia 6073
AUSTRALIA
www.hobbycentre.com.au

New Jersey Nostalgia Hobby - Imports Bauer HO scale cars to the United States
401 Park Ave.
Scotch Plains, NJ 07076
508-322-2676

Ninco (see REH, Stevens, and Imex for North America) - 1/32 scale cars, track, parts
Ctra. de l'Hospitalet
32, 08940 CORNELLIA
Barcelona, SPAIN
www.ninco.com

NorthWest Short Line - Gears, axles, and bearings
P.O. Box 423
Seattle, WA 98111
206-932-1087
www.nwsl.com

Nostalgia Raceways (see Mundaring Hobby Center) - 1/32 scale cast-resin bodies

Ozrace Models - Motors, 1/32 scale Holden bodies, and parts
18 Hampton Court
Wynn Vale SA 5127
AUSTRALIA
(08) 8288 8388 (Australia)
00618 8288 8388 (New Zealand)
www.ozrace.com.au.E

Parma International - 1/32 scale chassis, hop-up parts, motors, and controllers
13927 Progress Pkwy.
North Royalton, OH 44133
www.parmapse.com

Patto's Place - 1/32 scale clear bodies, decals, and wheels
9 Wesley St.
Oatlands NSW 2117
AUSTRALIA
www.members.optushome.com.au/pattosplace/

Pink-Kar (see Scalextric-USA and dealers) - 1/32 scale cars

Plafit (see MRRC and dealers) - Motors, gears, wheels, and tires

Playing Mantis - Johnny Lightning and Thunderjet 500 HO scale cars and bodies
3618 Grape Rd.
Mishawaka, IN 46545
www.playingmantis.com

Policar (see Pro Slot) - 1/32 scale cars, motors, and decals

Polistil (see Professor Motor for United States) - 1/32 scale cars and sets

Pre-Ad Bodies - 1/32 scale resin bodies
c/o Mac Pinches
30 Swallowfields Dr.
Staffs WS12 5UQ
UK
01543 871849
preadbodykits@talk2.com
www.preadd-bodies.tripod.com/index.htm

Professor Motor - 1/32 scale cars, controllers, electrical parts, decals, wheels, tires, and reproductions of vintage parts
38626 Reo Court
Livonia, MI 48154-1158
734-462-4226
www.professormotor.com

Pro Slot - Gears, axles, and other parts
www.proslot.com

Pro-Track - 1/32 scale chassis and clear bodies
158 Woodbury St.
Elyria, OH 44035
www.slotcar.org/protrack

Racemasters - Imports Tomy A/FX to America
5544 Vista Del Dia
Anaheim Hills, CA 92807

Racing Champions (available at larger toy stores)

REH Distributors - 1/32 and HO scale wholesaler; your local hobby shop can contact them
4415 Marburg Ave.
Cincinnati, OH 45209

Reprotec
s.l., apartado de coreos 28079
08080 Barcelona, SPAIN 00 34 933 712 085
www.reprotec.com

Revell (no longer makes 1/32 scale cars; see REH for track)

Revell-Monogram - 1/32 cars
8601 Waukegan Rd.
Morton Grove, IL 60053-2295
www.revell-monogram.com

Riggen (see REH) - 1/32 scale track

Scale Auto (see BSRT)

ScaleRacing (see Scalextric-USA) - Motors, gears, and other parts

Scalextric (see Scalextric-USA for North America) - 1/32 scale cars, track, accessories
www.scalextric.com

Scalextric-USA - 1/32 scale cars, track, and accessories
454 Court C
Tacoma, WA 98402
www.scalextric-usa.com

SCX - 1/32 scale cars, track, and accessories
www.scx.es

Silky's Custom Slot Car Tracks - Custom tracks
402-733-8570
402-896-6773
402-274-3499

Slot Classics (see Scalextric-USA, Monarch Lines, and other dealers)
www.telecable.es/personales/slotclassic

Slot Racing Accessories (SRA) - Cast-metal and resin 1/32 scale figures, pit buildings, and accessories
32 Jubilee Ave.
Headless Cross, Redditch
Worcestershire B97 5HE
UK
01527 545101
www.slotracingaccessories.co.uk

Slixx - 1/32 scale decals
7411 Garden Grove Blvd. #C
Garden Grove, CA 92841

Slot.it (see Scalextric-USA and dealers) - 1/32 scale motors, magnets, gears, and wheels
www.slot.it

Slottech - HO scale hop-up parts and bodies
28 Sandpoint Circle
Ormond Beach, FL 32174
www.gofastest.com/slottech

Speed Cast Slot Racing Kits
www.geocities.com/MotorCity/Speedway/2827

Stevens International - 1/32 and HO scale wholesaler; your local hobby shop can contact them
P.O. Box 126
Magnolia, NJ 08049

Strombecker (no longer produced; see REH and EJ's Hobbies)

Tomy (see Racemasters)

Top Slot (see Scalextric-USA for North
America) - 1/32 scale cast-resin bodies
IRB Auto Racing
S.L., Alba, 5
08700 Igualada, Barcelona
SPAIN

Trakmate - Lap counters and drag racing
timers for PCs
14624 - 102 Avenue
Surrey, BC V3R 7E5
CANADA
1-877-SLOTCAR
www.infoserve.net/oss/slotcar

Trix Trax - Lap counters and timing devices
P.O. Box 217
Coal City, IL 60416

True Scale Products - 1/32 and 1/24 scale clear
plastic and resin bodies, wheels, and inserts
www.truescaleproducts.com

Tweaker (see Scalextric-USA)

Tyco (see Mattel)

Umpfi's Slotbox - Bauer and other HO cars
Koelner Str. 102
51429 Bergisch Gladbach
GERMANY
+49 2204 952811

Wizzard High Performance - HO hop-up parts
148 Deer Oak Ln.
Bedford, PA 15522
www.wizzardho.com

Relevant Websites

1/32 Scale Model Car Racing

www.modelcarracingmag.com - *Model Car
Racing* magazine: a mostly color, bimonthly
that covers home racing exclusively (about
85 percent 1/32, 10 percent HO, and 5
percent 1/24 scale)

www.scaleautoracing.com - *Scale Auto Racing
News* magazine: publishes about 6 issues a
year, mostly commercial 1/24, 1/32, and HO
cars and races, but with occasional reports
on larger race events for 1/32 scale slot cars

www.oldweirdherald.com - Model car racing
'zine

www.slotcargarage.com - *Slot Car Garage*:
articles, news, reviews, how-tos, projects,
links, and forums about collecting and
racing 1/32 scale, HO, and 1/24 scale slot
cars

www.automodelismomagazine.com -
Automodelismo magazine (Spain)

www.slotrace.com - Tracker 2000 track design
program

www.cygnus.uwa.edu.au/~snowmanf/pages/sl
otcircuits.html - Tracks of the world in
Scalextric

www.Blueprint69.com - Automotive blueprints
(plans)

www.people.goldendome.com/~ken/slotwork
s.htm - Web ring

www.nav.webring.yahoo.com/hub?ring=sltcarr
g&page=2&list - Web ring

www.scalemodel.net - Website list

www.zagato.demon.co.uk/scalex - Dave
Cheesman's slot track, cars, and tuning tips

www.circuits-routier.asso.fr – French
enthusiast site

www.partsonly.com/slotlink - Links Mark
Gussin. Information about prototypes and
models

www.nscc.co.uk - National Scalextric Collectors
Club (UK)

www.derekcooper.co.uk - 1/32 scale cars

www.ukslotcars.co.uk - Catalog of out-of-
production 1/32 scale cars, plus a pictorial
library

www.origin8.com/bradstrack - Custom-routed
HO and 1/32 scale tracks

HO Scale Model Car Racing

www.modelcarracingmag.com - *Model Car
Racing* magazine, a mostly color, bimonthly
that covers home racing exclusively (about
85 percent 1/32, 10 percent HO, and 5
percent 1/24 scale)

www.scaleautoracing.com - *Scale Auto Racing
News* magazine

www.oldweirdherald.com - Model car racing
'zine

slotcargarage.com - Slot Car Garage

www.slotrace.com - Tracker 2000 track design
program

www.people.goldendome.com/~ken/slotwork
s.htm - Web ring

www.nav.webring.yahoo.com/hub?ring=sltcarr
g&page=2&list - Web ring

www.scalemodel.net - Website list

www.partsonly.com/slotlink - Links

www.spies.com/~ahm/ho-slotcars - Website list

www.members.home.net/bfergy - HO plans

www.origin8.com/bradstrack - Custom-routed
HO and 1/32 scale tracks

Index

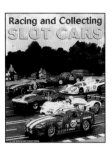

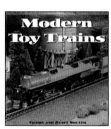
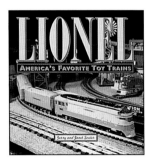